Bodily Reflective Modes

Bodily Reflective Modes

A Phenomenological Method for Psychology

Kenneth Joel Shapiro

The author and the publisher regret the following error: the diagram for figure 2 and the diagram for figure 5 were transposed. The correct diagram for figure 2 is on page 186; the correct diagram for figure 5 is on page 182.

Duke University Press   DURHAM   1985

Library of Congress Cataloging in Publication Data
Shapiro, Kenneth Joel.
Bodily reflective modes.

Bibliography: p.
Includes index.
1. Phenomenological psychology—Research—Methodology.
2. Body, Human—Psychological aspects. 3. Reflection
(Philosophy). 4. Introspection. 5. Structuralism.
6. Ambivalence. I. Title.
BF204.5.S53 1985   150.19′2   84–26018
ISBN 0–8223–0605–0

To: Ann, Debbie, Sabaka, and Elkie

Contents

Foreword

Phenomenology began in 1900 with the publication of *Logical Investigations* by Edmund Husserl. It was not born fully developed; rather, it gradually grew over the years, and one could say that Husserl was always catching up thematically with what he was writing prereflectively. The same would be true of the phenomenological movement as a whole: as it ventured into new areas, its application was ahead of its thematic articulations. Thus, we have Scheler extending phenomenology into the realm of values, Schütz into the social dimension, Heidegger into ontology and Husserl himself constantly speaking of the relevance of phenomenology for psychology. Yet each extension took place before phenomenology itself was fully clarified and each extension modified the self-understanding of its basic concepts.

Husserl was a rigorous thinker who was able to work systematically and methodically on long-term projects. He also had an uncanny ability to stay close to his own stream of experience, describe it faithfully, and turn each nuance into an important distinction. His approach was always a descriptive one and he kept pushing his descriptive methodology deeper and deeper into the obscure regions of experience. This was but a natural outcome of Husserl's program.

Husserl, as a logician and mathematician, was always a believer in universal, objective knowledge, but he was also interested in trying to understand how it was possible for humans to accomplish such absolute truths. Briefly sketched, we could say that in his first work of 1890, *The Philosophy of Arithmetic,* Husserl related objective achievements to the experiential acts of consciousness of the individual thinker. This justly made him vulnerable to the charge of psychologism. Consequently, Husserl began again in the *Logical Investigations* and tried to discern in consciousness a subject-object correlation that would transcend the acts of individual consciousness and thus clear him of any possible psychologistic critique. This he demonstrated by showing that an individual meaning could be the object of several different acts of an individual consciousness and thus the meaning could not be exclusively dependent upon them, and by developing a transcendental theory of consciousness that went beyond psychological reality. Most importantly, in the process of clarifying these problems, Husserl developed a method for analyzing the manner in which anything that is given to consciousness can be described and analyzed. That is what made possible a program of research on an infinite set of problems.

However, all of the above pertains to philosophy. Regardless of what the descriptive terms may be, the problems are philosophical ones and the methods devised to solve them are philosophical methods. But since phenomenology began as descriptive psychology and since the development of both disciplines has been intertwined in the twentieth century, many scholars have expected much from phenomenological psychology. It was thought that psychology would finally receive its adequate grounding in phenomenological thought. There have been such attempts, of course, but they have not taken hold across the discipline. The major difficulty was that there was no method.

For a long time, the phenomenological contribution to psychology was a theoretical critique of mainstream psychology's concepts and practice. However, the constructive alternative implied in such a critique was never articulated. It seemed, therefore, that phenomenological psychology was simply another version of the "armchair psychology" that contemporary psychology had just overcome with its labs and tests. This interpretation was reinforced by the phenomenologists' emphasis—especially while the movement was still an exclusive property of European scholars during the first sixty years of this century—on the idea of eidetic analyses and their removal from empirics. Since the sixties, however, and since existential and phenomenological thought took hold in America, a way of uniting empirical descriptions with phenomenological analyses has been developed both in therapeutic and research situations. In therapy there is the work of Rollo May and Eugene Gendlin and in research there is the work initiated at Duquesne University and, most recently, at the University of Michigan and the University of Alberta. Since these movements were initiated, the Utrecht School in Holland has been revivified along empirical lines as well.

Of course, as with traditional psychology, phenomenological psychology will need a family of methods that is as responsive to the many facets of psychological phenomena as the diversity of the field manifests. Only when this set of practices with its multiple procedures is in existence and ready-to-hand, can one speak confidently of the arrival of a mature phenomenological psychology on the psychological scene. That is why we welcome this work by Ken Shapiro that introduces another way to do empirically grounded phenomenological psychological research.

We said above that Husserl kept pushing descriptions to more obscure regions of experience. Shapiro bases his method on our ability to detect what is going on in one of these obscure areas, namely, our own bodies. Of course, following Merleau-Ponty, the body is understood here to be the "body-subject" and not the biological or physiological body. The "body-subject" is consciousness in its embodied mode. But it is still consciousness; thus Shapiro argues, it is capable of reflection and, indeed, it is the ground even of the obvious reflecting power of fully awake consciousness. Unlike most philosophers, Shapiro is sensitive to the fact that it is the nuances of our body that we must be in touch with, rather than our minds, if we are to do justice to psychological phenomena. The work of the mind begins at a later stage. Shapiro's contribution is to interpret these bodily nuances as forms of reflection that can reveal the meaning of psychological lived processes.

Shapiro realizes that the body-subject as a reflecting process is still an elusive phenomenon that resists easy analysis. Nevertheless, he presses on descriptively with a phenomenology of reflection until he is able to articulate, at least partially, how the body-subject is sensitive both to the atmosphere and structure of a situation and then how bodily reflection can grasp these aspects because they are appropriated by the body in its bearing, attitude, and potential for movement. The actual carrying out of this process

Shapiro calls "forming," which he describes as a "mode of experience that answers the call to be done implicit in a sense of structure by doing it." Thus bodily reflection can virtually enact the sense of a phenomenon and grasp it. The task of penetrating reflection was also facilitated theoretically by reinterpreting structures of experience in such a way that they could be made potential objects of experience rather than things external to experience or hidden so below it that they are inaccessible to analysis. Finally, Shapiro sets himself the challenging task of actually applying his method to an experientially elusive phenomenon—namely, ambivalence—and he comments on what he is doing as he proceeds. This manner of explicating his method seems to me to be highly successful.

Just how well interested psychologists will be able to practice the method Shapiro has presented by simply reading about it remains to be seen. The important point is that another variation of phenomenological psychological method has been introduced to the scholarly community. Ultimately, like all methods, its success will depend upon how well it can be applied, elaborated, extended, and even modified as various phenomenological psychologists attempt to probe the phenomena whose secrets they are trying to unlock. But it is a welcome addition to the expanding repertoire of phenomenological procedures.

Amedeo Giorgi
Duquesne University

This essay presents a phenomenological method for psychology based on a sensitivity to the experience of one's own body. In it I will show that recourse to the bodily sense of a situation is a possible and effective strategy in the attempt to recapture and explicate experience.

We are all familiar with dramatic moments when our bodily experience catches us by surprise: the way our heart stops and stomach sinks at the first ring of the telephone, even before we say to ourself that it is that long-awaited call; the way we are touched by a work of art, sometimes to the point of tears; the way our body anticipates the opponent's return on the tennis court and takes us to an advantageous position for the next shot. It would seem obvious that examining these bodily experiences would be helpful in a study of phenomena such as anticipatory anxiety, being "touched" or moved, and the mastery of complex athletic skills. However, it will be the burden of what follows to demonstrate that any human phenomenon has a bodily correlate, the rediscovery and exploitation of which can contribute to its study. Methods based on bodily experience need not be limited to moments when the bodily aspect stands out so poignantly as in these examples.

The intended audience of this essay is investigators in any of the social sciences seeking to broaden their approach to include phenomenological methods—sociology, anthropology, and history, as well as psychology. Several fields have already developed such complements to experimentalism. While this essay is more methodological than philosophical, it would be of interest to those philosophers studying the problem of the reconceptualization of the body.

Several contexts make the provision of a phenomenological method founded in bodily knowledge timely. In the past decade the study of language and the development of linguistic methods have increasingly been in the ascendant in virtually all fields. Often accompanying their focus on language is an assertion of the primary and pervasive influence of language in experience. By contrast, following the philosopher Maurice Merleau-Ponty, I will argue the position that meaning and understanding are originally bodily. Part of their being bodily is that they occur prelinguistically, before language and before reflective conceptualization. I will take very seriously the "wisdom" of the body as a possible guide both to how we engage ourselves in action and to how we eventually explicate in language what we already have been meaningfully living.

More generally, these language-centered methods often include a frontal attack on other mainstays of phenomenology such as the existence and importance of "presence." Roughly, this is the notion that meaning is immanent in immediate experience before the mediation of language or the distance of reflection. They also give a less determinative role to the subject or self than does phenomenology typically. For example, a poststructuralism associated with Jacques Derrida adopts the view that experience and its products from the outset are texts to be read.[1] The individual, an author for example, in this view is merely the vehicle of a particular moment in the historical evolution of meaning, of changes in language and concepts.

The present study opposes these developments directly. It rests on the assertion of an immediate, prelinguistic meaning in experience. In concert with Merleau-Ponty's position that the body and behavior are bearers of meaning,[2] I describe how meaning is known both immediately and reflectively by the body. I am the subject or agent in that I am a lived body. I am not lost in language, my meaningful intentions somehow irrecoverable in or superseded by texts, so much as any text, experience, cultural artifact, or historical moment consists in bodily intentions—both those it once invited and those it currently calls forth.

A second context supports the present approach and its pre-suppositions. A major shift in modern psychotherapy is its current emphasis on the body. Earlier systems of psychotherapy capitalized on the intellective and the verbal domains of experience, finding in them the primary motor for change. The psychoanalyst encouraged the patient to produce associative chains while he, the therapist, provided an integration of them by interpreting their meaning and connections. The Rogerian "reflected" the client's statement, turning it back on him to further his sense of and acceptance of himself. In recent times these "talk therapies" have been complemented by the emergence of "body therapies." [3] Increasingly, therapist interventions include pointing to gestures to develop the further assimilation of aspects of self or to enhance awareness of communications by the body, "body language"; or identifying, in some therapies physically manipulating, certain postures to unblock energy or to release hostility or sadness; or designing breathing and movement exercises toward similar ends; or directing the representation of personal or familial relations by positioning other persons' bodies.

The existence of therapeutic interventions at the level of the body that clarify and even modify the way a person lives corroborates the centrality in experience of the bodily modes that I will be examining. By describing how the body as we live it can bear affect and meaning, texture and structure, I hope to provide an intelligible explanation of the power of these interventions. It is striking to note, incidentally, certain parallel developments in the histories of psychotherapy and of phenomenology—from the "head" to the body, from the word to action and expressive motion, from a premature reliance on discursive thought and verbal modes to the possibility of lingering effectively in the prelinguistic regions of the bodily.

To some degree the direction of this task has already been indicated in the work of Eugene Gendlin.[4] More than any other contemporary thinker he has sought to clarify the role of the experience of the body, particularly in the setting of psychotherapy. He has described a way of doing therapy wherein the client is directed to "focus" on his or her bodily sense of situations. Through this focus the quality of the client's experience is vitalized; it is given body, if you will. The client moves beyond intellectualized and congealed understandings to a fresh sense of his life situation. For Gendlin, this attitude of "being in touch" is the critical condition for change in most forms of contemporary psychotherapy. He has offered empirical evidence supporting this contention. In his major work, *Experiencing and the Creation of Meaning,* he reconceived the body in a way that makes intelligible its important relation to personal growth and authenticity, and to the explication of meaning, the move to language.

It is on this last relation that the present method builds. It is my contention that attention to the body is a key to doing phenomenology as well as to the advance of personal meaning. I will describe how, through a bodily focus, an individual can explicate those structures of a given phenomenon that make it part of our common experience in a particular culture and in a particular era. Further, to Gendlin's emphasis on immediately felt or sensed bodily experience, I will add a description of the bodily aspects of our experience of movement or behavior.

A third context issues from a view of recent advances in the method of phenomenological psychology, which I shall critically review in the first chapter. In fact, the initial impulse to undertake this project was aroused by a felt lack in the method of phenomenological psychology. It is agreed in the literature of phenomenology that the center of a phenomenological method of inquiry must be reflection. While traditional data-gathering methods and the logical moves associated with experimentalism, such as deduction, induction, hypothesis testing, falsification, and the like, may play some part in a phenomenological method, that role must be an ancillary one and preparatory to a reliance on reflection. Only through reflection can the ultimate concern of phenomenology, faithfulness to the way phenomena appear in experience, be vouchsafed.

As the center of this method, then, reflection is the phenomenon most critically and perennially in need of explication. For a number of reasons that will be elucidated later, the literature does not provide that requisite account. Further, I believe it important that this phenomenology of reflection, which the field needs continually to augment, must be spelled out at the concrete level of its application, that is, as a method. To sustain a method for a viable social science we must not rely exclusively on systematic philosophic accounts, for they can only suggest or locate a method in general terms. While Merleau-Ponty's philosophy of experience as lived body–lived world is the most solid foundation to me as phenomenological psychologist, it does not tell me how to proceed. While on the other hand phenomenology cannot be method-centered, for its first allegiance is to the phenomenon, there is a possible middle ground. In the present essay I hope to provide an explicit description of method at the level of practice. I will try to show how an investigator can avail himself or herself of reflective modes and moves that are largely explicable in terms of a phenomenology of the body.

Of course, by the body I do not refer to that object of study of the anatomist or physiologist. Rather, I intend that body which is the embodiment of our consciousness. It is that body through which we live in the world, through which we know and affect the world, and, in turn, appreciate its effect on us. It is my connection to the world and how I am in the world. For example, at any moment I am in a certain mood that has a bodily aspect— as when my stomach is churning or fluttering. This mood and a correlative atmosphere, a tension in the air, affect and are affected by, constitute and are constituted by, my current situation. This bodily aspect is sometimes figural, as when I notice the butter-flies in my stomach. More typically, it is a background that is only known indirectly as a certain atmosphere, the tension in the air. However, at any moment I can be sensitive to that bodily aspect directly. Doing so is one way to begin to explicate that tense atmosphere. Hence it is a clue to the method of inquiry I shall present in this essay.

The body's appearance is by no means limited to ways I am being affected. At any moment I also have a bodily sense, whether figural or tacit, of the kind of space I am in (in a crowd or in a tight spot), or of the temporal frame (the burden of a recent loss or disappointment, or the buoying sense of a coming chal-lenge). Somewhat more subtly, any situation also invites me to take a certain course of action, to move in a certain way with respect to it that also has a bodily aspect (the tennis game, but no less the door, the typewriter, and your implicit invitation). Any relationship, whether human or nonhuman, is in part appre-ciated and known bodily. (I feel small and fragile vis-à-vis your dominance or stupid and slow approaching the new computer.) What I am suggesting is that the more direct recovery of these bodily aspects can be the basis of a portable, readily accessible, and powerful phenomenological method.

Further, I contend that certain bodily modes that directly intend these bodily aspects are the way the effective phenomenological investigator already proceeds. Explicit description of these as a method has awaited the lifting of certain prejudices such as the hypervaluation of the role of language and within phenomenology itself an overreliance on certain terms such as *intuition* which have remained packed. It has also awaited the establishment of a clearing within the conceptual thicket concealing the experience of our bodies.

To make the richness of the referent of that experience more graphic in these prefatory remarks, consider a performance by the French mime Marcel Marceau. With grace and economy that artful body creates objects, characters, and scenes—Marceau as David in the confrontation with Goliath, or as the wall of a prison, or as the circus performer on the high wire. Through the movement and protean form of his body he conjures a common world in which we can readily join him. Clearly, there is "knowledge in the body" at work here, but in what sense is this bodily knowledge prelinguistic? Is not Marceau's rendering of the wall merely a sign or symbol of a wall given in a language that consists of bodily signals rather than words? My position will be that Marceau gives us neither a symbol for wall nor, obviously, the object, a wall itself. Through the immediately meaningful movement of his body he invokes in us our own correlate of the experience of a wall. He shows us that implicit bodily sense of being at or up against the wall, of being trapped. That bodily sense is the way in which we originally lived and knew what it it was to be imprisoned.

While I generally must *see* his performance, the modality through which I am enabled to join him so fully is more akin to a kinesthetic empathy. I comprehend through my own bodily sense of the phenomenon. Haven't we all had the experience of being trapped in some way? In that I continually bear such bodily knowledge I have the potential to virtually enact a particular phenomenon—to create its space, relationships, and world without Marceau's aid. I shall show that the product of that enactment is a critical step in the explication of any given phenomenon.

A final context, although a personal one, may help orient some readers to phenomenology and my approach to it. Our experience of the body is generally of a backdrop or background. Since we typically live through the body to the objects of our world, our body itself remains implicit or tacit. It has been said that we "pass over" the body to "realize the landscape" but that in doing so the body informs that landscape or world. It has occurred to me that my research efforts on three apparently unrelated topics address a common underlying phenomenon—the tacit in experience. The presence of tacit significance, of experience's meaningfulness before it is explicitly captured in symbol or sign, has been and remains numinous for me, to employ a Jungian term. Each topic studied can be seen as a way of answering a particular question in regard to it. In my work on introversion an early attraction to the implicit keyed on the richness and opacity of its meaningfulness.[5] The introvert associates that richness with himself and he becomes the "object" to which he is oriented. In a second study, on elusiveness, I was impressed by the way the implicit is always beyond my reach, how I can never make it fully transparent.[6]

In the present essay I approach the implicit in experience by asking the question, How is it meaningful? Beginning with the lived moment, what is the nature of the object of experience, what is my relation to it, and by what modes do I apprehend it that allows its initial upsurge to be a meaningful one? From this first spectacle, how does the implicit allow an explication of itself? Here my inquiry is intense, searching, almost microscopic. It is not a simple matter of engagement immediately giving way to reflection, of an intention to mean realizing its meaning in one leap. The ways we understand are multiple and varied. To dichotomize them into two coarsely adhering lumps, the implicit and the explicit, would be a misleading if not a violent misappropriation. I intend rather to describe some of the complex and transient but distinguishable significant moments and modes as they appear. I anticipate that these ways of understanding will then emerge as a rich journey from the initial vague solicitation of the meaningful in any moment, to the incipient intention to grasp it more firmly, to the ways I begin to maintain access to it as lived; to moments in which it is first bodily felt and bodily reenacted, to its objectification anew as a reflective product of this bodily understanding, and, finally, to its expression through metaphor and language.

The plan of the book is as follows, by chapter:

1. *Introductory Concerns.* I provide a set of definitions, theses, and claims.

2. *The Method, Part 1: Reflection as Bodily Abstraction.* A bodily reflective mode that, although less critical to a phenomenological method, is more accessible and readily characterized, is described.

3. *Concepts of Structure.* Beginning with Lévi-Strauss, I describe critically one end of a spectrum of views of the locus of structure and correlative methods of its explication. The views are organized primarily in terms of the internality or externality of structure to experience.

4. *Toward a Phenomenology of Structure.* I present the possibility of structure's presence in experience through a consideration of Husserl and an original reading of Piaget.

5. *The Method, Part 2: Reflection as an Enactment of Structure.* I present this through, first, a comparison with more mundane modes such as perception, imagination, and behavior, and second, through a genetic phenomenology of the modes. This last begins with the description of a mode of apprehension of the immediate presence of structure in the lived moment, then of modes by which it is abstracted and prolonged, and, finally, a mode by which I make structure a focal object, thereby allowing this still prelinguistic formulation to guide me to language and metaphor.

6. *The Method in Practice.* I provide an example of the method by applying these modes to the phenomenon of ambivalence.

Acknowledgments

The primary individual to whom I owe acknowledgment is Maurice Merleau-Ponty whose philosophy initially inspired me to seek complements and alternatives to the experimental approach to the social sciences and provided me with the main metaphor guiding that effort.

I would like also to thank Eugene T. Gendlin whose work was also a strong influence and who offered me support in this project.

Others who read and criticized parts of the manuscript include David Kolb, Joseph Lyons, Bob Moyer, Howard Pollio, and Bob Romanyshyn.

I am indebted to Sylvia Hawks for typing and retyping various drafts of the manuscript over an extended period.

Kenneth J. Shapiro

Bodily Reflective Modes

To understand is to experience the harmony between what we aim at and what is given. . . . and the body is our anchorage in a world.
MAURICE MERLEAU-PONTY

If we do not have the felt meaning of the concept, we haven't got the concept at all. EUGENE T. GENDLIN

I regard knowing as an active comprehension of the things known, an action that requires skill. MICHAEL POLANYI

For we do live in space, and there is no physical, nor even spiritual, affair which does not enact itself in space. J. H. VAN DEN BERG

1

Introductory Concerns

THE PROBLEM OF METHOD IN
PHENOMENOLOGICAL PSYCHOLOGY—A SURVEY

Since recent advances in the method of phenomenological psychology are in part the occasion for the present contribution to phenomenological method, the background to those advances provides a convenient starting point. The history of phenomenological psychology began with an extended period of critiques of the predominantly positivistic approach of academic psychology. These largely prescriptive and programmatic efforts railed against that approach to psychology for the reductionism inherent in its objectivistic investigative stance, a product of its, from phenomenology's view, misdirected desire to ally itself with the natural sciences. For the phenomenologist this association maligns the person as an experiencing being in that it seeks to exteriorize experience, to naturalize it, to portray it as it would appear from nowhere or from everywhere, forgetting the individual and situated perspective in which it is given. In the works of this period the phenomenologist argues for a reconstruction of psychology as a human science that would restore the integrity of experience and, thereby, of the person.[1] Undergirding this general critique is the view that a psychology built on the stilts of a Cartesian dualism requires regrounding. It is argued that this divided base accounts for psychology's various leanings, all necessarily overcorrective and precarious, from the subjectless world of behaviorism to the worldless subjectivity of some "depth" psychologies. At this level of philosophical tenets, the phenomenologist offers the possibility of crossing the great divide, the Cartesian legacy, through a notion of experience as being-in-the-world, as an embodied consciousness, and, thereby, transcending such dichotomous categorial distinctions as physical/mental, objective/subjective, and behavioral (in a behavioristic sense)/experiential (in a prephenomenological sense).

This early work attacks the prevailing natural scientific or experimental paradigm through this critique and through appeal to a presumedly shared evaluation that human experience is diminished by that approach. In this way, the "normal science" supported by the traditional empirical paradigm in psychology might be shown exhausted, to have encountered "puzzles" it cannot solve, "anomalies" for which it cannot adequately account.[2] The relatively monolithic approach of positivistic science might make way for, or at least make room for, a paradigm based on an existential-phenomenological perspective.

After and to some extent overlapping this initial period devoted to critique, to the introduction of its own "concepts" (in the new paradigm, "constitutive features of human experience"), and to reformulations of the subfields of traditional psychology for the new perspective,[3] phenomenological psychology increasingly left its armchairing position. It began to generate solutions to the problems to which it gave currency, to constitute its own normal science. At present, the literature in phenomenological psychology consists primarily of substantive contributions; the phenomenologist plies his own product.

Its content reveals more concretely the components of the dissatisfaction of the psychologist who would be a phenomenologist, a clarification of what was missing for him from the products of established psychology. In this growing body of literature the phenomenologist studies the taken-for-granted, the sedimented and commonplace aspects of experience, and lifts them out so that we may recognize them, research them, approach them afresh, in a sense know them for the first time. For example, F. M. Buckley describes the sense of being "at-home," [4] an important aspect of daily experience which we seldom posit. In a related but more problematic area, he studies phenomena that bear a theoretical burden, phenomena stretched out on a theoretical frame, reified as constructs which forget their original referents as lived. For example, W. F. Fischer takes us back to a more immediate sense of anxiety, before its theoretical association with energy, impulse, defense, or repression.[5] Impelled by a third phenomenological thrust, the investigator also "discovers" and discloses aspects of experience gone unnoticed, the subtle or intangible, the ephemeral or transitional. My study of elusiveness is an example of this. Or he attempts to approach the aberrant, the "pathological," the fringes of experience to which most of us have only limited if any access. For example, A. Burton provides a description of schizophrenia as a way of life.[6] Or he explicates "new" phenomena, aspects of experience that are historical emergents or at least that have become more salient in a particular era. J. H. van den Berg makes this claim about certain forms of neurosis.[7]

A final area, research on research, functions partly in the service of the critique of the experimental paradigm. By applying a phenomenological perspective to the situation of the experiment, to the research itself,[8] and to the experience of the subject,[9] the phenomenologist demonstrates the tunnel vision of the official view, the arbitrariness and artificiality of taking "data" as the only object to be understood. Part of this critique, also, is the assertion that a paradigm cannot examine itself. Research on research within the experimental paradigm, it is argued, simply isolates more variables, which, then, may be controlled or may be themselves the object of experimental manipulation.[10] Such research cannot be a genuine self-examination for it presumes precisely what must be held in question—its own approach. Consequently, rather than reforming itself, it results in additional content, more variables constituted and functioning within the paradigm as any other variable. But beyond a further strategy in its critique, this area of the phenomenological literature can explicate phenomena important in their own right: epistemological concerns such as the experience of being understood or of gaining certainty of understanding;[11] generative and investigative postures; the structure of the interpersonal relation between investigator and investigated.

The sine qua non of all of this work is the regulative ideal that it return us to, evoke, and firmly grasp through its description the phenomenon as lived. On the face of it it would seem that the phenomenologist's product can be judged within this concern. But it also can and must be judged for its espousal of this concern. Of course, to make this judgment requires a perspective outside the existential-phenomenological one. While this judgment awaits the construction of yet another viewing platform,[12] I offer here a brief and personal comparative evaluation, between the products of the experimental and the phenomenological approaches. From a point of view of personal satisfaction and edification, the evaluation falls along the following lines.

The most successful phenomenological study changes me and my view of the world by locating aspects of my experience formerly disembodied or dim or misconstrued. I subsequently "see" that phenomenon in my experience as if for the first time, or I am more affected by it, or I see it differently. The structure of my world as I live it has changed. An occasional experimental study locates a relationship between two or more conditions (phenomena that have been objectified or operationalized) of which I was unaware or held to be other than the relation that obtained. In such a case, despite the lack of direct explication of the phenomena, I now experience that connection in the world and may live toward it differently. Often, however, even if the relation is novel to me, I do not find it credible, for the operationalization, instrumentation, nature of statistical inference, and logic of the experimental situation all appear as impediments—as a sophisticated set of strategies that unintentionally construct a world that, being ingrown, can never reach, let alone illuminate, mundane reality.

The phenomenological study has its own pitfall, a negative reaction induced that is peculiar to it. Particularly the less effective study, although it is to some degree a response inherent in the approach, touches me briefly but then is quickly forgotten. Reading it engenders a kind of "high" as I find that to which it is pointing; but it does not truly inform me. The evocation, the arousal, is there but without any furthering of my sense of the phenomenon. I doubt that I live that aspect of experience or experiencing differently as a result of my reading. There has been no gain in understanding of the structure of the experience for me and hence no change in how I live it. The impact of the study on me is like that of eating a certain cuisine, delectable in the act but not ultimately filling.

Given the importance of the criterion in phenomenological psychology that the description be faithful to the phenomenon as lived, recent literature in phenomenological psychology increasingly has addressed questions of method. Through what investigative stance and procedure am I assured that this criterion of faithfulness is met?

Until recently, a typical phenomenological investigator limited himself to what is now called an "individual reflection." [13] By recourse to his own experience he attempts to "return to the thing itself" and then, through a series of reflections, to explicate the structure of that prereflective appearance, its constitutive features. This is a journey familiar to phenomenologists and I shall describe it more fully in various contexts later. My point here is that reflection, itself the vehicle of that itinerary, remained largely unexplicated in this literature. The focus of recent methodological advances has been an examination, buttressing, and systematization or even standardization of the investigator's "own experience." Formerly, an investigator relied on his own experience, his own personal run-ins with the phenomenon of interest, poignant moments of its presence to him. To allow this return, he stripped away postreflective theoretical layerings and sedimented cultural and linguistic habits—again, a familiar enterprise in the writings of Husserl and others. Having gained a prereflective view of the phenomenon of interest, he then made explicit his own personal perspective on it to arrive at its more general structure.

A retrospective view of studies of these early and middle periods in the brief history of phenomenological psychology suggests that the weight given in them to the dissolution of theoretical and cultural accretions was a necessary concomitant of the introduction of an alien existential-phenomenological perspective and critique into the heartland of an objectivistic psychology. This center now has shifted as both general and phenomenon-specific critiques have revealed the typical style of the objectivistic mode, its peculiar idealization of a phenomenon as a "thing" within the Cartesian dualism, and certain subjectivistic correctives, notably the construction of a fantastic region of "mental things." A general familiarity with the style of these constructs allows the investigator to more readily dispense with these theoretical layerings. Both he and his reader have become familiar with the ways various psychologies, for example, behaviorism and cognitive psychology, "lose" the phenomenon as lived. As a result he is able to replace the dialectic between the theoretical and the prereflective with a dialectic between his own experience and other persons' experience of a particular phenomenon. The methodological focus shifts to devices that might supplement his own experience, that upon which he eventually reflects to reach the structure of the phenomenon as lived.

The literature of phenomenological psychology refers to this development as a turn to an empirical phenomenology.[14] The use of the term *empirical* is problematic. It cannot refer to recourse to experience as opposed to theory, since phenomenology always is necessarily that. The more modern usage, as an adjective descriptive of methods that facilitate such recourse, again necessarily embraces a phenomenological method since it has a similar concern. Rather, the term is employed to refer to methods that are characteristic of the particular ways current scientific methods go back to or gather experience (data) as distinguished from the ways of a phenomenological method. Empirical phenomenology borrows with modifications certain data-generating and -gathering techniques from that tradition, partly motivated to effect a working relation with it. Following a period of confrontation and critique, phenomenological psychology apparently feels secure enough about the distinctiveness and significance of its own position to examine objectivistic psychology with an eye to adoptions from it to serve its own ends.

More broadly, this development bespeaks a more positive strategy—from the tactic of defining itself through its critique of objectivistic psychology to that of approaching any material, theoretical or substantive, worldly or laboratory bred, in order to extract from it whatever experiential truth it might contain. From this point of view any text, whether experimental study, theoretical construct, clinical lore, or personality theory, despite the approach or paradigm from which it issues, may be scrutinized for its experiential bedrock. For example, one might review theories, traditionally accumulated empirical data, and clinical lore on anxiety to locate in it approximate descriptions of that phenomenon as lived. The reorientation in this strategy is a subtle one. The earlier approach treated the product of any theory or study for which it could lay bare an objectivistic or dualistic set of presuppositions purely as an encumbrance to leave behind.

Instead, it is possible for this critical analysis to function as a dialogue that aids in the location and description of the experiential referent of interest. An investigator approaches the text open to the likelihood that, notwithstanding its reductionistic treatment of it, it still retains some relation to the phenomenon as lived. A reading of the text, then, is a likely occasion for evoking and advancing the phenomenological investigator's as yet unexplicated sense of the phenomenon.[15]

It is a short step from this use of extant materials or texts to methods whereby the investigator generates his own, from this transitional empiricism to what is a more genuine data-gathering empiricism. Now he can supplement his own experience through these concrete and, from an objectivistic perspective, tried and true empirical procedures. He can construct "situations" and exercises which more or less evoke the phenomenon of interest. Then, he can obtain descriptions of other people's experience of that phenomenon through interviews, questionnaires, or the like. Once the investigator moves from exclusive reliance on his own experience to a concern for other persons' perspectives on the phenomenon, the methodological gambits open to him are vast and again call on those methods developed by psychology the laboratory science. To study the experience of learning, he can place people in a situation that demands that they learn a task.[16]

The investigator provides a circumstance or task intended to generate an experience of the phenomenon of interest. He then orchestrates each participant's return to that moment, for example, through a semistructured interview. In effect, the investigator teaches his subjects to do phenomenology, to locate and to describe a phenomenon recently lived through. He can ask what it was like for them to have just learned something.

There are clear gains here in the compellingness of the procedure, although the final test of any phenomenological study is the effectiveness of its description to advance the reader's sense of the phenomenon. The use of an evocative task or "situation" gives more immediate access to the phenomenon of interest. Further, it diminishes dependence on language to locate the phenomenon. In earlier studies the investigator might have asked the subject for examples of his or her experience of learning. In effect a word, "learning," was given the burden of the initial location of its felt-meaning. Only then could the sense of the phenomenon lead the way to a fresh explication, to other words. More recently the investigator, while still employing discourse to direct the subject, is not fully dependent on a common signifier. He can more or less point to the phenomenon, as it was likely occasioned by the contrived circumstance. He has provided a moment of learning for the subject. The use of the evocative occasion seemingly does some of the work of the stripping away of linguistic and theoretical accretions accomplished in earlier studies through the investigator's reflective moves, phenomenological and eidetic *epoches*. Individuals, including the investigator, now have more direct and concrete access to a phenomenon as lived. Presumably this lessens the distortions of encapsulation in certain favored linguistic categories, and of the reliance on habitual ways of understanding the kind of phenomenon. The use of other people, while borrowed from traditional empirical psychology, is modified. The subject is treated as truly that, as a subject rather than as an object, as only a source of data. He is not "run" through the investigator's paraphernalia and measured on already constituted dimensions or variables. The relationship of subject and investigator approaches that of coinvestigators, as the subject is given the opportunity to describe his own experience in a relatively open dialogue.

To establish a social science as this more freewheeling enterprise of mutual participation is consonant with the goal of attempts from various quarters, notably the third wave, to humanize psychology. Within phenomenological psychology it represents a move away from total reliance on the investigator, on his peculiar and personal sense of a given phenomenon. While the investigator is always informed in his own experience by the experience of others as one horizon of his own perspective, here those other perspectives are available to him more directly. Particularly as he seeks to facilitate the other person's explication of his experience, he can empathically realize other perspectives and eventually a more intersubjective and a less idiosyncratic formulation of the phenomenon.

There is clearly a gain here toward a more likely acceptance of the phenomenological study into traditional empirical circles. From that point of view, the phenomenologist may be said for the first time to be "doing studies." He has moved out of his armchair into the laboratory. The use of subjects in dialogue with the investigator makes the phenomenologist's procedure more public, more "observable," less mystifying. Of course, this entrance into the world of interviews and questionnaires opens the phenomenologist as empiricist to a host of problems associated with these data-gathering techniques in empirical psychology. At the same time, the phenomenologist settles, in the experimentalist's view, for soft and fuzzy findings at best. More critically, these tactics, the evocative situation and the assay of subjects' experiences through interviews or questionnaires and the extraction, thematic analysis, and collation of this material, do not free the investigator from an ultimate reliance on reflection. However aided, his final move must be a reflection on the lived presence of constitutive features of the phenomenon of interest. An empirical phenomenological psychology is obviously not simply a controlled method of content, thematic, or even structural analysis. However creative and sophisticated these evolving data-gathering techniques, they cannot replace reflection. For it is reliance on reflective postures which defines the methodological departure of phenomenological psychology from the objectivism of the dominant natural scientific method.

In sum, then, while I read these methodological incursions as ground gained, largely by omission they highlight the critical problem in any phenomenological approach—the provision of a description of reflection. Although not denying the centrality of reflection, these methodological advances do not provide an adequate account of reflection as a way of experiencing, or of reflective modes for explicating phenomena.

More subtly, they begin to imply their own displacements from the pivotal position of reflection in doing phenomenology. In particular they enhance our ability to evoke a phenomenon of interest, partly by utilizing procedures from traditional empirical psychology. Further, they add the participation and the contribution of other individuals and their experience in the investigatory procedure. In these ways phenomenological psychology both becomes more public, by operating more directly in an intersubjective realm and availing itself of intersubjective checks, *and* accomplishes a rapprochment with natural scientific psychology. However, the danger in the former is the substitution of description by consensus for description through reflective dialogue with the phenomenon as lived. The latter threatens to accept (or give the impression of accepting) operationalizations or situational concomitants of a phenomenon as criteria for its "presence" rather than its actual presence in experience. The touchstone for a phenomenological method must be a reflective posture through which I experience myself engaged in a particular phenomenon while I am looking at myself so experiencing. Let me be clear that the literature has not provided a description of this methodologically critical way of experiencing reflectively.

What does it mean to reflect; what is this peculiar posture or attitude or mode of experiencing; how do I assume it; how do I describe it as a method? Rather than providing a systematic description of reflection, a phenomenology of reflection, this literature typically either defers to philosophical literature or offers only brief and facile treatments of reflection. These latter key on and overuse terms such as "dialogue with the phenomenon," leaving them packed and unexplicated. For the traditional psychologist this results either in a view that reflection is mysterious, metaphysical, and inaccessible, and therefore unscientific, or, at the other extreme, in a view that it plays no critical role in phenomenology, that this peculiar empirical phenomenology is merely some watered-down laboratory-based method of content analysis.

When I turn to the philosophical literature it does not offer the requisite treatment of reflection or of method more generally. The classical descriptions are not readily applicable to phenomenological psychology and particularly to the evolving enterprise that I have been describing. A primary intent of the present work is to avoid the twin dangers to a phenomenological psychology—its assimilation into the dominant natural scientific perspective and its continued alienation as a somewhat obscure and "philosophical" field of inquiry. My reading of its current position and needs suggests that this can be accomplished through an exposition of reflection at a level that fits snugly between phenomenology's origins in philosophy and its offshoots in psychology and other disciplines.

The literature is not without efforts in this direction. In his monumental account of the history of the phenomenological movement in philosophy, H. Spiegelberg describes a reflective procedure on a concrete level that is readily understandable and applicable to a phenomenological psychology.[17] Although it is helpful as an approach to the operation of reflective postures, it has problems that stem not from Spiegelberg's presentation but from his primary source, Husserl's rendering of reflection. As I will show, Husserl's description equivocates and even misapprehends reflection to varying degrees, particularly in regard to *noesis,* his own term for way or mode of experiencing. There are also problems in his identification and exposition of the essence of the object, the *noema,* which reflection intends, although his description of this is clearer.

R. D. Laing and D. G. Cooper[18] provide a similar service with respect to Sartre's contribution to the elucidation of reflection by rendering his critique of the dialectic in concrete contexts such as social psychology and psychotherapy. Again this is helpful in bridging the gap between the use of reflection as a means of examining traditional philosophical concerns such as ontology and epistemology, and a more applied use, the explication of particular phenomena in a phenomenological psychology. However, the emphasis here and elsewhere in recent existential phenomenological philosophy on various versions of the dialectic fails, from my perspective, to provide a clear referent for reflection. The predominant approach has been to define reflection as sets of systematically variable relations of the investigator to the phenomenon, such as Sartre's interiority/exteriority/totalization sequence of shifts in perspective and level, and the double negation so masterfully executed in the writing of Merleau-Ponty. To describe reflection is to explicate these particular relations of investigator to phenomenon and the changes in them that constitute a dialectic.

This focus on the dialectic aspect of reflection, while helpful, describes where I move, my itinerary as investigator, but not how I move, the requisite vehicle of my movement. I demand a description of the reflective moves and how I can assume them. Following Merleau-Ponty, I take the lived body to be precisely the requisite vehicle. This essay may be viewed in part as serving the same function for Merleau-Ponty as Spiegelberg's work does for Husserl and as Laing and Cooper's do for Sartre. While my strategy in approaching reflection is Husserlian in that it emphasizes the way an object appears and its correlative mode of apprehension, the particular modes to be described are derived from a reading of Merleau-Ponty. In his descriptives, "living through" and "taking up," in his notions of a motor physiognomy and of a motor space, and, more generally, in his ontology of the lived body—lived object, of consciousness incarnate, we will find metaphors as well as a foundation for the present theses about reflection.

DEFINITIONS

In this section I provide definitions of some of the key terms in what is to follow. From them I can then move, still in an introductory way, to a glimpse of the method and to a presentation of the theses and claims upon which the method is built. More precisely, the definitions are an indication of how terms will be used in this text. In the main, the usage is consistent with, or at least in the spirit of, the philosophical tradition, particularly the writings of Husserl and Merleau-Ponty. However, I make no claim that taken together they constitute or even belong to any one systematic philosophy. In the final analysis, my claim is only that this selection of terms and their usage is descriptively faithful to the modes, moves, and postures of the method as they appear in experience.

Phenomenology is a rigorous and systematic attempt to explicate the meanings of experience. The guiding ideal of a phenomenological method is to develop a description of a given experience while remaining faithful to the appearance of that experience as it is in the living of it. The *implicit* or tacit in experience refers to the meanings of an experience that have not yet been put into words (*explicated*). *Tacit knowledge* is the immediate understanding of an experience before it has been explicated. The *lived moment* or lived experience is the plenum of meanings in any moment of experience prior to their explication. *Presence* refers to the immanence of those meanings, to the fact that meaningfulness appears immediately, without the mediation of language or thought.

Experience is a system in part constituted by my body as I live through it to participate in (or take up or be at) objects in the world. It is a two-pole unity of this body as I live it (the *lived body*) and the world as it is constituted through my participation in it (the *lived world*). A situation is any such coconstituted moment. It is coconstituted in that it is the product of both the potential object's invitation and the way my body takes it up. A *phenomenon* is a set of features of any such moment that is typical across situations. For example, it is those features of anxiety common to a certain set of anxious situations. The *structures* of a phenomenon are those relations among objects and parts of an object that are present across situations. The *textures* of a phenomenon are those atmospheres or emotional climates that are common to it across situations. For the most part, phenomenological psychologists seek to explicate phenomena at a certain level of typicality or generality. The way an object and the contexts in which it occurs (*horizons*) appear are called the *noematic* features of a phenomenon, while the ways in which it is taken up and the person of the experiencer is implicated are called the *noetic* features. To put it another way, the noematic features are on the side of the object and the noetic are on that of the subject. Again, any situation or phenomenon is coconstituted dialectically by both sides. *Dialectic* refers to a relation between two unified entities involving their mutual implication.

Neither is the cause of which the other is a result, rather, there is a circularity of influence.

Occurring on the noetic side, *modes* of experience refer to the variable ways of apprehending any object of interest. Any particular mode and the object taken up have a *correlative* relation. For example, seeing the object has as its correlate the object-as-seen. This correlative relation is grounded in the fact that any experience, here in a perceptual mode, is coconstituted by subject and object. Any mode is *bodily* or incarnate in that experiencing consists of the lived body–lived world. Experience is not somehow only a direct presentation of the object, nor is it merely subjective or mental. It is bodily in that the *body-subject* or individual must actively participate or engage himself in the situation of any moment.

However, certain modes are bodily in a restricted sense (*bodily modes*). For example, one bodily mode features the way an individual is affected. More than simply seeing or hearing, he feels or senses bodily the impact of a situation. Another bodily mode is a kind of kinesthetic empathy in which the individual feels or senses his own potential movement. These bodily modes are tacit ways of knowing the world. *Abstraction* refers to the way the only felt or sensed impact or potential movement lingers in the aftermath of a given moment of its occurrence. The body is the vehicle of this carrying from or taking apart from. Of course, this abstraction is only relatively disengaging, for every moment of experience is an involvement in the world. *Reflection* is a mode in which there is at once an awareness of that which has been abstracted and of the self implied in that abstraction. It is a holding of a lived moment at arm's length in a way that allows the meaning itself to be posited, particularly that meaning that illuminates the self which coconstituted a given situation or phenomenon.

THESES

I borrow some of these theses directly from the philosophy of Merleau-Ponty. For others more peculiar to this essay or more critical to the method, I provide argument, or, rather, in the manner of argument of phenomenology, exposition of their experiential referents. So that this section can be an aid for what follows, particularly for readers less familiar with phenomenology, the presentation sacrifices the rigor of a full and qualified argument for direct and bold statement. It will remain as the task of the body of the essay to guide the reader to experiential referents for the different modes and aspects of experience that constitute the method. Here I adopt the less strict criterion of locating these theses in an imaginable or conceivable space rather than the better-trod space of lived experience. Again, such an initial anchoring may be helpful in finding the way to the latter.

1. The lived body is a protean being. It consists of an indeterminate number of potential shapes and movements. In any engaged moment, I take up an object and coconstitute a situation by assuming certain of its shapes and movements. This participation in and at an object is lived experience. Through this participation these forms are changed; the lived body is further informed or informed differently.

2. The informed body is a locus of meaning. Meaning is not somehow out there already given in the object. Rather, meaningfulness first arises in the dialogue consisting of an invitation from an incipient object and the response of my lived body.

3. The meaning of the lived body is always an implicit knowledge. Its meaning does not have the structure of language. It is not intelligible as a bodily grammar or semiology. Its forms are always only potential forms, always only in the act of being formed through my continuing experience.

4. The lived body bears the bodily pole of situations once lived through. It is those moments of which it is informed. This bodily pole is horizontally present as a *sense* of situations once lived through. This sense of situations is not somehow merely pure emotion but rather is always a felt-meaning.

5. I can attend to this bodily sense. When I do so I discover that my lived body is protean in the further regard that I can take up any presently sensed aspect of it. I am then relatively disengaged from other potential objects at hand. When I posit this bodily sense as an object, it appears as a way my body was affected in some prior engagement. When explicated this impact reveals as its correlative the atmosphere of that situation.

6. Any bodily sense is also present as a potential move that I can enact virtually. I can attend to any present bodily sense in such a way that I live through certain of its potential moves. I can do so without the actual presence of the incipient situation that would invite those moves. This way of intending a bodily sense is more active than focusing on the way my body was affected. Through virtual enactment, that is, an enactment in which I do not actually move, I realize the bodily sense as the articulation of a space. The virtual moves cut through and thereby *form* an abstract space. To suggest how this space is meaningful and of what its meaning consists will require several additional theses.

7. *Any situation as I live it means through its structure.* Structure refers to how parts are organized. It denotes that organization or those relations as such—not the particular parts, but the relations among the parts. Any aspect of experience can mean through its structure, whether objects like things, ideas, or personal relations or ways of intending objects. In that structure refers to relations as such, it attains the level of generality of a phenomenon; it refers to a set of constitutive meanings across situations.

8. *Structures have a presence in the lived moment.* Structures originally are coconstituted through an appeal to the mobility of my lived body, for any relation as such is a dynamic entity. It is the way parts stand one to another as, for example, one part encloses or supports another. Any structure's presence in the lived moment is known by taking up its call to make the move implicit in its dynamic relation. Part of what the body bears in the aftermath of a lived moment are these structures present as the bodily sense of a potential move.

9. *Forming is a bodily mode through which I virtually enact a structure of a phenomenon.* The act of forming posits those moves I once lived through to originally constitute a structure of a particular situation. The abstract space formed in this way is, then, a presentation of the noetic correlate of a structure as it appeared in lived experience.

10. *Forming is a bodily reflective mode.* I can intend the abstract space so formed as an object. When I do so I become aware of an aspect of myself, for that space is the product of a move I once made to coconstitute a lived moment. Since that move is a way of knowing a relation as such, it is a way I lived the structure of a phenomenon. For example, it is the way I am anxious across situations. More generally, a bodily mode becomes reflective when through it I posit the pole of experience that is the lived body for I am my lived body.

THE METHOD

If these theses have a theme, it is, of course, the marvelous capabilities of the lived body. In these powers, I find a method for doing phenomenology. The general thrust of that method may be suggested here, while it is the task of the remaining chapters to describe it more fully and more systematically.

In the tradition of phenomenological methods, the initial move is a return to the things themselves. In doing phenomenological psychology the return is specifically to instances of the particular phenomenon under investigation. I describe a posture that can be adopted in making this return. This assumed attitude is an "abstractive" one through which I sensitize myself to the bodily pole of experience. Through it I can focus on the bodily felt residues of the textures and structures of these instances. Becoming sensitive to the way I was affected yields the bodily correlate of the target phenomenon's texture, posited now as a certain impact on my body. Focusing on this impact provides a guide to a description of that texture.

I can also abstract and continue to bear the structures of the lived moments present as the sense of potential moves. Their virtual enactment is possible through the bodily mode I call forming. Forming that incipient or unfulfilled intention to move yields an articulated space. The form defined by that space is the noetic correlate of a structure of the target phenomenon. It is a presentation, here for the first time as an intended object, of the moves of my lived body in originally coconstituting an instance of the phenomenon. I can preserve that form as an actual diagram that is available as a primary source of the structures to be explicated. For this reflective schematization shows the relations as such that are constitutive of the phenomenon of interest.

I can only suggest here the further power of these bodily modes. Sensitivity to the bodily correlate of a structure or form and to the potential act of forming is also a way both to locate further instances of the phenomenon of interest and to discover related phenomena that have a particular structure in common. In addition, the informed body is a seeker of metaphor. Through sensitivity to a particular form I am primed to find phenomena that, although apparently disparate, have that structure in common. These metaphors are helpful in describing features of the target

phenomenon and in contrasting that phenomenon with related
phenomena.

CLAIMS

In the final analysis, the present contribution to phenomenological
method must be judged by the effectiveness of the products of
its application. Any cohesiveness and intelligibility of the claims
and positions implicit in the descripton of the method are subor-
dinate to that criterion. However, it might be helpful to conclude
these introductory remarks with a list of certain philosophical
claims and disclaimers.

    1. With respect to meaning I claim that meaning can mean
through implicit relations. Meaning can arise through the appreciation both of the relations among parts constitutive of an object
and of the relations between that object and potential objects
that form its background. This position is close to that of Merleau-
Ponty in *Phenomenology of Perception*. It also has some affinity,
though less, to the concept of meaning held by the early Gestalt
psychologists[19] and to contemporary views of meaning as contextual.
It is distinguishable from another current view that meaning
means through contrast, as, for example, in Derrida's notion of
"difference." [20]

    I do not need to claim that this is the only way meaning means.
I claim only that it is a predominant way meaning arises when
we are actively engaged.

    2. Structure can be known through and be present in the living
of relations. It is therefore a site of meaning. I do not claim that
structure is only known in this way, nor that all structures have
a presence in the lived moment.

    Further, I relate structure to behavior in that implicit knowledge
can be coconstituted through the active taking up or living through
of relations. This focus on behavior is not a behaviorism since
I refer to behavior as lived rather than to an objectivated behavior.
Nor does this focus on structure imply a sympathy with those
loosely confederated intellectual currents called "structuralism."
In particular, I dissociate my position from structuralism to the
degree that it conceives meaning to originate in language and
denies structure any prelinguistic presence in lived experience. The
approach to structure here is phenomenological in that I supply

a description of the appearances of structure from their original implicit upsurge in lived experience to their eventual explicit formulation. My finding is that structure has a presence in the lived moment as a shape or as a deformation of space that is given as meaningful.

3. While the bodily knowledge that is the focus of this essay is prelinguistic, this is not the case for all bodily knowledge. Certain bodily movements through which we directly communicate to each other, gestures for example, have some of the features of language.

4. Positing the bodily pole of a lived moment is necessarily reflective since I am always implicated in the way my body takes up objects. However, I do not claim that all reflection posits the bodily pole of experience. I only claim that adopting bodily reflective modes is an effective way to do phenomenology.

Further, I am not saying that I can take the lived body as an object for it is the ground for the possibility of taking objects. But I can posit the way my body has been affected or the space through which it has moved.

5. Reflection through the adoption of bodily modes is typifying, for through it I explicate relations as such. In explicating experience through these bodily reflective modes I can reveal my characteristic self to myself. However, in doing so I also can learn about the culture and times in which I live. Any particular way I coconstitute a phenomenon is a way generally available in the cultural setting in which I am presently embedded. For example, the way I grieve is both recognizable as a way characteristic of me and as an option in the culture.

I claim that these bodily modes can explicate phenomena at a relative level of generality suitable to the study of individual personality or of a particular culture. This claim excludes the view that experience is radically ephemeral and context-bound, an ever-changing flux such that our awareness is limited to successive "nows" or even to the past only as it appears now. Explication of experience is not limited to an understanding of a particular moment in an individual's experience. On the other side, I do not claim that phenomena consist of ahistorical and unchanging essences. My position is intermediate here. While not denying that the structures of phenomena are historically conditioned and that structures change through the way I live and reflect on them, I claim that the target phenomena of a phenomenological psychology can be treated as relatively congealed. My grief this year and five years ago and the possibility of this form of grief in the present cultural setting are relatively stable.

6. Related to this is the problematic status of lived experience itself and of its relation to bodily reflective modes. While occasionally my language suggests that situations already have their own structure which somehow is transferred to me in the moment, my position is that my active engagement in situations is partly determinative of them. The meaning of situations is never prior to that engagement. However, I recognize that here I seem to want it both ways. I conceive of phenomena as fixed enough in their structures so that through my body I can retain them as a bodily sense and reactivate or revivify them. At the same time I leave an opening within both lived experience itself and reflection on it that allows and indeed locates change in the creative acts of individuals. My position here is close to that of M. Natanson's in his assertion that lived experience always consists of two moments—an individual, particular, or existential moment and a typical, essential, or "phenomenological" moment.[21]

In like manner reflection also is both a transforming and a typifying agency. Without denying reflection's implication of the knower in a dialectic, I assert that the investigator as phenomenological psychologist is relatively secure within a culture and within a present historical period. While it never yields transparency, reflection is the effective center of a phenomenological psychology for through it I can achieve an explication of the typical structures of a target phenomenon, bounded by historical and cultural contexts.

7. A related problem is the possibility of exhausting the structures of a given phenomenon. Here the claim is the modest one that the investigator can never exhaust the meanings of any phenomenon both because they are historically evolving and because the perspectives through which they are known are indeterminate in number. The adequacy of a phenomenological description is not in some measure of its exhaustiveness. Rather, it lies in such criteria as the power of each explicated structure to evoke that and only that feature and the degree to which those structures explicated together refer to this and only this phenomenon.

8. The present method in part consists in a description of reflec-

tive modes, in particular of those modes through which I can apprehend and posit structure. Any object, situation, or phenomenon is originally meaningfully present, as I live it, in that it consists of a set of relations as such. To know that lived meaning as an explicated or formulated meaning requires reflection. A phenomenology of reflection provides, then, a general hermeneutic, a description of the ways that any "text" means.

While I intend this degree of general applicability for the methods to be presented here, yet I maintain that the level of discussion need not be as abstract as that of a philosophical treatise. I present here no philosophical system, although one is implied. This essay will be an instance of doing phenomenological psychology. That the phenomenon that I shall describe happens to be a way of explicating phenomena, that that which is my object is not an object but a way of knowing objects does not in principle introduce any greater problem, any more stringent criterion for its execution or its judgment. I must be true to the phenomenon. To do so, to be so, requires that same sensitivity and familiarity, the same rigorous adherence to appearance exacted by the description of any more "substantive" phenomenon. I must continually refer to it, live it, be it so that I may describe it. Again, that I must be a phenomenological investigator, that I must continually refer to that, that I can only refer to that by being that subjugate me to no more inherent circularity than that encountered in any phenomenological project. As phenomenological investigator I am always radically embedded in that which I would study; I must return to it, live in it, be it, continually have access to it. Here in a sense my return to the thing itself is a shorter hop, for I am already there, as I am a phenomenologist, as I am doing phenomenology, as I am already reflecting. The hermeneutic circle, the dialectical spiral, the opacity of knower to known are my stock in trade, my occupational hazard. Entering those circles, being tainted by that blinding, incestuous relation between me and what I would know are the way I work, whether I study grief or reflection. The same point may be put in the other direction: as phenomenological investigator, whatever I describe is inseparable from the way I am, from how I am, in describing it. Any substantive contribution is always also an effort at a methodologic contribution.[22]

2

The Method, Part One:

Reflection as Bodily Abstraction

THE PROVISION OF A PHENOMENOLOGY
OF REFLECTION

As propounded by Husserl, the "central figure in the Phenomenological Movement,"[1] phenomenology's original project was to found knowledge. Husserl's strategy was to define the problem of knowledge as the problem of the structure of experience. If I can only know something in or through my experience of it, I must begin with and build my understanding of it on an understanding of experience, of how I know in and through experience, of the relation to things that experience constitutes and that constitutes experience.

An antithetical strategy maintains that the ground of knowledge is a peculiar relation to things in which that relation is not in any way implicated. It is the view that the thing itself can be known outside of my perspective on it, my approach to it, my "experience" of it. The heart of this alternative belief is a faith in reason and a concomitant skepticism of immediate experience, variously rendered as "sensory experience," mere appearance, subjective or biased involvement. This epistemology, which is the basis of the traditional natural scientific approach to understanding, argues that through reason I can objectify the thing and so have it outside of my perspective on it, outside of reason itself. Reason is a way to a pure knowledge of the thing, a way that can leave itself behind.

Husserl and later phenomenologists' critique of science and

modern technological culture find this peculiar objectification of things a way of knowing that forgets our original knowledge of the world. In their view, reliance on intellection to lift us out of ourselves and to give us a transparent access to things is a bootstrap operation that results in an idealized and a fabricated understanding of the world and our relation to it.

In place of the ideal or myth of achieving a view of the thing from nowhere or everywhere at once, phenomenology has had its own ideals and myths. Ironically, despite his concern with returning to the thing itself as lived, part of Husserl's work is informed by an ideal that is akin to a romantic escape to the self. The ground for knowledge at times seems to be sought by effecting a hermit's journey out of the world and into the self—eventually, to some transcendental plane beyond both self and thing. A second ideal, associated with phenomenology more recently and one more consonant with a return to an original knowledge that would be prior to the distortions of science and intellection, is the belief in a primordial relation between person and thing. The ground for knowledge is gained by the explication of this originary relation. It involves an absorption of self in things, a participation that allows the thing to disclose itself, "a letting be of what is." [2] It is a return which leaves behind peculiar cultural ways of knowing the thing, or finds the basis of such ways of knowing. This relation may be likened not to a Western romanticism but to an Eastern mysticism. The ideal is a participation in the thing that is totally self-absorbing, but more: self-dissolving, a radical belonging to or oneness with the world.

That my goals in this essay are less ambitious than working out a systematic epistemology allows me merely to point to these positions and to characterize them, as I have here, almost metaphorically. In that I seek only the description of a method to explicate the structure of certain relatively stable phenomena as lived, I need espouse neither ideal—neither the inflated self with its emphasis on a universality reached by a reflective journey back into the self, nor the lost self, a focus on an originary or inherent or universal relation to things which lets them speak with radical directness and transparency. The method that I shall describe claims only a "prereflective" participation in things, a way back to an appearance of a thing at any moment, an appearance that need not be originary or precultural. In fact, this method

accepts that that appearance, even as I participate in it prereflectively, is a historical and dialectical phenomenon. On the other
side, that of the subject, following this return, reflection on and
explication of this appearance of the world need not transcend
my peculiar self. Indeed, it will find that appearance in me—
not represented in me as in a dualistic representational realism,
but borne by me.

Both Husserl and Heidegger, along the way to their respective,
more ambitious concerns, attempt to capture descriptively the
thing itself as lived. For both, this refers to the appearance of a
thing prior to that peculiar idealized objectification that is the
dominant, scientific, technological way of being in the world.
Both also understand this project by the metaphor of the "return";
and they believe that they can effect this return through reflection.
Reflection supplants reason, the scientist's path to knowledge,
and takes as its first task cutting it away. In that reflection, in a
most general way, is an awareness of the structure of our awareness, of our relation to that which we are experiencing; through
it we can "bracket" reason's peculiar objectification of the thing.
In this way we can return.

To return to experience as lived requires a certain posture
which reflection must effect and which we must describe. But this
is half the task, only half of reflection's burden. Experience is
ongoing. To know it as such we must participate in that immediate flow. It is not enough to return, for we must explicate
that appearance—how it is in our unreasoned, immediate participation. But how can we live in it and describe it at the same
time? James likened this dilemma to that of seizing a spinning
top in an effort to capture its motion.[3]

This is the other side of the problem of intellection. Having
stripped away reason's approach to and rendering of the world
to reach a prior world, a closer approach to the immediate
upsurge of the world if not to being as such, the phenomenologist
must leave that to describe it. Undoubtedly, part of the impulse
that led to the ideal of the externality of reason was to achieve
this very separation. But the phenomenologist, of course, would
take this prereflective world with him to make precisely it explicit.
Having returned through reflection, there is the problem of
keeping being and knowing coterminous—of staying with the
experience as lived that I might know just that explicitly. If

reflection is an awareness of awareness, perhaps through it I can both be there and know how I am there. I intend to describe how reflection is a form of knowing that permits being and knowing at once. To accomplish this requires a phenomenology of reflection—a description of the object in reflection, the mode of its appearance and of the form of intentionality, the posture and implication of self in reflection.

We must describe a way of experiencing that can both return us to experience as immediately given and grant us retention of some moment of that original appearance that that original might be explicated. To reiterate some disclaimers—this project does not require that I freight "original" with the originary, with a primordial relation, or with a search for being as such. The method I shall describe operates comfortably within the dialectics of history, of culture, and even of that more local dialectic between my engaged and reflective experience of a given phenomenon. Finally, while accepting the radically pervasive presence of such dialectics, I believe that this description of reflective modes need not, really must not—if that description is to be grasped by the reader—directly engage these dialectics. To do so would force me to deal continually with the powerful sirens peculiar to the dialectic, the temptation to follow it into ever tightening spirals that eventually crash on circularity and regress. Being so occupied, I would fail, as I believe much literature on the phenomenological method does, to describe reflection as it and what it intends appear at any moment. Rather, I propose to stay with those momentary appearances until reflection is located and explicated as a set of modes and postures.

POSTURE AS AN APPROACH TO EXPERIENCE

To begin to move from a program for reflection to its phenomenology, I intend, initially, to keep to one aspect of it. In this still preparatory effort to grasp reflection itself, I define and exemplify generically a feature of experiencing that I shall refer to as *posture* or *approach*.[4] From there, I can discriminate a reflective posture. Eventually, I shall distinguish posture from mode.

A posture is a peculiar relation of a person to the objects of his experience. Although postures variably seem to demand for their description, as I shall illustrate, vocabularies of motivation or purpose or organizing principle, all as lived are a certain *relation* to an object or situation. The term posture refers to the way I hold myself, the way I am being at any such intended object. Posture's affinity to relation is not incidental given our earlier suggestion that reflection is a certain set of relations of knower to known. Nor is its affinity to body, as we will find that reflection, in company with all postures, is a bodily relation.

A posture is present also as a *possible* relation to an object. It is a way I am more or less free to assume at any moment. Clearly, that it is a possible way of being at or approaching things suggests that any given posture can be appraised critically as a "return." Does a particular possible posture provide us with the return to things as lived that is requisite to a phenomenological method?

This feature, posture or approach, is not without its hazards even as a beginning point. At first glance it seems to invoke a dualism, a discrete separation between subject and object. But as will be clearer below, any posture is ensconced or radically embedded in the world. Subject and object are conceivable not as distinct entities but as two poles that constitute the world as lived. No posture is knowable except "in action," as already engaged with the object it would take or is taking. No approach occurs except within a dialectic of present invitation by an object, of ways I have already approached and am about to approach— within a system that already includes me. I am never outside experience about to enter in a certain way ex nihilo.

To illustrate most broadly what I intend by posture, consider these possibilities. I can relate to the world as a thing to be known or to be mastered, as a thing in which to lose or to find myself, to join or to distance, to help or to violate, to take as it is or to impose upon. For these global postures motivation and purpose are salient. While for all a self is implicated, for some more than for others, an "I" is directly served.

More examples: at certain stages in his or her development, a child approaches the world as a set of things that are more or less graspable, to borrow from a Piagetian scheme. Or, later, he is apt to enter situations that he constitutes as occasions for things to be placed in piles—his blocks and french fries, or, regrettably, his father's papers and files. In these postures an organizing principle or an operation is definitive. The approach is a way in which I put things together, relate them to each other, or manipulate them, either actually or virtually.

I can also relate to any moment of my experience by organizing it or by operating on it temporally. I cut my day into pieces delimited by the time I allot to each of them. I allow a certain amount of time for any given activity; I continually time my experience and feel the burden of the time yet to pass or the guilt of the time already elapsed. Some of these postures are recognizable for their prevalence in certain cultures or subcultures or in certain personality types.

These few examples demonstrate that posture is of endless variety. It is also evident that any given posture may be assumed habitually and that it may become habituated. This is to say that it may be always already assumed, assumed unwittingly, "forgotten"; or, on the other hand, that it may be deliberately and knowingly adopted or that it may be there to be assumed only upon a certain invitation, such as on the occasion of the presence of a certain object or circumstance that invites it.

Any posture is necessarily a way of knowing the world, but that it is so is typically incidental. However, some postures seek knowledge focally and systematically. The objectivistic or natural scientific approach is one such that phenomenology has assailed critically in its effort to found knowledge anew and on a more solid ground. As we have suggested, it is a peculiar relation of knower to known in that it denies the necessity of any relation. It systematically attempts to exclude any implication of how it approaches to know in what it comes to know. It is an approach or posture that would be approachless. From any classical phenomenological perspective, this "approach" remains exterior to phenomena as lived: it never returns. In the context of this discussion, it is in practice a habituated posture that returns only to that world which consists precisely of objects lived in its own way. The natural scientist lives through or engages in an exteriority of objects.

There are other prevalent approaches that systematically and focally seek knowledge and that retain their own brand of exteriority. One family of approaches, an example of which I shall consider more fully below, rests on the argument that knowledge is fundamentally linguistic. Knowledge begins with and is inseparable from language. In this view, if a return to a prelinguistic, prereflective relation to objects were possible at any moment, it must remain a dumb one for there is no prelinguistic relation to the world that is a way of knowing the world. Experience is like a text that only becomes intelligible when I begin to read it. To do that I require a set of rules or a grammar; but the text in no direct or simple way "contains" those rules. Experience bears no tacit or felt meaning that is prior to some process of its interpretation. There is no ground for my reading, only the possibility of a reading of that reading.[5] Again, from a phenomenological point of view, this posture, habituated, retains an exterior and distanced relation to lived experience. Were its exclusive assumption possible, what I would live is a radical intellectualism. In this world I would not be participating in a way that permits my experience to be furthered or advanced that it in turn may be or need be explicated anew. I assume a protected stance in which I prevent myself from touching or being touched, from moving or being moved. My experience is restricted to further renditions of itself, to yet another interpretation. Phenomena, in the perverted sense in which there are such in this posture, would consist exclusively of those meanings, categories, and "differences" that I impose upon them.

One other posture may be briefly noted for contrast before I turn to those that apparently approximate, rather than fly in the face of, a posture that would make a genuine phenomenology possible. Susan Sontag offers a compelling description of photography as a posture.[6] The peculiar relation to things and events implicit in taking their picture or intending to do so is a complex one that involves a certain aesthetic and a certain sentiment but also a certain way of knowing. The picture that I presently hold in my hand is at once an artful form, a piece of nostalgia, and a testimony. It is a "pseudo-presence" of the thing itself; it "furnishes evidence" of the thing.[7] But even before I have that product, the posture assumed in taking a picture and, as well, the approach implicit in looking at the world at any moment as to-be-photographed is a seeking after knowledge, after an understanding that is in the form of evidence, of what is evidently there.

To acquire this form of knowledge I require a passive, nonintervening relation to things and events. As Sontag argues, in that as photographer I must refuse to intercede, I gain this evidence through a form of passive aggression—I "shoot" them.

More subtly, when I limit my experience to the photogenic, when this approach is pervasive and forgotten, my experience itself is constituted by the fact that my relation to things is to photograph them. That experience bears heavily my particular conception of a "good picture," a certain style, composition, way of cropping and framing, taste for drama, and the like. More generally, that I would relate to things by understanding them in that way, by "capturing" them rather than participating in them or directly engaging them, becomes the limited way in which I live.

What might appear at first glance to provide a technology for phenomenology,[8] a way of returning to and staying with a version of the thing itself by carrying away its direct impress, is yet another brand of externality. The photographic posture toward things is an imposition of self and tool that typically fails to recognize the constitutive level of that implication. Rather, as photographer, I believe that that which is evidently "out there," separate from me and unrelated to me or my approach, is now duplicated by an image, recorded. The imposition so denied is one that makes "having an experience identical with making a photograph of it." [9] As a habituated posture, photographing knows only its own way of living, a peculiar aestheticizing, passivating, and disengaged form of exteriority.

How do I begin to locate a posture or set of postures through which I can return to, stay with, and eventually explicate a fuller, more involved, more participatory, and more dialectical relation to things, a more genuinely lived experience? Obviously, phenomena as lived consist in and are constituted by a relation between experiencer and experienced. Knowledge is relational in this sense and reality is perspectival. To recognize this is to accept that the posture we seek can neither stay in itself, external to things, nor lose itself or leave itself behind in some self-dissolving relation to things. In the vocabulary of the present discussion, the posture must accept its own *implication* in that which it seeks to know, and in turn the dialectic that this implies. This is to say that such a posture must be reflective; it must be aware of itself, turn back on itself.

Phenomenology recognizes—for in fact it has brought to light—these requisite features for a reflective method. Husserl's bracketing and reducing, Heidegger's "letting be," and Sartre's "totalizing, detotalizing, and retotalizing," his version of the dialectic—all are systematic descriptions of a set of relations to phenomena as lived which intend to meet these requirements. Other postures found in the literature of phenomenological psychology are typically less fully explicated and may be understood by reference to one or more of these three postures.

Those that rest on the early Heideggerian posture tend to reduce it to the possibility of a direct and immediate return. Propensities toward dualistic thinking and layers of meaning resultant from them and other postreflective postures, those attendant sedimentations so assiduously addressed by Husserl, are bypassed in one move. Postures such as reliving, entering into, conjuring, fully engaging oneself—all seem to displace reflection. Even if such an unencumbered return were possible, it is as if they assume being so returned were synonymous with the description of what appears in that moment. The problem of staying with the phenomenon while explicating it, of how to move to a posture that allows description and yet does not slip back to the presumably divested postreflective prejudice, is not addressed. However, having the phenomenon again, at the extreme achieving an engagement so absorbing that horizons of self are eclipsed and I become the phenomenon, perhaps does give a fresh sense of a particular phenomenon. As investigator, I might then take that as a starting point for subsequent reflection. I might then be in a better position to describe it in a way that is not a reconstruction from the outside. But the critical additional posture whereby I might accomplish this is not indicated.

Another general solution more consistent with Husserl than with the early Heidegger does not involve becoming the phenomenon, but merely being at it, returning *to* it. I am not in it but neither am I external to it; I get into a position to know it directly. For Husserl a series of reductions or *epoches* puts me in a position relative to it where the phenomenon may be intuited. I need not presently be in grief or even presently re-evoke a moment of it; rather, I am enabled to "see" it, to have it appear in front of me. (I shall critically review Husserl's reliance on analogies to perception when we consider *mode* below.) In the phenomenological psychology literature there is the possibility of being, as it were, at the lived edge of the phenomenon: *return* is merely access to the phenomenon—I can be in touch with it, be in sympathy with it, focus on it without yet yielding to the temptation to be in it again. The implicit distinction here between entry or reentry and access perhaps suggests that the latter is a more effective beginning point. Perhaps simply being in touch with the phenomenon puts me in a better position for the eventual task of explication. Through it I might keep postreflective formulations behind me and a direct but nonabsorbing presence of the phenomenon as lived in front of me. Again, the description of the shifts in posture that would effect this explication is not provided.

The tensions between an analytic posture that would stay outside of the phenomenon in an attempt to be clear about what is there, and more phenomenological postures that would either relive or be so close as to sympathize directly with the phenomenon may be "resolved" by letting just those possibilities occur in turn. In the method described by Sartre,[10] the investigator moves in and out. He is not participant observer so much as participant then observer in an ongoing round of these positions. I have indicated earlier what is lacking in this description of the dialectic. In the phenomenological psychology literature "dialogue with" and "commune with" the phenomenon function as code words that refer to this complex and elusive set of investigatory postures without unpacking them.

The reflective modes that are the subject of this essay involve a basic posture that is distinguishable from all of the above. I believe that this posture can provide a ground for a dialectical phenomenological method and indeed can lead us to a fuller description of some moments in that critical dialectic between experience as lived and its explication.

AN ABSTRACTIVE POSTURE

Of course, "abstractive," "abstract," and related forms carry a considerable baggage of references within the philosophical tradition as well as connotations from everyday usage. Both of these build on that which is abstracted, that is, on the noun forms. From this beginning the abstract comes to refer to the quality of a thing without reference to the particular thing, the attribute "honesty" without the subject "honest man" of whom it is predicated. The abstract is a quality that is a disembodiment; it is an ideal distillate of the substantial and of the particular. Its conceived separateness from the original establishes a duality, such as idea and thing, and renders a dialectic impossible. Having established this as the region of the abstract, the act of abstracting becomes a cognitive or mental operation, a moment that begins and ends in a linguistic and explicitly conceptual domain. Such an abstractive posture operates postreflectively; it fails to be a turning back on the phenomena as lived. From the point of view of the description to follow, it fails to be abstractive for it does not "take from" the original. It is not reflective for we will show that reflection necessarily begins in an abstractive act.

If we begin instead with the active form, with the act of abstracting, we can locate a different region of the abstract and eventually travel more lightly and effectively in doing phenomenology. The abstractive act must originate in the lived world, not in the "abstract." It must be an embodied act that participates in the immediate engaged moment of lived experience. That which it abstracts can be an object of reflection in the sense that it reflects or retains "attributes" of the original as lived. In being aware of the abstracted I am aware of the original and of its origin. The region of the abstract consists, then, of objects we can or must know by a form of reliving or reenactment. I constitute them through an active and bodily sense of them, that same sense through which the original was coconstituted. That moment is a reflective one because it constitutes a derivative object that continually points back to an original that included me. Hence, we must describe how a reflective posture can be abstractive and yet partake of bodily modes. Also, we must describe how such a posture can constitute an object that at once carries a particular original object or situation and has a certain generality or contextlessness which will lead us to phenomenological descriptions of the structure of phenomena.

Let us turn to a moment in mundane experience when we find ourself "taking away" or withdrawing some aspect of that experience. In this way we might discover how the abstract is constituted and how, then, an abstractive posture may be assumed intentionally.

Consider a moment in which I am walking through a museum. I find myself standing in front of a particular painting. I become engaged in it: various features, first the prominent human figures, then certain other details, in turn catch my eye. Some I quickly survey while others gain my attention and become new objects of my engagement. One such feature, some strikingly colorful orange patches, I stay with longer. As I do so, they begin to lift from the painting. They seem to appear in slight relief. What is going on here?

At this moment the orange splotches are no longer simply another object of my attention, the last object in a series of shifts in attention. The way this feature is present has a more complex and clearly distinguishable structure from that of an object of my attention. The latter is present as the point in a point-horizon structure that constitutes my phenomenal field.[11] I inhabit such a point.[12] I am absorbed in it while the horizon is like a surround, a faded background which is present only as it is implicated in the way the focal, posited object appears. A subsequent shift in my attention is my active acceptance of an invitation from within that horizon to take it up and establish it as a new abode.

The orange is not an object of my attention if attention has that structure. I do not go into the orange patches or take them up so much as they come out. Rather than implicating their surround, they appear against it. The point-horizon structure is retained only in that the raised-orange-against-the-rest-of-the-painting is the new point or object of my attention. This object has its own peculiar structure. It is a two-story affair—the orange raised above the rest of the painting. We will explicate this two-story structure as the first moment in a genetic phenomenology of the abstract, through the descriptive: a part taken apart.

A PART TAKEN APART

The orange patch appears above the original as at a second level or story. It is a part taken apart, taken away from. The way it is apart is given first and most directly through a spatial sense. It is above the painting. But in being above, it appears away from the main body of our present concern, the painting. It is at a remove from that with or within which we were and still are relatively engaged. In the present example, the sense of this being at a remove is striking, for the popped-up orange, as we stay with it, takes us out of the region of the perceived. In this first moment, it appears in front of the still present spectacle of the painting. It is no longer part of the flesh of the perceived for it floats above it, although still loosely anchored to it. However, a shift in modality is not necessary to effect this incipient moment in the birth of the abstract. In fact, when we turn from this description of the abstractive posture to bodily modes of abstraction, we will show that this first moment is not modality-specific. In general, the part apart is present as "a sense of" some aspect of the original. It is not yet an image or a concept. We will show that the spatiality of the two-story structure is first apprehended as a bodily sense; it is not yet seen or imagined. What is critical at this point is the sense of the part being at a remove, as occurring above and in front of some original of which it was and is a part, an aspect.

Another disclaimer reiterates the point that the abstract here is such only in that it is constituted through an act of abstraction, in its being a part *taken* apart. The second story of the part apart here is not yet a shift in conceptual level, a level jump as from membership in a class to that class, from orange to the category *color,* or from a particular something to an instance of something, as one of a certain kind or type. The orange patch lifted out need not be posited as orangeness. The part apart is not a "property" as distinguished from a "part." [13] Although an abstractive posture often consists in such a conceptualizing act, as looking for a color or a certain class of objects or properties, it need not be so ladened. Of course, this is a relative statement. That which strikes me, that which pops up, can only do so if it speaks to some possibility of which I am already partially informed. But I can approach a situation relatively open to that which emerges as removable. On the other side, I do not burden the abstractive posture here with the task of exploiting an essential feature, some *eidos* that emerges only when I am radically "letting be what is," when I somehow utterly forget the history and person that I bring to it. What is critical for this abstractive posture that it might serve us in doing phenomenological psychology is that through it we stay with the incipient moment of the abstraction—with a part of the original that is only an embossment of it, a part of it not yet torn away and transformed by conceptualization. We must assume precisely that posture which does not miss this natural flaking off from the main body by skipping directly to a categorization of it. We must continue to have it against the original, as a part of the original, not yet as a member of a class that I bring to the original.

To put this important feature another way, the part is not taken apart in the sense of its being analyzed. It is merely at a remove.

I have not yet located the part dimensionally. I do not have orange in its place in a spectrum of hues, or with respect to variable saturation. The orange splotch is still "of a piece" with its original setting, as a part of that painting. The second-story remove is "contained" in the first-story original. The second story is a mirroring of the first in that it borrows from it directly, without mediation, yet is not of its flesh. Through the abstracting posture I can lift out some part of the original without transforming, conceptualizing, dimensionalizing, or typifying it, and without depleting the original, for it is still completely present to me. Were the second story to be given alone it would be more a partial presentation than a commentary or interpretation of the original. As we shall describe, indeed it is precisely a potential presentation.

It remains to say how it is possible for me to take and to have a part apart without analyzing it in relation to the whole and without classifying it in relation to other things. Here I intend only to lead you to the experiential referent, that moment which is an incipient abstraction, and to prolong your stay in it. For the possibility of the prolongation of this preconceptual moment itself will be a critical ground for a phenomenological method. Here I wish to suggest that the general character of the intended object in that moment, that which I abstract, is more that of a mirror than a lamp, more a potential presentation than a transformation. To describe the kind of act that makes this possible, we will need to move from posture to mode and to trace from that act through which I coconstitute the original to the abstractive act. We will need to show how that original act is at once creative or originating *and* imitative; how, then, it grasps and retains what is already there.

A second example will broaden the arena into which the abstractive posture may enter and will further help to establish the experiential referent. Turning from the painting, I am engaged in a conversation with my companion. We talk of impressions of the painting, of impressions of our impressions, and the like. Beginning by sharing our own positions, we eventually further each other's positions as he finds in mine what I did not quite know was there and vice versa. We reach a common position, then a fresh divergence, and so it goes. At different points in the conversation, my experience threatens to take on the structure of the abstract. That two-story structure begins to form, as some part of the experience lifts out against the ongoing moment: some aspect of the moment, some nuance of the discussion or its gist, or a sense of how we are together.

If I attend to any such aspect focally, I can explicate it. When I do I can bring it back into the conversation. In this way I select a certain highlight of the original which then is present as a certain possible direction for further discussion. However, more typically, I remain more fully engaged in the ongoing moment. While the part does not yet appear apart, there is a slight swelling, a quickly passing wave. I find that I can ride that wave back into the conversation without disengaging. I do not fully shift attention to it or posit it as an object. I find myself about to get onto it; it is that which I am about to say. It can be my unfulfilled intention at any moment. Riding each successive wave, then, is how I can advance the conversation without the disengaging move of a reflection on it. The waves are parts of the conversation which both issue from it and continually constitute it. They can be how it moves.

But as another possibility, I can let the two-story structure congeal. I neither explicate it at the moment nor ride it into the conversation. I notice this possibility most strikingly when, the interaction ending, my partner and I go our separate ways. I carry away some particular aspect of the moment which had been lifted out as the orange splotch earlier, and which remained as such, that is, with the structure of the abstracted. It is a part apart which I am carrying with me. Its presence to me is meaningful but unexplicated. It is present as something about that moment, some meaning of it as yet only felt; it is present as something to be understood. More generally, when I have assumed an abstractive posture, there is this possibility. A sense of some aspect of the moment can be lifted up, thereby constructing a two-story structure. I can carry the part away with me in a bodily way (which I have yet to describe). I can embody the meaningful sense without positing or explicating it. Through this abstractive act I can prolong the preconceptual moment.

PARTICIPATION AS ACCESS TO MEANING

This may not seem like much but let us see how far we have come toward a posture or approach that would make a phenomenological

psychology possible. Following Husserl's original call, such a posture must begin with a return to the phenomenon as lived. While
Husserl's own method sought to fulfill this requirement by an
access to or being at the phenomenon, for Merleau-Ponty the
phenomenologist must first take up a habitation. He must be
in—not merely at—that which he seeks to describe. As van den Berg
refreshingly puts it, "To understand swimming, I must go for a
swim." [14] With Merleau-Ponty and van den Berg, the first moment
of the abstractive approach necessarily finds me embedded and
engaged as an active participant. To describe the painting or my
interaction with my friend and, at the same time, some more
generic phenomenon of which these might be instances, for example, the structure of the aesthetic experience or of dialogue,
I must first become a participant in it. Participation is distinguishable both from the Husserlian looking or looking through and the
Heideggerian "letting be what is," letting it speak to me. In participation as an approach I am included not as observer or audience,
nor even as that passed-over self, that self transcended in the
object; I am a partner in the moment of the phenomenon that I
seek. I share or partake in the phenomenon, take a part in it, and
become a part of it. But at the same time *I form a part of it.* I do
not simply take on what is there; as one moment of the same act,
I impart to it. My participation is coconstitutive of the moment,
situation, or phenomenon. The phenomenon as lived is not out
there to be discovered or disclosed in the Heideggerian sense. It
consists in an object acted upon; it is an actor-object relation. My
involvement is coconstitutive of the phenomenon when that involvement is a genuine participation, when it is an active, bodily
engagement that is formative. A return that is not a coconstituting
participation is not a return to the phenomenon as lived.

While a response to Husserl's call for a return, this is a sig-
nificantly different execution of his program. Husserl's principal
strategy in attaining the return was to put the investigator in a
position of uninvolved or disinterested access. In this position he
could reduce or strip away postreflective accretions to the meaning
of the phenomenon. Leading back to some unmediated, intuitive
apprehension of the phenomenon in this way was the road not to
the structure of that particular phenomenon but to more general
structures which would then constitute a transcendental philosophy.
A phenomenological psychology is a less ambitious undertaking

and requires or perhaps can indulge a less aloof method, one peculiar to its own project.

At least initially, it is also less burdened with those concerns of a "critical theory" approach to the social sciences.[15] While acceding to the historical embeddedness of human phenomena, in particular to the formative influence of current social and political institutions and, in turn, the ideologies upon which they are built, the tactic of a phenomenological psychology is to return to phenomena as lived and from there to their description. Such an initial program does not preclude, indeed it demands, the eventual explication of any formative horizons of that phenomenon traceable to such contexts. In fact, recently several writers, perhaps influenced by critical theory, have examined the possibility of an extension of a descriptive to a normative phenomenology.[16] I believe that the program of a phenomenological psychology justifies a method that is independent of those concerns peculiar to a transcendental philosophy and that is consistent with the eventual explication of typified social realities that are derived from any peculiar ideological bent.

For a phenomenological psychology, given that the primary region of its investigation is phenomena of a middle range of generality, the return can be to a genuine participation in the phenomenon as lived. But while beginning in a coconstitutive reentry, it is critical to the return that it stay with some moment of that lived experience. An approach that forgets that aim, the prolongation of the phenomenon precisely as it is when it is in motion, never catches that flow. The abstractive posture is itself a paradox constructed to resolve that problem. It is a return that intends to take away. But how can it take away the lived moment, the ongoing stuff of a phenomenon as lived, without arresting it in such a way that the motion that constitutes it is forever lost? This question is the guiding query for the rest of this essay. In part the abstractive posture begins in my becoming a party to, a part of, a participant in that motion; that part which I subsequently take apart is a moment of that participation. In this abstractive act there is the incipient structure of reflection, for that part taken apart initially appears against the original, as a mirrored flaked-off piece of it. It begins to be an awareness of an awareness. It is also reflective in that it is a movement to the self. The part that lifts up is a product of my participation which, however, is both myself and the other, the object, for my participation is coconstitutive of the object, of the phenomenon.[17] To take a part apart and for that part to be part and parcel of the original as lived, I must first myself have formed a part of it. Further, when I eventually posit that part, it will be indistinguishable from taking a part of myself as object.

MEANING AS BODILY

Undoubtedly the description to this point raises more questions than it answers. If I can anticipate, two problems will concern us in later sections. One is the question of equivalence. How can, and in what sense is, a part taken apart similar to the original moment; and, the prior question, how is it possible for my participation to be of a piece with the original? Secondly, if the lived moment is dynamic both in that it is a flux and in that it consists of relations in motion, relations being lived, how can a "part," a seemingly static entity, carry it away while retaining that life? We require a species of reflection that, to be true to lived experience, knows it as an enactment, as motion or movement.

For the moment, we consider a third question: How, and in what sense, is that part apart meaningful? We claim that abstracting bypasses the mediation of intellection, that the abstracted is not yet in words nor in an image, that it is present only as a potential presentation—and yet that it is meaningful. This is possible because meaning means through the body, the lived body. We can show this position by contrast to linguistic theories, for which meaning is centered in and has its origin in language.

In classical linguistics a direct relation between a conventional sign and an object, event, or, in general, an intended meaning constitutes meaning. Language, and therefore all meaning that obtains and may be conveyed, consists in a set of punctate relations between the signifier and the signified.[18] In this view, an intended meaning cannot stand alone meaningfully because it requires a signifier to mean. Further, linguistics as a science is primarily the study of the structure of signifiers—of phonemes and how they form words, and of how words in turn, governed by certain rules of syntax, form sentences.

In this enterprise the signified requires no further description. Two contemporary theorists carry this inattention to its extreme as, for them, the role in meaning of the already deprived signified is further reduced. Derrida, in his own terminology, "deconstructs" the structure signifier/signified by placing the latter under "erasure" and replacing it with a second signifier.[19] More simply, meaning consists in the structure signifier/signifier. There is no meaningful region prior to conventional signs; rather, the world is meaningful only in that it consists in signifiers. Experience is significant only in that it has the structure of a text. The world or our immediate experience of it is not tacitly meaningful and present as to-be-explicated. From the outset we are at the world as at a text. Meaning is not grounded in any originary lived relation we have to the world, nor even in our ongoing participation in it from moment to moment. Without such ground, there are only texts and our readings of them, more texts.

Lacan's creative recasting of these ideas within the molds of psychoanalytic thought provides further illustration of the modern plight of the signified. For Lacan, the analysand's dreams and associations, by extension your and my phenomenal worlds generally, consist in "chains of signifiers."[20] The signified, that lost ground that in Derrida's deconstruction is simply the false ground built by a philosophic tradition hankering after metaphysics, is the child's original wish to be with his mother. The signified is an unreachable state, an originary prepersonal relation, Freud's oceanic feeling. The child accomplishes the critical developmental task of relinquishing this desire by entering into the symbolic order, distinguished by Lacan from the real and the imaginary orders. He "forecloses" that wish for the mother (actually, to give more of the flavor of Lacan's thought, his wish to be the phallus of his mother, phallus being the symbol of wish, intention, the primordial signified) by accepting the *name* of the father. This adoption of the symbolic order, this accepted substitution of signifiers for the actual object of desire, precludes an otherwise psychotic resolution of that wish.[21]

In Lacan's modification of linguistic and Derridean terms, the signified goes "under the bar." Signifier/signified becomes signifier/signifier. The original signified is now irretrievably unconscious and what we have left to fill that gap are vague reverberations of it in endless chains of signifiers.

If accepted, these contemporary linguistic viewpoints on meaning result in a fundamental openness of human phenomena to interpretation and have profound implications for method in the social

sciences. They may themselves be variously interpreted as marking
the inauguration of a poststructuralist zeitgeist à la Derrida, or,
on the other side, as the peculiar reverberating signifiers of an
academician's lost signified—a game preserve with an open season
on meaning. Or they may signal the rediscovery of the "word,"
not as the deliverer of salvation but as therapeusis à la Lacan; or,
the other side of that, they may be interpreted as a reconstrual
of the schizoid position—withdrawal or retreat into words as
symptomatic of a failure at genuine relatedness to the world.

I do not accept a conceptualization of meaning based on the
structure signifier/signifier, for it denies the presence of tacit
meaning in experience. It does not deal with the fact that my
immediate lived experience is implicitly meaningful prior to my
assumption of a relation to it of linguist to language or reader
to text. To take action in the world requires me to be present to it,
embedded in it by taking part in it, again, by being a participant.
Not only do I know the situation that I am in (and hence how
to act in it) without disengaging from it, without reflectively
explicating it, at any moment I know more than I could tell. For
example, I recognize and distinguish more faces than I could
describe. I am incredibly informed as to the gist and nuances of
any ongoing situation in which I am engaged—well beyond any
immediate or reflected reading of it.

This is possible because the primary vehicle of experience's
meaningfulness is not language or any structure that is intelligible
as language. Rather, it is my body as I live it, my body as it is called
to action and as it is actively situated. The ringing telephone inter-
rupts my present activity and grips my heart well before I posit
that it is that long-awaited call. In a conversation I have a sense
of what I want to say before I have the words. What I intend to
say I find lodged bodily in me. The implicit meanings of situations and, as well, my own intended meanings are felt; they are
present bodily. Even in speech, I do not proceed in meaning or to
mean by moving from signifier to signifier. I must continually refer
to an implicit sense of what was said and what I would say.

Phenomena are immediately meaningful because they have the
structure lived body–lived world.[22] My bodily implication in situations is how they mean and how they are coconstituted. A situation
is not a set of objective facts to be read, but rather a moment that
I must live in a certain way. Through this requisite active commit-

ment meaning arises. In a sense, the structure lived body–lived world is the signified.

If I had to reply to the linguistic theorist of meaning in his own terms, I might say that meaning from moment to moment, as I am engaged, is more like a chain of signifieds than the traditional signifier/signified or the contemporary signifier/signifier. Phenomena, the world as it appears when we are living it, consist of signifieds, of layers of implicit meanings. It is because of this that the explication of human phenomena cannot begin with a method of linguistics or of interpretation. Again, we require a method that begins in a return to the world prior to language.

To borrow from M. Polanyi, we know more than we can tell.[23] We know in a way that does not yet invoke language or its structure—a way of knowing that, though meaningful and intelligible, does not intend to speak itself. To insist that it must is to begin to espouse what I might call the new reductionism. It is the attempt in several quarters to reduce social phenomena not to microbiology or to physics but to linguistics, semiotics, grammar. Here we counter that a key to the explication of phenomena is the lived body, not language. As one pole or moment in the constitution of phenomena, it is a ground of meaning. Meaning arises through the body as we live it, not that body according to natural science, the physiologist's body, but the lived body. Bodily participation in the world issues in and is itself an embodiment of that world.

The lived body is the *bearer* of meaning. It does not mean as a signifier does by referring to or symbolizing some intended meaning. It is itself the bearer of an intended meaning, a meaning present as to-be-understood, as to-be-explicated. It bears an equivalence to the original for it was one moment of it. To develop the distinction between equivalence and symbolization, it will be helpful to move from this description of an abstractive posture to a first mode of abstraction.

To summarize to this point, through rendering reflection as bodily abstraction, we have begun to suggest a method involving the sequence participation, embodiment, abstraction. We have also suggested that the lived body, the centerpiece of Merleau-Ponty's ontology, is the vehicle of that abstraction, that through it there is possible a kind of splitting or flaking-off, a meaningful parceling of the moment. We have yet to indicate what is carried away, how it is a meaningful although preconceptual and prelinguistic presence, and how that original part apart may be posited. To do so, we will continue to carve out a region of experiencing between the lived moment and its eventual explication.

THE AFFECTED BODY: AN ABSTRACTIVE MODE

To accomplish its task, an abstractive posture requires modes of experience that can embody knowledge of the world, that can carry meaning bodily. Of course, among such bodily modes are touching or feeling and grasping. Both of these are ways of exploring the world that immediately, as part of their respective forms of action, can both know and carry knowledge. When I touch or feel an object, as one moment of that experience I am touched. The touching of the object immediately impresses me in a certain way; I can carry that impress. In the most poignant instance, we say, "I am touched." When I grasp an object, I must "accommodate" my hand to that object's shape, to use Piaget's term. Having grasped something, my hand itself becomes an imitation of that object, or of an aspect of it such as its shape or size. I can show you a version of the object in its absence. I retain the "knowledge in the hand."

More generally, action both gives me and requires knowledge in the body. My action is a bodily mode of knowing the world which subsequently allows me to embody that knowledge. I can mimic what I have done; I can "act" or do mime. The performing arts, whether mime, dance, or theater, all feature the knowledge of the body.

The mode with which we will be concerned here is closer to touching and feeling than to the more full-fledged action of the latter group. "Feelings may be said to be that aspect of consciousness which most proximally draws attention to our bodiliness." [24] We will begin with a bodily mode of feeling, for it more readily demonstrates the bodily pole of experience and is itself more readily located and described. While such a mode is useful as part of a phenomenological method, we will discover that recourse to it limits explication to a broad-stroked description. However, this mode provides a model of what we seek. Through it, I can introduce a more subtle mode based more directly on action. This latter mode will yield a more articulate phenomenological description.

To establish referents in a preliminary way, consider this example: I am listening to recorded music in the company of my daughter. The band strikes up a marching song. My seven-year-old is immediately strutting about the room, furniture no obstacle. The record changes but she continues the same lilt into the kitchen. Having already enlisted the dog, she would now draft her mother. A second variation: the record stops and I go to the window. It seems brighter out now, the world is somehow lighter. Reflecting on this, I notice that I myself am buoyed and that, although not marching, I have partaken of the spirit of the march. A final variation: I am following the melody of the marching song. In doing so I am not imagining the music for this score, being ignorant of such matters, so much as I am following the movement of the music—the gathering power, the denouement, the regrouping. I do so, also, without yet resorting to the particular metaphor I have just offered, nor any other. There is just the movement of the piece and my following of it, which is the way I am participating in it. Of course, I am moving with it without leaving the chair. Further, I can anticipate its movement through my own. My own virtual movement in the ongoing moment and in the aftermath itself has an appearance. It is a tracing, a forming of an illusory space that somehow articulates the movement of the composition.

Each of the three variations exemplifies a distinct bodily mode, and each can subserve an abstractive posture. The first is familiar as a kind of imitative behavior; the third, forming, we deal with extensively in chapter 5; the second we treat here beginning with the descriptive: the affected body.

We approach this mode in those familiar moments when we directly take on the expression of a person with whom we are engaged. His smile is contagious and I find myself smiling. His mood is now seemingly mine. But sometimes, particularly as the moment shifts, my smile seems tacked on and I readily discard it. The mood has not really affected me. Having only worn it, I do not bear it away. Other times I take it with me. He affects me; what we had together lingers as a kind of halo which intermingles smoothly at its periphery with the atmosphere of another, a different kind of moment. Or, as I leave the movie theater, the heavy matinee immediately crashes and fractures against the mundanity of life in broad daylight. However, sometimes what I carry wins the day, as when I finish the exam with a flourish and find the world outside the classroom, apparently sympathetic, comes to receive me and makes its way to my doorstep.

Any moment can affect me. It can lay hold of me, touch me, flow into me; I am touched, moved, influenced. Having been affected, what I feel is affect, feeling, disposition. M. Scheler describes several "strata" of the "emotional life." [25] While we need attempt no phenomenology of feeling here, what we refer to as "being affected" is closest to his "vital feeling" and most distinguishable from his "sensory feeling." In vital feeling, there is a "unified consciousness of the body" rather than the localizable awareness of a separable part, as in sensory feeling. Rather than the pain in my knee after a fall or the gustatory pleasure in my stomach after a filling meal, there is a generalized feeling of weariness or misery, or vigor, zest, or elatedness. Further, while the vital feelings do refer to me, to my vitality, to my life, through vital feeling I also am exposed "immediately" to the world and events, "even when I do not in any way grasp their intellectual meaning." [26] In vital feeling, "the *value* of phenomena is given to us before the phenomena themselves" (Scheler's emphasis).[27] Here Scheler points to the way in which we are always receiving through these feelings the register of the world's impress without yet positing it as such. We are a "radical opening" onto the world;[28] we are threaded to it.[29] In the terms of the present exposition, we are an affected body.

What we are adding here to the sympathetic union between person and world described by numerous phenomenologists is its bodily prolongation after the fact. In what way is the bodily pole, one moment of a previous union, present after the fact? After a long day's work, I return home to my share of the preparation of the evening meal and to my participation in the life of my family as if they are tasks, as if they are burdens that threaten to strain me. Eventually I am asked by a discerning wife, "How was your day?" As I answer, the landscape of the home begins to reveal itself as, in a sense, counterfeit. I see that it is a continuation of a workday in which I had overextended myself. Failing to acknowledge or own that overextended, strained, stretched, and irritated lived body, I had let it be present as a landscape which I then attributed to my home. The simple question shook that present frame. The landscape pointed back to that passed-over, previously unposited, commuting bodily pole of my day at work. Finding itself no longer supportable, that landscape collapsed. The atmosphere of the evening became the possibility of a respite, indeed of a replenishment. Sometimes I manage to "forget" that landscape in another way, still without quite knowing how I have been affected by the day. In the course of working, I begin to sense a tightness in my shoulders. At first only occasional, it begins to establish itself as a pain to be reckoned with. Arriving at home, I lie down on the couch with a throbbing headache. As I focus on it now for the first time directly, again there is a sense in which it reveals itself as a counterfeit. It is a stand-in for a more general tightness, a more global, "vital" feeling of strain and overextension. Too much having come at me, I had tightened to protect myself from the overload of the day's work.

In this instance I have reified the original situation as the somatic symptom, headache. While I have a symptom, a sign of the original, it functions precisely to keep me from rather than to lead me to a more direct consideration of my apparently threatening work situation. In a like manner, in the previous example, the extension of my workplace into my home prevents me, paradoxically, from staying with it or returning to it, from eventually positing it as it originally appeared. By focusing on the landscape as counterfeit or the headache as a symptom, I can discover that sense of my lived body which, being forgotten, made each possible. From that tacit bodily sense, I can then return to the original. I can posit the particulars of that aggravating day, that indeed it was a Tuesday, my heavy and anxiety-provoking day. This circuitous path is useful in a clinical setting, for it is a way through the "defenses." It "works through" them to show them and the "psychodynamics" of the moment that occasioned them.

However, I can circumvent these pathologies and arrive more directly at the bodily sense of a situation as lived. If I assume an abstractive posture, a bodily prolongation of that situation is possible. Through the intention to take a part apart, I can locate or discover in the phenomenal field the tacit presence of the bodily pole of experience. At any moment I am being affected by the situation in a bodily way. This is not to say that the situation is there, outside of or prior to my entrance. To the contrary, the way I enter, how I take it up, is coconstitutive of the situation. For the day at work to strain me, in a sense I must assent to its invitation; I must overextend myself in concert with it. Yet at the same time that the lived body is one moment of the bipolar affair that we call experience, that body is horizontally present as the way it is affected. When I answer the invitation of that horizon, I find myself turned to it and for the first time positing the body as it has been and is affected. As we have described, that move does not have the simple structure of a shift in attention. The new object has the general structure of the abstracted. A residue of a previous moment presents itself as the second story of a part apart.

Here what lifts itself up is the way I have been affected. As I participate, I am moved, touched, impressed, affected in a certain way that is now part of me. The body that can, indeed must, be so affected is itself a first mode of abstraction. It is a way I embody, a way experience means to me. Under the auspices of an abstractive set, I am bearing it as part of me. While I might notice it in the heaviness of the landscape or in the lilt of my gait, it is present as a more general bodily feeling. When I take that body as an object, I can directly receive its embodied meaning. In Gendlin's terms, when I "focus" on "bodily felt-meaning, words [can] come from it." [30] Positing the affected body, explication of the way my body is, of how I am and how I was in that situation, of how I was situated, follows immediately.

Here we are faced with a regress with respect to the lived body. In a radical sense, on the level of the ontology of experiencing beings, I believe that regress is unavoidable. While illuminating if followed to a limited extent, it is a spiral in which we as phenomenologists are inherently caught. Fortunately, that we are so is not critical to our methodological concern here. The lived body cannot take itself as an object. "The body is the point of view on which there cannot be a point of view." [31] This is to say, with Merleau-Ponty, that the body is the basis of reflection *and* that there is no possibility of pure reflection.[32]

The affected body as abstracted is not the equivalent of the lived body through which I abstract at that moment. Nor to abstract do I adopt a second lived body from a store maintained for such purposes. In any moment, whether in an abstractive or engaged posture, how I live is through the lived body. But as I am living, I am being affected in a particular way. That way, essentially a bodily feeling, has a protracted effect. We say I carry it or bear it. In a sense, it is a former lived body. More precisely, it is a necessary residue of it, its inescapable product. Again, as I live, I am necessarily being bodily affected. The subsequent residue is a relative congealing of the bodily pole of a previous moment of living. I carry it as the earth contains the frozen cells of a former inhabitant. They are ready to show us their life if we only know how to approach them. Of course, when I do so a circularity is operative. The meaning they embody is never transparent to me, for I must take up that affected body in a certain way which is then part of what it means and which itself issues in a further affected body. But in that a particular affected body is an embodiment of a moment as lived, in that it has the double-story structure of the abstracted, that is, that it takes that embodied part apart, and in that it is, at least in its origin, an unmediated prolongation of that moment, it can serve us well in doing phenomenological psychology.

THE PREPERSONAL UNION: THE ORIGIN OF BODY-WORLD

Aside from the phenomenological gain, when we assume an abstractive posture we can posit an awareness which, as adults, we often have lost or know only as it is distorted in pathological variants such as the projection or externalization and somaticization illustrated earlier. The literature in developmental psychology, whether psychoanalytic, cognitive, or phenomenological, suggests that there is an early precursor of the affected body and of bodily abstractive modes more generally. While only a rough assay of the structure of the infant's world is possible, the various literatures converge on the idea that there is a period early in development when the child makes no distinction between the self and the other.[33] Experience does not yet have the structure of intentionality, of a subject taking an object; nor does it have the basic structures of temporality, of a before and an after. Piaget describes how the child must learn the concept of object through a period in which his activity does not yet have the structure of action.[34] H. S. Sullivan refers to a prototaxic mode of experiencing in which self and world are undifferentiated, as are moment from moment.[35] Following H. Wallon, Merleau-Ponty refers to the "syncretic system of me-and-other."[36] If the child's relation to his or her mother in this period is "symbiotic,"[37] this does not mean that the child lives an attachment of self to other; rather he lives a primary "unseparatedness."[38] For the child, there has been no attachment, for there are not two entities. Following psychoanalytic literature, we may speculate that he experiences this state as fullness or perfection or bliss.

In any case, there is only the comprehensive, prepersonal, and, of course, unposited entity, *child-world*.

That the child's experience has this structure, or, more aptly, this lack of structure, makes intelligible his apparently prodigious sensitivity in this period. In particular, he seems exquisitely sensitive to the expressive and emotional aspects of his surround. Sullivan notes that the mother's "emotional disturbance" immediately registers in the expression or performance of the infant.[39] The child is attentive to facial expression and responds in kind with roughly imitative expressiveness and gesture—a smile for a smile. With explicit reluctance Sullivan writes of a "communication of anxiety" or a "kind of empathy." [40] For clearly these attribute to the infant capacities that are well beyond him developmentally. But our language fails us, being itself built on the existential structures of subject and object. "Contagion" and Sullivan's "induction" are closer although they retain a remnant sense of two entities. The child catches the mother's anxiety because "there is not one individual over against another but rather an anonymous collectivity, an undifferentiated group life . . . an initial community." [41] Given being-in-common, there is no need for communication.

Analogous to this inescapable "precommunication" based on a "syncretic sociability," the infant's "action" is a primitive act. Without agency, his movements are "primary circular reactions," [42] simply motoric exercises. Initially, the infant repeats a particular movement of his own body; later, he acts to repeat the effect of an object external to his body, as for example shaking the rattle that someone shakes before him. Again, we must not understand this as one person imitating another. "At first the child imitates not persons but conducts." [43] In a sense, initially there is only conduct and, later, conduct-in-common. Even the attribution of imitative action is too strong. As Piaget's language suggests, the early repetitive character of the child's reactions reflect more a biological function than a personal intention. The early sensorimotor schemata have an inherent property to exercise themselves. Through motoric bodily functioning in interaction with the "aliment" provided by his environment, the child-world begins to crystallize into object, action on it, and agent of action. The child can now genuinely imitate a world from which he is relatively distinct. At the same time, his imitation is a version of the world which is his own.

Before this emergence the child was not merely embedded or situated in the world, he was radically a part of it. There were not self and spectacle but only happenings and the climate of their occurrence. The child was of a piece through his body. Through both its affective and expressive aspects and its potential for movement, he was radically exposed to that climate. The infant's sensitivity is really an indiscriminateness, an undifferentiation, a bodily being that is part of a greater body. He moves in relation to that larger body as an organism, adrift at sea with no demarcating anchor of its own, follows the current.

The personhood of the child, then, issues from certain bodily connections to the world: what we have called the affected body, and certain simple motor reactions. For Piaget, the child achieves this integrity through a complex development of sensorimotor schemata which culminates in the presumption of the "constancy" of objects and, correlatively, of self in the posture of the self as agent. This development proceeds through an interactive process wherein the child simultaneously and continually becomes like the world ("accommodation") and shapes it to fit himself ("assimilation"). By means of this process the child learns first to imitate objects and their movement in their absence, as when in play he lets one object stand for another. Eventually he can imitate these at will, without props, through images which being in their likeness begin to constitute a mental representation of the world. This gives the child some mastery of the world by reducing his prior vulnerability to its immediate bodily effect on him.

In psychoanalytic accounts of this period, this "separation" requires the playing out of a drama in which certain needs and wishes of the child are frustrated. The child resolves his conflict by a compromise in which he at once relinquishes the object of his needs and "identifies" with certain aspects of that object. Through variable modes of taking it in, "aspects of internalization" such as incorporation, introjection, and identification,[44] the child separates from the world and attains "individuation" by becoming like it. In a stage transitional to this he relates to the world as if it were part of himself. In this narcissistic orientation, "objects" in the world are as "self-objects."[45]

Building on Lacan's observations, Merleau-Ponty finds that the critical moment when the child is "drawn from this immediate reality" is the discovery of his body as a unified object.[46] This is demonstrable in the child's fascination with the mirror. The child is torn away from the immediately felt "introceptive body," "this immediately lived me ... [to] a me that is visible at a distance." [47] Between the affected body and the world with which it was once one flesh, there arises that "corporeal schema," that unified body, which is me as others see me and I as I see myself. The immediately felt me, which formerly was a me indistinguishable from its setting, is now in conflict with a visible me, the mirror's image of me. Through this viewpoint on myself, I objectify myself and the other person. The visual now predominates over the affective, permitting me to control more readily both things and people in the world and their bodily effect on me. Corporeal unity diminishes corporeal dominion; but, as well, it reduces access to and awareness of bodily affectivity.

In these rich and seminal accounts, only sketchily indicated here, the several observer-theorists grapple with the problem of how the child comes to distinguish himself from, while maintaining a fundamental affinity to, the world. Whatever the differences in their resolutions, they all point to a radical bodily equivalence as an original state out of which the person emerges. Before there is a self, even before there is a unified sense of my body and my body for others, before phenomena assume the structure of experience by becoming the way the world appears to me, and before there is the possibility of abstracting from the world in which I act, all that I am is "of a piece"—a radically embedded body. In each account, this bodily undifferentiatedness serves as the ground for a separation which then can be only relative. The original indistinguishableness makes possible the resemblance, the equivalence between myself and the world. Building on this ground, for each observer-theorist I become a being that carries the world with me. For Piaget I recreate the world in the form of an image by abbreviating, internalizing, and transforming my own action, itself initially merely an echo of the movement of a surround in which I am only latently present. In contemporary object-relations psychoanalysis, those persons from whom I must separate become part of me as I incorporate, introject, and eventually identify myself with them. I carry that interpersonal world in the form of internalized personifications that goad or punish me, or as structural features of my psyche, their origins forgotten.

For Lacan, "I" become how the world sees me. I carry a

mirrored me, an alienated me. While for Piaget my relative connectedness to the world is through an isomorphic representation of it, and for much psychoanalytic thought it is at least a partially gratifying personified version, for Lacan the alienation is intractable. It can only be assuaged by reverberations through language of the lost prepersonal union. In language, we have a common discourse and may be reunited at least in our alienation from the world out of which we all emerged.

As I have indicated, each of these descriptions of the birth of the self recognizes its origin in an indiscriminate, prepersonal bodily connectedness. Further, each only partially severs that connection for, being originally a part of the main, the self necessarily carries some vestige of it. Each utilizes some form of imitation, in the broadest sense of that concept, to maintain a similarity or equivalence and, hence, a bond of kinship. However, while they begin with a bodily union and maintain some loose association and identity in effecting a self, eventually they abandon the bodily as a dominant mode of that connectedness. Reunion with the world, continued sensitivity to it and knowledge of it, comes to rely on cooler, more distanced modes—abstract formal concepts, imagistic representations, linguistic associations and categorizations. Lacan's emphasis on alienation, on the "gap," is apt in that these modes provide duplications, models, and schematizations rather than direct access.

That bodily equivalence is a primary possibility adds compellingness to the present thesis that I both can know the world in the moment and can carry it with me in a bodily way. Given my origin as a bodily embeddedness, as of-a-piece, what I become is a bodily prolongation of the world. This origin and its prolongation are the conditions for the possibility of my imitation of the world. While I can imitate the world dramatically by producing discrete replicas or even paragons of it that, surpassing it, allow me to ameliorate or destroy it, the way I know it originally and at every moment is more quiet and more intimate. Following the self-constituting rift with the originary "world," my experience becomes that quiet, unnoticed coconstituting dialectic lived body–lived world. The bodily pole, then, is an embodiment of any and every moment. Through it I know that moment by merely being a prolongation of it—without yet resorting to the distance of representation or imitation or the violence of reconstruction or symbolization. Being incarnate is how I originally knew and in every moment know the world. Only through the fact of my embodiment can I become armed and, ambivalently, armored with these other modes.

The abstractive posture effects a return to a forgotten bodily sensitivity, to the presence of myself as an embodiment. It is not something I need to learn; rather I need both to rediscover it, as it was an original possibility, and to uncover it, for it is hidden by the predominant visual and intellective modes. Ironically, taking a part apart in the way we have described serves to reinstate my awareness of my being of-a-piece. Far from being a disembodying act, abstraction returns me to my bodily participation and to my embodiment. In the context of the purpose of the present essay, it is in the service not of recovering my early childhood (although it harks back to the bodily equivalence of that period), but of revealing how the world or any phenomenon appears to me as I live it.

ABSTRACTION OF THE TEXTURE OF PHENOMENA

We have been discussing one bodily mode, one means of conveyance, within the abstractive posture. This mode of embodiment carries an effect which is the prolongation of how I was affected by a phenomenon as lived. When I assume an abstractive posture, it is precisely this way my body is being affected that can lift out, which I then begin to notice, and which I eventually can carry away as a part apart. But what aspect of any particular moment immediately affects my body, touches me, and impacts on me? I am not affected by any aspect in particular but by all aspects, by the phenomenon as a whole. Before I say what it means, all that it means affects me. The whole experience weighs on me or lightens my way.

However, a particular experience or phenomenon as a whole as I live it is already an *aspect* of that phenomenon. The entirety of the phenomenon is present as that phenomenon's atmosphere. By the atmosphere or ambience of a phenomenon I do not refer to its particular momentary setting. While a phenomenon may be said to appear in variable settings in that it has variable appearances, that which constitutes it as a particular phenomenon is what appears across all its settings. A phenomenon is the theme in the variations on a theme. Every phenomenon intends a world. We as readily speak of the world of grief as that of the dance, of drug addiction, of seeing, or of the beautiful. As a world, a phenomenon has a general atmosphere or ambience or tone or style or way or physiognomy. It is that aspect, the feel of the phenomenon, that affects me. It is because the lilt of the marching song is a world that I can so readily surpass it and realize it in the lightness of the day. However, when I realize it more directly, what lifts out is the buoyancy of my affected body. Atmosphere and the affected body have a correlative relation. One is not the stimulus to which the other is response. Together they form one moment in the coming into being of a particular world. Their relation may be likened to that between Husserl's *noeme-noese,* where the atmosphere approximates the object, the *noeme,* of the *noese,* the affected body. Here, however, atmosphere, remaining just that, is not posited as an object. Rather, in the aftermath of the moment I can carry the atmosphere as an affected body which eventually itself may be posited as an object.

It should be clear that this atmosphere of the whole is a constitutive feature of a given phenomenon. I will refer to it as texture and distinguish it from a second constitutive feature, the structure of a phenomenon. A major task of chapter 3 is a critical examination of contemporary concepts of structure. For the moment, structure is the set of relations among the parts that constitute a phenomenon, while texture is the "feel" of the phenomenon, including, critically, the feel of those relations. The distinction is in the neighborhood of the oppositions content/ form and figure/ground. The metaphor flesh/skeleton is also helpful.

Both texture and structure are associated with a particular and correlative mode of their respective apprehension and abstraction. As we have described, the texture of a phenomenon is an atmosphere that affects me as I live it. I can abstract that bodily pole as a vital feeling which I then can posit as a feeling. The structure of a phenomenon is its dynamic relations, how the parts stand in relation to each other. In the lived moment these dynamic relations are present to me as a field of forces, as a certain potential movement. Correlative to this, I live the structure as a virtual conduct of my own body. I can abstract that bodily pole as a motor intention, as the possibility of a certain movement.

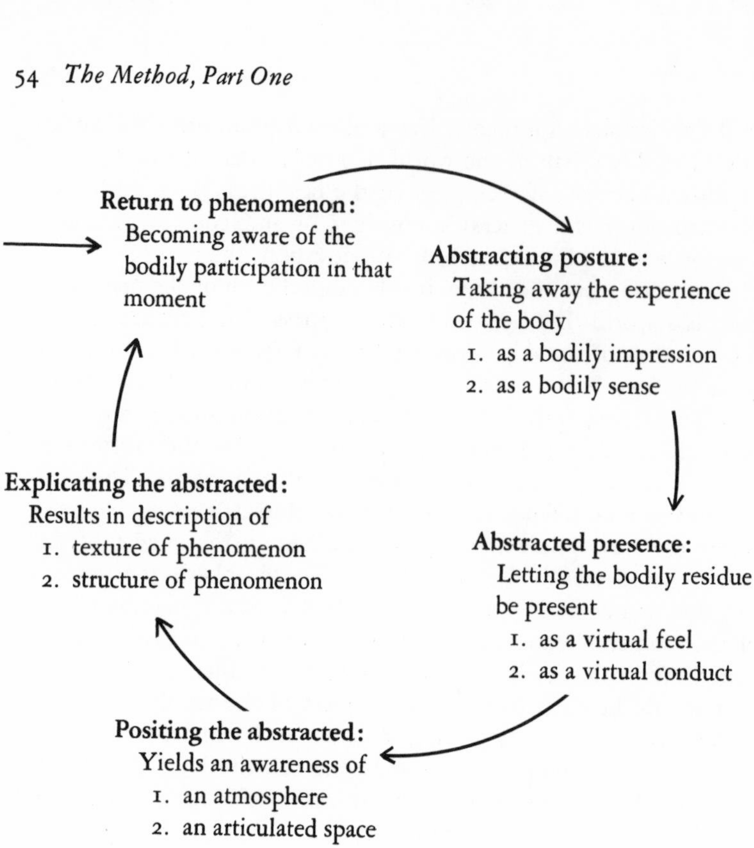

Return to phenomenon:
Becoming aware of the
bodily participation in that
moment

Abstracting posture:
Taking away the experience
of the body
  1. as a bodily impression
  2. as a bodily sense

Explicating the abstracted:
Results in description of
  1. texture of phenomenon
  2. structure of phenomenon

Abstracted presence:
Letting the bodily residue
be present
  1. as a virtual feel
  2. as a virtual conduct

Positing the abstracted:
Yields an awareness of
  1. an atmosphere
  2. an articulated space

FIGURE I

While the texture of a phenomenon moves me, to know the
structure I must move with it or through it. I call this mode of
abstraction *forming*. In that forming is a kind of doing, it is
participatory, "a living of." As a mode of reflective abstraction,
however, it is a potential reliving that can know what it does.
Hence it is at once a being and a knowing, a living and a "seeing."
In it we will find a behavioral mode of the apprehension of
structure which provides sharp contrast to the classical modes of
Husserl with their reliance on the visual and its virtual counterparts, the imaginative and the intuitive. Further, its postponement
of the entrance of language until a relatively late moment in the

reflective journey distinguishes it from certain contemporary linguistic modes.

Through these bodily modes of abstraction, we reassert the meaningfulness of the immediate and the bodily prior to language. In particular, with forming, we describe how a phenomenon has a presence, a tacit meaningfulness which I know through virtual conduct. I participate in a behavioral space which has an equivalence to the structure of a given phenomenon.

This latter thesis extends the description of phenomenologists such as Merleau-Ponty and Scheler for whom behavior is our access to each other. For Merleau-Ponty, the other person, being himself "not a 'psyche' closed in on himself but rather a conduct, a system of behavior . . . offers himself to my motor intentions."[48] For Scheler, as interpreted by Schütz:

The Person, as the correlate of different forms and categories of acts, manifests itself exclusively by performing the acts in which it lives and by which it experiences itself. . . . [A]s far as the other persons are concerned, they can be experienced by coperformance, reperformance, or preperformance of the other person's acts.[49]

We will describe the sense in which I know not only the other person but, as well, the structure of phenomena as "the correlate of different forms and categories of acts."

In doing so we will add to our description of reflection as a bodily abstraction, a bodily taking away which begins in the constitution of a double-story structure. We will show reflection as a bodily mode which makes it possible for me to reenact and posit the structure of a phenomenon as such. Through the description of this abstractive mode, the in-and-out movement of the dialectic will be more fully explicated as an ongoing succession of returns and abstractions. It will be shown to consist in a circle of bodily participation, embodiment, bodily abstraction, thematization of the bodily pole, and participation anew. Figure 1 schematizes our presentation to this point and the task of the ensuing chapters.

3

Concepts of Structure

Having described an abstractive posture and one mode of abstraction
with its typical object, we have other business before we can turn
to the second mode. Before we can describe forming, we must
deal critically with that object which, we argue, it intends—
structure. Does that object have an appearance in immediate
experience? To the extent that it does, a phenomenological
approach to it can be justified. Here we construct one end of a
spectrum of concepts of structure which vary from those that
limit its location to regions exterior to experience to those that
allow or require its inherency in experience.

There is considerable agreement that when I refer to the
structure of an entity, whether that entity be a condition of the
natural world, a situation, a human relation, or a way of experiencing, I intend relations among parts.[1] With respect to structure
parts are substitutive, while the way things are together is
constitutive. Divergence of opinion sharpens when I attempt to
specify the locus or region of being that "contains" structure.
These discrepancies are not simply a function of the phenomena
peculiar to a given field of inquiry, the anthropologist's gift-giving
ceremony or the physicist's quark. Rather, they are a derivative
of general epistemological and ontological assumptions peculiar
to different disciplines. Critical to my concern here, region of
structure immediately implicates mode of apprehension of structure:
the kind of "thing" structure is limits it to certain ways of
knowing it.

LÉVI-STRAUSS'S STRUCTURALISM

In that it locates structure exterior to experience, "structuralism" [2] is necessarily a critique of existentialism and phenomenology.[3] The primacy of subjectivity, emphasized by existentialism, is overthrown as analysis shifts from the level of the subject's intentions to that of linguistic structures.[4] Intended meaning and any meaningful presence of structure are relegated to linguistic systems outside of experience. An examination of structuralism, particularly of the structuralism of Lévi-Strauss, provides the exemplar of the extreme "exterior" end of our spectrum.

While it has been called by some a pseudoschool,[5] structuralism has a loose unity in at least three regards: (1) it largely emanates from a French intellectual tradition with roots in rationalist philosophy, particularly that of Descartes;[6] (2) if there is any common core to a structuralist method it owes its modern origin to the work of Saussure in linguistics;[7] and (3) it shares certain presuppositions about cultural phenomena and mind, such as a kind of isomorphism between them and, at the same time, a certain priority of the latter over the former.

Structure as Sedimented Strata

Lévi-Strauss credits geology as among the determinants of the direction of his thinking about structure.[8] To the geologist, a landscape of valleys, plains, mountains, and ravines is only the apparent, the surface. Such features are extremely diverse and have no final boundaries. While it is immediately visible, the landscape is not really intelligible, or at least it is equivocal in meaning. If the landscape itself has any structure, that structure is superficial and functions as much to conceal as to reveal the deeper structures that underlie it and give it its shape. A truly unequivocal account of the landscape requires a description of this deeper structure, this concealed undergirding. The geological strata below the landscape are the structures through which the landscape means.

For Lévi-Strauss the features of the landscape are like social facts which constitute a culture but only its veneer. They all fit together, one giving way to the next, but with no explicit cohesion. Any understanding of a feature or features is largely local and is limited to a realization of apparent relations, as the way the hills surround a vale. There are strata hidden beneath these social facts and their merely contigual and adjunctive relations. The inhabitant of a culture is largely unaware of these geological strata. He cannot see them, for they are hidden, and he typically does not look for them. He takes as the objects of his experience the features of the landscape, a set of social facts. He traverses the landscape, thereby gaining varied perspectives on it but always operating from within it. Its explicit meaning to him is limited to the local and contigual relations of its features. The culture is organized at a level below this surface but he does not know this organization.

From this typically structuralist perspective, structure is not conceived as tacitly present or intimated but rather as profoundly buried. While the inhabitants impose a structure on some givens, presumably ecological in origin, to constitute a cultural world, this world is one of which they are "unconscious" [9] both as to its organization and as to the mode by which they organized and, in an ongoing fashion, organize it. The inhabitant does not live through the organization and in that way gain knowledge of it, as the phenomenologist would assert. While it guides him in the construction of his world, it remains always a hidden foundation of that edifice. It is always external to that life that he lives and knows.

Enter the anthropologist. Unlike the inhabitant he is a stranger even to the landscape. He does not know how to live in the culture, how to traverse from one object to another or to anticipate what is on the other side of a hill. Like the inhabitant, he is a stranger to the particular deep structure that underlies this particular land-scape. However, he believes he has the tools to lay bare that stratum. When he does he confronts both a set of features formerly concealed and a peculiar organization, a layered organization, again one that was not immediately apparent in the surface relations of the social facts. This organization consists of layers of structure arrayed such that deeper strata provide more inclusive and general organizations, from "surface" to "deep" structures. The identification first of these features and then of their layered organizations constitutes the primary work of the anthropologist as geologist. A final move is the comparison of one stratum to that of another region, another culture.

Here we begin to surpass the usefulness of the geological metaphor. The strata are not directly laid bare as in certain circumstances
they are for the geologist, nor is any direct sampling possible.
The strata are intrinsically hidden and must be fathomed indirectly.
Again from a structuralist perspective, the buried geological strata
are in the region of the "rational" as distinguished from the merely
"sensible," those shimmerings of the landscape that are the inhabitant's immediate neighborhood. There is here a more discrete
distinction between the sensible and the rational than a phenomenologist finds descriptive. The former is considered largely elemental, that is, devoid of structure and of meaning, a kind of brute
reality. The latter is then the only meaningful access to the sensible
or the real. This rationalistic way to social facts or appearance is
through an understanding of underlying structure. To understand
this local, preconceptual, and inarticulate mass of sense-data, the
structuralist must plumb that subterranean region which is the locus
of structure. However, if structure is in the region of the rational,
any particular structure cannot be self-evident, cannot be known
immediately or immanently.

Structure as rational is as a foreign language that requires translation or as a code that must be deciphered. The strata are linguistic categories, a hidden lexicon; the relations among strata are
a kind of syntax; and the relations among sets of strata are a set
of rules of transformation. The structural anthropologist is a linguist and a metalinguist. As such he operates against overwhelm-
ingly adverse conditions. In a foreign land he yet cannot ask directions for those who live in the culture do not know what he seeks
to know. He has only the shape of the land but that conceals or
at least is equivocal as to its underlying and meaning-giving nature.
The structural method must be a potent one.

Before we turn to an exposition of the method that follows from
a conceptualization of structure as linguistic, a further point can
be developed within the present discussion. The geological metaphor illuminates the peculiar and complex structuralist handling
of the temporal. If structure is likened to underlying strata, it has
a certain temporal stability which at increasingly deeper layers
approaches the ahistorical.

While it would be granted by the structuralist that all structures
are laid down in time, at the deepest level they are considered
universal, timeless features of culture (and of mind, as we will see).

But even at the middle level of structure between the surface landscape and this deep structure, analysis emphasizes the stability both of strata and their relations. While it is not denied that the layering of the strata imply a history, description is of present nexes. The present layering is a relatively fixed one. While the layering refers to a past and implies a future, relations among strata are all there now. This present network may be described without centering on it as a set of inherently temporal relations—as the network of retentions and protensions of Husserl's analysis of inner-time consciousness. While for Husserl and more radically for later phenomenologists, notably Heidegger, this intimated temporal system is itself foundational, for the structuralist the present strata can be treated as structural, not temporal. Certain principles of *their* organization provide an essentially atemporal foundation. Again, even at a middle range of depth of structure, the layering is of relatively congealed strata that are there now. Somehow a structure has a permanence which is not simply its history. A structure is not its history nor is it a history of its individual elements at the superficial level. In structuralist terms, the synchronic is a more fundamental level of reality than the diachronic. The latter merely reflects the former. "Each act [is] as an unfolding in time of certain non-temporal truths." [10]

That structure in this middle range of generality, that is, at the level of cultural phenomena, is relatively congealed is consistent with our own position. However, for the structuralist these relatively fixed structures have no presence. Though the underlying structure is likened to the geologist's rock, it may only be approached in the region of the insubstantial, of the rational. Having no phenomenal presence, it must be inferred. Fixity refers only to a relative ahistoricity for the structuralist. It is almost as if to escape the embeddedness of the historical, the structuralist presumes he must go to the rational. While he calls himself structuralist, the structural anthropologist is more comfortable with a linguistic and syntactical model to describe this layering. He cannot begin with it as a form or a shape, as a "structure" in that original sense. Rather than begin with the presence of the temporal in the way it appears, as a certain shape, and reflect on that, he denies its presence as such and deductively leaps to discover it or some version of it in the region of the rational. We maintain that while structure is relatively congealed and therefore knowable as shape, it contains and includes a temporal organization. This is to say that part of that which is congealed or fixed is a temporal patterning.

Structure as Language

To make the anthropologist's project possible, Lévi-Strauss requires additional assumptions about the structure of culture. He invokes a bedrock or deep structure for which he claims an invariability that is in contrast both to the shifting contours of the landscape and the relatively gradual evolution of its immediate structural underpinnings. The basis of the invariability of this deep structure is an assumed isomorphism between culture and mind. The isomorphism operates within the culture between it and its inhabitant. With this presumption an understanding of the artifacts of a culture, their meaning and organization, is equivalently an understanding of the mind of the user and creator of the artifact. The image suggested by this, that the inhabitant in pointing to an object also points to himself, is termed *redoublement* in structuralist writings.[11]

Like culture, at its deepest levels structures of mind are universal and ahistorical. In fact, as universal structures of mind, they are operative in and limit and guide the formation of all cultures. But what is our access to these structures which govern culture formation? Fortunately, according to structuralist lights, the operation of language manifests the operation of mind:

> The emergence of mind coincides with that of language; together they constitute an intellectual and qualitative mutation in time, and, even more important, represent a priori and generic givens from which all further historical events and human creation may be deduced. Lévi-Strauss characterizes this universal *esprit humain* as follows: Like language, the human mind differentiates empirical reality into constituent units; these units are organized into systems of reciprocal relations; and these systems enunciate rules to govern their possible combinations.[12]

This complex and rather inelegant ontology, at once joining culture and mind isomorphically and identifying mind with language, allows Lévi-Strauss to borrow for his own purposes aspects of theories of language. In classical linguistics,[13] language is conceived of as a set of hierarchically related systems such that, for example, a change in one phoneme changes the set of phonemes that is a word. The phonemes of a language are a limited set of elements that are meaningful only in combination. Without rules for these possible meaning-giving arrangements, phonemes present only a bewildering array of meaningless sense-data. To discover these rules requires moving beneath those meaningless elements to a deeper level, an underlying structure, which here is a kind of lexicon. Contemporary linguistics extends these relations between hierarchically related systems, mutatis mutandis, for words and sentences. An underlying structure in the form of a grammar provides rules for the meaningful ordering of words into sentences. These rules are themselves undergirded by universal rules which are indistinguishable from the structure of mind.

For each pair of systems constituting language, it is the discovery and application of underlying similarities which makes a seemingly haphazard array intelligible. In each case the underlying structure has the character of an operation of reason on the sensible, for it consists of rules or principles of organization. Again, as in the geological metaphor, structure is extrinsic to that which it organizes. In particular it is an operation from below; structure is underlying. Superficial elements or parts in and of themselves are merely sense-data that must be arranged according to a rational structure to attain meaning. One must probe below the surface, below appearance to underlying reality, below the sensible to the reasonable, below differences to similarities. This is the basic structuralist move whereby structure is located. Of course, this is one way to think about understanding—for example, the kind of insights that Freud and Marx gave us involve a comparable move. A vast array of seemingly disparate phenomena are given organization, made meaningful by a limited set of underlying principles.

For Lévi-Strauss, culture may be treated as a language because social facts, social relations, and cultural artifacts, like phonemes, are meaningful only through the consideration of a structure, here a social structure, that underlies them. Like language, culture is or is built on a layered affair. At the deepest level its foundation is relatively universal, providing requisites and setting basic limits on the formation of culture. A particular culture is made intelligible primarily through an understanding of a middle level which is at once limited by a deeper level and itself limiting or organizing a superficial level, the particular existing set of social relations, including institutions, mythology, and all the artifacts of a living culture.

However, these relations between the structure of culture and language are not intended metaphorically. The structure of culture consists of the same entities that constitute language: a set of categories, a matrix of rules of syntax, and superordinate rules governing that matrix. Culture's structure is inseparable from symbolic thought.

A Linguistic and Logico-Mathematic Method

Given this conceptualization of the problem of structure, where would Lévi-Strauss have the anthropologist stand; with what postures and modes can he begin to locate and describe the structures of interest? A phenomenological method is ruled out because the structure, being underlying, has no presence in the cultural phenomenon. Lévi-Strauss relinquishes the possibility of any lived grasp of the structure of the phenomenon, any form of understanding based on the phenomenon as lived. He is prevented also from an empirical inductive method, from simply moving by inference from the data, for it is equivocal as to its meaning and, again, its organization is an underlying, hidden foundation. The culture is a gelatinous mass floating loosely and opaquely over its structure. This leaves at least partial reliance on some form of rationalistic or deductive method.

Lévi-Strauss describes two methodologic moves as follows: "define the phenomenon under study as a relation between two or more terms, real or supposed . . . [and] construct a table of possible permutations between these terms." [14] The two moves may be described here as categorizing and formalizing.

Investigating a cultural phenomenon such as the family or a set of myths, the structural anthropologist's first move is to locate a set of elements comparable to the linguist's set of phonemes. These elements are only meaningful through categories that organize them. Initially the posture is an observational stance, a view of the arrangements of the sensibles from an external vantage point. But that arrangement is assumed to be categorical. This is the case even though the culture is in a sense mute to itself. The inhabitants form the culture through the operation of a set of categories of which they are largely unconscious. The primitive mind employs a "concrete logic," builds its culture through a "science of the concrete." [15] Unreflectively, sensible qualities guide the basis of classifications, giving content and form to a given culture's familial relations and myths.

More particularly, then, the anthropologist's posture is one of category finding or concept formation. From this posture he locates salient features of the culture and organizes them into categories— where on the body certain items of clothing are worn, divisions of relatives along certain dimensions. Lévi-Strauss's anthropologist stands in the thick of the categorical reaching up from it toward the phenomenon which is a certain arrangement of elements. The approach begins with language because Lévi-Strauss believes the emergence of culture and its expression in language are the same moment. The search for categories is then a necessary and effective way to find similarities among disparate elements, of encompassing apparent differences.

But it is not simply a matter of thematic analysis. The observed array does not yield the categories directly or unequivocally. The culture as a code is sloppy and inefficient, ambiguous and polyvalent. The anthropologist requires not only a dictionary but a grammar to understand the cultural phenomenon of interest. As the categories are a structure external to but supporting the concrete features of the culture, they in turn are supported, guided, and limited by deeper structures. For example, one deep structure is the property of the human mind to limit categories to binary opposites, such as raw/cooked, near/far, container/contained. Because of their isomorphic relation this qualifying rule about categories also will operate in the formation of culture.

The logico-mathematical character of this particular deep structure, binary categories, is typical. It lends itself to a cultural analysis through tabular presentation and reduction to formal signs. For example, all the "near" elements (close relatives) can be listed as "+," while their respective "far" counterparts are listed "−." In this way a thematic analysis gives way to a more formal one. All possible combinations and permutations of the terms within the categories can be generated logically. The formal signs can be further organized or operated on by rules of transformation or transposition. For example, near/far rendered as "+/−" is further organized by a rule such as "If the relations between brother/sister and father/son is "+," then that between nephew/uncle and husband/wife is "−." [16] The formalization allows transpositions or translations and hence comparisons within a culture across apparently disparate phenomena, and across cultures.

The formalizing posture assumed to effect the construction of these tables and rules or formulae is a second turn of the linguistic screw. Lévi-Strauss can stand in the thick of the categorical from the outset because he believes he is supported by a bedrock of certain a priori universals. This bedrock is the set of rules for all possible grammars, for all possible arrangements of a set of categories. The structure of a culture is both a set of linguistic categories and a matrix of rules of syntax. Lévi-Strauss would have the anthropologist apply relatively formal logico-mathematical operations to get at these latter. He would have structure or form be known only as "formal," that is, as a logico-mathematical entity. This is the case despite the fact that structure also involves shape for Lévi-Strauss, as his reliance on an assumption of isomorphism makes clear. Isomorphism implies that structures that are similar are so in shape or form. But given his distrust of the "sensible" and his complementary, or is it compensatory, faith in the rational and the linguistic, the formal is never a description of shape or form. It is formal in that its expression is through formulae, mathematical or logical statements or rules.

In the final analysis Lévi-Strauss stands by his faith in the rational. Categorizing and formalizing are possible and requisite postures because for him the structure of a phenomenon is in the region of the rational from its beginning. A structuralist method does not seek to abstract structure in our sense, for structure is originally abstract, having the rational as its birthplace and permanent residence. It is not a matter of locating structure in experience but of deducing and inducing it. If the structure of phenomena is already abstract and if that structure is grounded in structures of mind, then the application of rational systems is a compelling method of choice. By comparison to the phenomenologist, the structuralist investigator must do more than or other than have a certain relation of regard to the phenomenon, a return to it, a living manipulation of its aspects, and a crystallizing of what was already immanent. Believing that a full, almost tangible grasp of structure is possible, the phenomenologist attempts to move toward that grasp while and by never letting go of it. The structuralist's relation to structure does not so involve him for he does not allow the possibility of such intimacy with it. A rationalist at heart, his faith necessarily is in the rules of his own logic, the structures and structuralizing tendencies of his own mind. The leap of deduction is a relatively sure step for him while the purportedly indubitable givenness of the phenomenologist's intuitive embrace is a chimera, or, to give him some benefit of the doubt, an as yet vague intimation of steps leaped over but not yet explicated, of rules not yet worked out.

From a phenomenological viewpoint the structuralist conceptualization and its concomitant approach is likely to result in a method that imposes structure on the phenomenon rather than in one that allows structure to rise from the phenomenon or from a coconstituting dialogue with it. We are suspicious of the turn to the linguistic and particularly the further turn to a logico-mathematical formalism. The former is troublesome when it comes prematurely in a method for it then truncates analysis by placing itself between the investigator and the phenomenon. The latter gives up access to the phenomenon, settling for a location of understanding in a region that is distinctly thought, not life.

STRUCTURE AS "IN THE 'UCS' "

From this extreme band, exemplified by structuralism, we can move toward more central bands on a spectrum of concepts of structure. The movement is from those positions that deny direct access to those that at least begin to assert the immediate presence of structure. In its theory, psychoanalysis parallels the structuralism of Lévi-Strauss in finding structure extrinsic to and, in particular, beneath the phenomenal.[17] In fact, interestingly, both geological and linguistic metaphors also abound in this literature, evidence respectively the important place of such terms as "depth psychology" and "interpretation." However, on the face of it the psychoanalytic solution to the problems of structure that arise when externality is a presumed starting point, by contrast to the convoluted ontology of structuralism, is simplicity itself: a region, "ucs," is posited outside of the phenomenal as the source of its organization. In its fullest and most facile use, this region can be the origin of form and meaningfulness and of intention or drive and content as well. Once positing this region, the status of the phenomenal becomes peculiar. Its importance lies not in itself but in that it is the primary access to its own hidden structure, to an understanding of itself. The richness of conscious life, dreams, fantasies, and even everyday concerns is a function of what is latent to them.

The posture of the psychoanalyst as investigator has the same mixed or divided allegiance as that of the structuralist. He sits outside of the phenomenal, inferring from it to its structure and at the same time deducing to that structure from general laws governing the unconscious domain, house rules for the structure. Accepting certain rules of association and of symbolization as given, the analyst treats the phenomenal (manifest content) as a foreign language, as a communication that, since it is assumed to mean other and more than its speaker "consciously" intends, must be decoded.

Listening to Structure

However, while to be true to the central tenets of his metapsychology the analyst as investigator must disavow any posture or mode that claims immediate presence to structure, it is part of clinical lore that the expert clinician can transcend translation and inference. The expert clinician hears the voice of the unconscious immediately in his patient's disclosures and resistances. Is the posture here still one of a very competent bilinguist for whom the rules of translation are so ingrained that he does not so much decode as immediately receive the material already translated?

There is a suggestion in the literature that the analyst is a listener, not a translator.[18] Through practice he develops or discovers a sensitive organ, a third ear, which makes possible a direct receptivity to the analysand's unconscious. A direct line replaces the relatively cumbersome mediation by translation. This more immediate apprehension distinguishes the project of the analyst from that of the structural anthropologist. The analyst does not sit with code of symbols in hand, translating "mountain" to "breast"; he hears "mountain" as "breast." More important to our purposes than the mode of transmission or reception of content, the analyst operates in the same way in matters of form or structure. As the client describes his current relation to his spouse, the analyst "hears" its structure; a particular variant of a psychosexual or psychosocial relation between two people appears. For example, he immediately apprehends without inference or translation that the relation consists in one person receiving succor from the other, or more generally that the relation is one of "taking from" or of one person "using" the other person. The current relation immediately appears as an instance in a context of other such instances in the patient's history. By a kind of auditory intuition, the analyst immediately knows the form common to such a set of human relations.

Listening with the third ear is a way of immediately apprehending structure. The psychoanalytic literature does not indicate why the critical organ is ear rather than eye, why it does not utilize the more traditional inner or third eye. But it does insist and largely rest on the assertion that structure originates in the unconscious and that that structure can be directly known by a trained élite. The psychoanalyst in practice is a burrowing geologist, one who comfortably or at least effectively lives underground amidst and at the source. Lévi-Strauss was attracted to and accepted the hidden and underlying location of structure while rejecting any of the connotations of its underground or subterranean character. He rejected the possibility that one must be covered by structure or in the midst of it to know it. The psychoanalytic choice of the auditory over the visual accentuates the necessity for this relative proximity. What I see I see over there while what I hear comes over to me.[19] Etymology suggests that hearing is related experientially to obedience.[20] Hearing or the world heard is one in which I am by force more intimately related. Both Lévi-Strauss and the Freudians give structure a deep location removed from while directing the traffic of everyday life. Both give it at once a universality and an inaccessibility. However, the practicing analyst gains the power, in his own view, of the immediately evidential by living in the depths as subterranean, as a region where one knows by a kind of grovelling, a kind of passively being surrounded by, an obeisance; while, in his view, Lévi-Strauss retains the power of distance, the space and control assumed by inferential knowledge.

The analyst resolves the problem of the externality of structure by positing a region of mind and an organ for immediate access to it. Of course, conceptually, his solution is contradictory on the face of it. If there is such a direct access-giving posture, even one presupposing certain training or initiation, what does it mean to call the region the unconscious? If I immediately can know the unconscious structure implicit in the patient's description of his involvement with the spouse, in what sense are we dealing with or do we require a region "ucs"? It is not enough to say that it is unconscious to the patient and immediately evident only to the analyst. If there exists a posture through which structure is immediately apparent, then structure has a presence, is not unconscious, and we are left with the question, How and where do we stand and through what modality do we apprehend it? Do we perhaps hear it? The suggestion implicit here that the psychologist as investigator only need undergo his own psychoanalysis to gain direct access to psychological structure, while intriguing, is not very helpful. Yet I believe that the posture of the highly practiced psychoanalyst *is* a direct access to structure, at least to the structures of human relations. Whether or not therapeusis follows such apprehension, the analyst is immediately privy to the actual form of human relations. His metapsychology aside, the analyst operates in a way that the phenomenologist must understand. When he forgets his metapsychology, the analyst is a practicing phenomenologist. We must attend more closely to how he manages to live directly in a world where structure is immediately salient— unencumbered by his overreliance on a reified region of unawareness.

STRUCTURE AS MICROPHYSIOLOGY

While much of the metapsychology of psychoanalysis centers in the region "ucs" with its structuralizing structures and its rules of their movement, expression, and development, it still rests all of this on another region. Freud believed that the final explanation of psychological structures would refer and needed in principle to refer to a physiological substrate. This view has been a recurrent feature of psychoanalytic theory, whether offered as a serious argument for the necessity of a final reduction, or merely given lip-service amidst the often preoccupying proliferation of yet more psychological paraphernalia. Of course, this view is not one peculiar to a theory centering on a "cs/ucs" distinction. It would seem that most modern psychological theories, particularly the recently mushrooming cognitive psychology, yield or at least nod to reliance on the physiological as an ultimate level of explanation.

There is more to this resolution of the problem of structure by reduction to the biological than the important idea, which we have examined in the context of structuralism, that it lies beneath or undergirds the phenomenal. If structure is the relation among parts, then it should be evident at the level of the building blocks of the real. True structure is microstructure; it is how atoms join together. The units of physiology and their joinings have priority over the phenomenal not simply because they are beneath but because they are the more elemental unit. Part of the search for and the appeal of the more elemental is that it is concrete, unalloyed, and knowable as such. Ironically, the original impulse of the natural scientist, here the physiological psychologist or biologist, parallels that of the phenomenologist. It is to achieve a tangible grasp of the structure of phenomena by approaching it directly and locating it concretely.

At the physiological level the investigator might actually witness the genesis of structure, the way the parts fit together. The desirability of observability and the micro-unit are related in a peculiar way in the early modern history of psychology with its reaction against introspectionism and its espousal of empiricism. The prevailing idea was that an introspective posture did not open onto a public domain. It did not because it was not a direct seeing. Empiricism is public because its modality is the purest, clearest, most objective, most at the real; its primary modality being the immediate givenness of the visual. Of course, the history of psychology has followed the lines of the history of the more "basic" natural sciences in that for it also the concrete, the visible, and the "micro" or elemental are found to diverge quickly. The original impulse to be directly present at the birth of structure within such a region gives way to an enterprise that is much more inferential and abstract. In physics the search for ultimate particles and their joinings has followed the progression of a Chinese box, a regressive reduction which continually repeats itself on a smaller scale. The attempt to find structure extrinsic to the psychological or the phenomenal in a physiological domain, the presumed external and publicly accessible locus of its formation, gives rise not so much to a transparent givenness of empiricism as to a brand of heavily mathematical and technological logico-empiricism. At best, in this enterprise, structure is known by the implications of the tracing of its parts on a medium other than its own. More generally, the more elemental or micro the particle, the greater the remove from its actual presence and the larger and more sophisticated the machinery required to furnish these increasingly shadowy apprehensions.

STRUCTURE AS HEURISTIC DEVICE

Given the technical and inferential elaboration of such a method, it is a small step to the assumption of a locus and an ontology of structure that is more consistent with it. If structure is external to the immediately phenomenal but not recoverable in an unconscious and if it is lodged in the biological but in a way that is beyond our reach, nothing is lost by giving it the status of a hypothetical construct. Structure may be conceived as a device of our creation, as part of a heuristic program. The project becomes one of constructing models of the phenomena that may have predictive value but that presume no referent to structure in reality. The search for structure itself and hence concern with modes of its apprehension are abandoned as misguided, as an instance of asking the wrong question. At the opposite extreme from the reduction to the level of concrete, ultimate particles, this peculiar move reduces structure by taking it out of existence.

A complex variant of this way of thinking or not thinking about structure can be seen in cognitive psychology, particularly as practiced in the United States. In this setting it has partially withstood the epistemology and the method of Piaget's developmental psychology by retaining a more behavioristic approach. In fact there are currency and high hopes for the amalgamation "cognitive behaviorism." [21] This cognitive psychology is behavioristic in that the primary datum is the result of the performance by subjects of certain tasks. The subject is asked, for example, to judge the similarity of the shape of two states in the United States,[22] or to match figures that have been spatially rotated.[23] From data consisting of measures such as reaction times the investigator constructs a model, often in the form of a simple mathematical function, describing this data.

The approach by and large rejects "subjective reports," any elaboration by the subject of his own experience during the performance. When collected such material receives minimal weight, serving a collaborative function or, in a post-facto analysis of behavioral findings (particularly those counter to the hypothesis), a corrective or generative function for further research. Once the investigator selects an operational definition of the phenomenon of interest, there is no recourse to the phenomenon except through that operation. However, while this general procedure follows that of a radical empiricism or behaviorism, the phenomenon operationalized is not a behavior. The object of the investigation is a cognitive process or a cognitive structure with its associated process. The location of this phenomenon ontologically is complex. In practice, the results of the task delimited by the operation are the only indication of the cognitive process, and we have a behaviorism in which the language of theorizing is in terms of cognitive process. This practice is, then, consistent with holding "structure" to be merely heuristic, a theoretical net which refers only to observable behavior. "Cognitive process" or cognitive structure sustaining cognitive process is a set of ideas that account for or explain a set of data. The explanation is external to the observable and itself has no existence except as a model.

In theory, however, cognitive process is vaunted as "the way the mind works" and its status surpasses that of an explanatory construct. We can know this cognitive process or structure indirectly by our observation of how, as it were, it has us perform certain memorial or cognitive-perceptual tasks. It is assumed that this way the mind works, this mindfulness of which we are unaware, is grounded in brain function, in physiology. The presumption is that at some time in the future one might begin to make meaningful statements having the following form: the description of a certain physiological process, built on a specifiable brain structure, accounts for and is predictive of performance of a certain task. Here mind or mental process may be omitted, at last having been shown for what it is—brain function. The structure described in such a statement is located neither in the subject's behavior nor in his phenomenal field. The structure of behavior itself is not of interest; rather, the investigator seeks an accounting of the aggregate results of the performance. Whether or not in the future or in principle such statements based on knowledge of physiology can generate such behavioral predictions, it is evident that they do not do so now. Neurology and neuro-psychology supply little descriptive or conceptual advance in the study of these cognitive tasks of memory, coding, concept formation, or the like. Advances in the field occur rather within the cognitive behavioristic research enterprise itself, and through borrowings of concepts from other fields, such as cybernetics.

We can appreciate the complexity of cognitive psychology as an approach when we look between the enterprise in practice, in its resemblance to a radical behavioristic empiricism, and the theoretically desirable but unattained and perhaps unattainable rapprochement of behavior and physiology. To some extent cognitive psychology has its own language and implicitly asserts its own ontology and general location of structure. Cognitive structure and, through it, mental process function to create an internal representation of the world, or internal models of the environment. The primary product of mind is a reproduction of world, an image of objective reality. This view that the mind comes to contain or mirror the world assumes the possibility of an isomorphism between mind and world. But since mind in theory is reducible to brain function, the isomorphism must be extended to include world-mind-brain or behavior-mind-brain.

In all of this there are parallels to the structuralism of Lévi-Strauss. For both, the scaffold that is the structure or the locus of structuralizing is in a different region than, a region extrinsic to, the surface phenomenon; and that region is "unconscious"— it is beneath that which is the only apparent region. Structure is the hidden underlying reality and the extrinsic source of mundane reality. The mental activity of cognitive psychology is analogous to what we have described as the middle region of Lévi-Strauss's structuralism. It is the focal level of explanation. It has no direct appearance but is inferred from a performance in the physical world which is observable from an objective stance. Further, analogous to the universal properties of mind of structuralism, it is contingent or built on a deeper level which here is a presumed final reduction to brain function. Both approaches rely on a mixed methodology which is logico-empirical at the nexus of the two upper levels and largely deductive from a fairly obscure and presumptive lowest level to the middle level.

STRUCTURE AS COMMON STRUCTURE

Both also rely on certain assumed isomorphisms to deal with the problem of structure. The device of positing parallel forms, analogous or homologous structures in different regions, slips the question of locating structure in a particular region of being and describing a concomitant mode of its apprehension. Structure is neither extrinsic nor intrinsic to a particular locus; it occurs in more than one.

Taking as a starting point in approaching structure the observation of isomorphisms, methodological implications drawn vary according to the strength of the isomorphic relation. A strong or pure variant, such as Hegel's identity theory, assumes an identity between subject and object, or mind and matter.[24] While typically implicating a transcendental region, in Hegel a region of the spirit, this kind of isomorphism stays with the fact of identity and presents a harmonious universe built on it. There is no question or problem of movement among or access to different regions: being in one is being in all.

Some system builders stop short of this assertion of a unity based on identity but are still impressed by structural homologies in various apparently disparate regions. For such an investigator there is a certain methodological license implicit in the fact of isomorphisms. If regions are homologous, he may explore the more remote by way of the more accessible. At least at some critical points, the structuralism of Lévi-Strauss utilizes this methodologic retreat.

In weaker versions of isomorphism, there is movement beyond the celebration of or methodologic exploitation of "identity" to problematics in the fact of "same forms" in different regions. For example, must not there be a relation between the two regions beyond their similarity of form that makes that similarity intelligible? Perhaps one region is the cause of the second, or the second may be reduced to the first, as, respectively, in a causal positivism or in a physiological reductionism. These supplemental relations refuse the given parallelism and opt for assymmetries among regions. The simple parallelism of isomorphism is hybridized and diluted, and we have positions that are midway between an identity theory and the strictly dualistic oppositions that are the Cartesian legacy. Relations between regions vary from identity to correspondence to contingency to polarity. At the latter pole there is really no semblance of a notion of isomorphism. The emphasis is on a denial of similarity; different regions consist of different kinds of things. With dichotomous regions as a starting point, "resolutions" tend to absolutize the one region to the diminution of the other, as for example the absolutizing of fact in empiricism and of idea in rationalism.[25]

Yet another response to the observation of isomorphism assumes that if two regions have forms in common, then it is possible to transform one into the other. The equal status of each, if retained in that translation, is possible in either direction. However, the focus on rules of transformation and on the process of moving from a first structure to a kindred second structure begs the question of the nature and mode of apprehension of structure. In less considered instances it calls structure process, in Orwellian fashion. In more thoughtful settings it leaps to a postreflective concern with the explication of rules. The rules describe a process. In the case of the anthropologist the process is a way to transpose among cultural phenomena at the level of their structure. The similarities among such structures is said to be demonstrated and made intelligible by a description of the rules of transformation. In place of a description of the structure itself, or here the structure in common, I am asked to accept a description of rules for changing structure. Again, there is a confusion between structure and process. An account of how the conductor transposes the musical score into a set of bodily gestures that are somehow equivalent to the score, or how the musician transposes from those to his performance, is not a description of that which is equivalent in, say, a "performance" by the conductor and the symphony as heard.

Isomorphism proclaims a rather dramatic, since apparently independent, parallelism between radically divergent regions of being at the level of structure. Given the observation of isomorphism one may seek to corrode or undermine it by focusing on the peculiar character of the two particular regions. The similarity is a function of a peculiar relation between them, one being the cause of the other, one being merely epiphenomenal to the other, or the like. One may rest in the unity, asserting it or capitalizing on it methodologically by assuming access to one region is access to a second. Or, one may proceed by exploring the phenomenon, here the observation of isomorphism, more directly.

An experiential referent of the fact of isomorphism is the immediate sense of similarities among structures—similarities in shape or form. If what is common among structures is their shape, it follows that structure itself is a shapeful entity. It further follows that to ground structure in a conceptual, linguistic, or abstract region is wrongheaded. The frequent observation of isomorphism supports the thesis of the present work that we can locate structure in a preconceptual region. It leaves open the possibility that we can describe a mode through which we can apprehend that shape immediately.

The fact of isomorphism also suggests that when structure is salient, similarity or likeness is afoot; somehow, structure lends itself to likeness. Structure, a certain form, and *similarity* of form seem inseparable, as if the latter were an inherent feature of the former. In that it consists of relations as such, it is obvious that structure reduces differentness. Structure as the way that sundry parts are together, structure as organization, averts chaos and is the ground for the emergence of meaning. Relations as such are more general than any particular set of parts that they hold together. The structure of a situation is that which constitutes it as a phenomenon. Any instance of grief, any particular lost object, is only meaningful in that it consists in a generalized or typical set of relations and, as well, a typically grievous world. Structure is the relatively congealed, the more general, the typical that is part of our experience of any particular instance or situation. Hence when we focus on the structure of a particular instance, we are unhinged from it and immediately find ourselves open to situations of similar structure. Through focus on structure we move from consideration of a particular instance to the phenomenon of which it is an instance.

Of course, concepts and language have a similar function with relation to likeness. Through them particular instances are organized, classified, and typified. But the prevalence of isomorphism suggests that similarity on the level of conceptualization—for example, common class membership—can be grounded preconceptually through the common shape or form of structure. We can know that preconceptual similarity inherent in structure through the body. Earlier, we suggested how the body carries a residue of particular situations and how the ground of that possibility is a radical bodily equivalence which is the original state out of which personhood emerges. In that the lived body can carry a certain equivalence or similarity across situations, through it we can abstract the structure of a phenomenon—as we will show more fully in chapter 5.

From the survey of concepts of structure to this point, we have a growing set of demands for this bodily mode of apprehension of structure: it must be able to carry and to articulate shape, in particular the original presence of the shapely, elusive entity structure. It must lend itself to or partake of that certain generality or relative contextlessness which is a hallmark of structure.

A third demand is still largely implicit. Eventually we shall find in the isomorphic proclivities of structure the ground for metaphor. While structure provides the framework of a particular situation, it surpasses that moment at the same time, inviting an open horizon of possible applications of itself. By taking a structure focally, we can promote the generation of such applications across regions of being. Such an application, we will show, results in a metaphor, a linkage of two apparently disparate entities through a common form. The third demand, then, is for a mode that while beginning as an apprehension of structure as shape can facilitate these applications, can guide us to find metaphors. In turn, these metaphors will augment the explication of a phenomenon under investigation.

The present critique of several concepts of isomorphism in approaches to structure reveals that to understand structure we need invoke, not the special creation or parallel operation of duplicate worlds, but rather an inherent property of structure itself. The review reinforces the importance of similarity and its apprehension in the problem of structure.

From a phenomenological point of view it is clear that a sense of similarity is a powerful indicator of the salience of the structure of any phenomenon, and hence is a guide toward that structure. When two entities strike me as having something in common, an explication of this similarity reveals, in our terms, either textural or structural commonality. The former are felt directly as a bodily impact. As we described in chapter 2, the basis of their similarity is readily explicated. The latter are more complex and subtle; their explication and the mode of accomplishing it are more problematic. They often leave us stuck in a haunting familiarity, as in the experience of déjà vu. There is a sense that a personal relation or the course of such is somehow a duplication or a rerun, or that a line of thought is paralleled elsewhere but in very different terms. Structural similarities that occur across modalities are particularly striking. For example, the structure of a building may remind me of the structure of a musical composition.

CONCLUSIONS

We began this consideration of concepts of structure oriented by our peculiar concern with modes of apprehension of structure. Within the more general question of a definition of structure, we wanted to clarify how and where we might stand to know structure and, the correlative questions, how does structure appear and where, in what region of being. We have found that concepts may be readily organized as attempted answers to a question of the invisibility or externality of structure. A common response to the fact that the structure of any given phenomenon is not immediately or originally *perceptible* is, to us, the overreaction of locating it exterior to experience. These denials of any apparentness of structure in the given moment permit the investigator to presume that he may forfeit without penalty an approach to the phenomenon as lived. He may claim to be in a position to understand the structure of that phenomenon without entering into it. He is privy to its organization, the relationship among its parts, its meaning, all that we intend by structure, at the outside, for that is structure's location. Correlatively, for that investigator structure's first appearance is necessarily through an external posture and, with respect to the original phenomenon, the mode of its apprehension is necessarily indirect or inferential in the broadest sense.

Within these conceptualizations of structure as extrinsic, the most typical further specification of its relation to the phenomenal is that it is beneath or underlying. Such notions of the depth of structure versus the superficiality of the phenomenal tend to carry something of the Kantian distinction between reality and mere appearance. Connotatively, the phenomenal is flimsy or weightless or chimerical, without standing of its own. The major ways in which structure is said to be underlying include the following: it is the cause or determining anchorage of which the phenomenal is the effect; it consists of the linguistic categories or organization of categories of an appearance, which only it can help decode;

or it is the organization of the microstructure beneath the gross macrostructure which is appearance. Other resolutions that are extrinsic but that do not imply the further spatial metaphor "beneath" assert that structure is merely a heuristic, an investigator's way of organizing the given, or that structure is in a region of unawareness, or describable only as a process.

Isomorphism as a resolution somewhat begs our distinction between extrinsic and intrinsic. The strong isomorphism seems to accept structure's inherency in the phenomenal, but, taken with the observation of parallel forms across phenomena, simply rests in the assertion of such parallels.

From our point of view what the extrinsic concepts as a group give up at the outset they cannot recover, at least in principle. By searching for the structure of a phenomenon in some region outside it, they divest the phenomenon of its meaning. Given this starting point, any organization "discovered" is an imposed one. Being itself meaningless, the phenomenal in this "extrinsic" position requires such an imposition. Since the phenomenal has no shape itself, since it does not consist, in part, of its own frame, the ground to its understanding must be outside it or beneath it. It must submit to a supporting context of which it itself has no intimation. The presupposition is that as investigator I can or must find such a formative context through my own device, that is, without direct recourse to the phenomenon that I initially undertook to research. I must lay some kind of foundation upon which the phenonenon may rest, whether that ground be a set of categories, a syntax, a governing process, or a micro-anatomy. I am forced to bring to my aid some system which, with reference to phenomena, is conceived as a metastructure, a system that structuralizes. These are various linguistic, logical, mathematical, and, in general, rationalistic systems.

Ironically, these grounds or regions beneath are better described as above. Extrinsic concepts of structure are topsy-turvy with respect to the ground and origin of structure. All organization, all meaning, originates in the phenomenal and must be explicated and advanced through dialogue with it. As Merleau-Ponty and others have pointed out, systems typically taken as ground are rather postreflective products of such dialogue.

The investigator's faith in such systems is misplaced when he forgets that origin. That faith is blind when the investigator utilizes such a system to provide structure or to impose structure since structure is already there in the phenomenon. For while it is not visible, it has a presence to which the investigator's faith would seem to strike him insensitive. A phenomenon needs no external frame, for it itself consists in an inexhaustible set of layers of meanings, of contexts. It is thick with structure though that structure is originally only adumbrated or sensed or felt. While utilizing a postreflective system or even some commonsensical considerations can be an effective generative strategy in the explication of the structure of a phenomenon, any organization that does not eventually refer to the given phenomenon is an imposition, a false ground and a false understanding. A structure *refers* if and only if it is in some sense, however dimly, already there in the phenomenon as lived. Since structure has a presence in the original living of the phenomenon we are not dependent on some external system with its own criteria, logic, rules of deduction, or procedure for grounding or for knowledge. For the phenomenon "contains" its own ground and itself delivers or dictates the "rules" for our understanding of it. Any undergirding that is not intrinsic is alien and distorting, again a false ground and a false understanding.

While leaving the phenomenon to eventually return to it is a possible strategy, it is not a necessary move unless the investigator is closed to the immediate presence of the structure of the phenomenon. Of course, it is an uneconomical move on the face of it, leaving only to return, and, more importantly, it invites distortion. In practice, however, the situation is more insidious. If the investigator does not believe that the structure is inherent and accessible, he has no reason to return. He believes he can or rather must find another ground, and he rests on it. The description of the phenomenal and its structure built on this ground and governed by its rules is necessarily a construct and a reification. If there is any dialogue between this "reality" and the world as lived, it is an unacknowledged one since, again, the latter being merely phenomenal has really nothing to say and can only speak, as a kind of marionette, meanings spoken through or for it. More likely, there is little dialogue and the constructed reality communicates largely within itself.

4

Toward a Phenomenology

of Structure

INTRODUCTION

Here we consider approaches to structure at the opposite end of our spectrum—those that locate structure within experience, that give it some presence in the phenomenal field. Beginning with Husserl, we will then turn to Piaget the structuralist, in whom, ironically, we will find an incipient phenomenology of structure.

A reading of Husserl suggests, to put it dramatically if loosely, that he believed he could *see* structure, "seeing" a mode requiring qualification provided below. Husserl clearly built his philosophy on the premise that structure or eidos[1] is immanent in the immediate appearance of the world. If structure is interior to the phenomenal, then the starting point of a philosophy seeking a ground for knowledge must be a return to things as they appear. Husserl's general program is to lead back from that original given, having first bracketed all theoretical, linguistic, and even existential post-reflective presuppositions as to the lived world, to the constitutive features of consciousness, for example, from the object, to its various horizons, to the mode of its experience, to a constituting agency, and, eventually, to a transcendental ego. In the context of a phenomenological psychology, the structure of a particular phenomenon or mode of experience has a presence in immediate experience. To explicate it the kind of inferential leap characteristic of Lévi-Strauss's method is unnecessary. No position in some rational region of being need be constructed, as structure now has the opposite grounding in the prelinguistic immediately given. For Husserl, as for later phenomenologists, all organization or meaning originates in the phenomenal and must be unfolded and advanced through dialogue with it.

The following brief treatment of Husserl focuses on selected points that, through their critique, highlight further demands on the present bodily reflective method and possible gains in meeting those demands. The critique notwithstanding, the indebtedness of this work to Husserl should be clear. His seminal description of the basic structures of experience provides a ground for any phenomenological method. More particularly, this philosophy grounds and his own phenomenological method demonstrates that we are immediately in the midst of meaning and that a necessary correlative of that fact is the availability of modes through which that meaning is immediately apprehensible. Husserl's method itself is an early and seminal account of modes of apprehending structure.

HUSSERL

Reduction and Return

For Husserl all phenomenology begins with a return to the things themselves, a return to the world as it immediately appears, to the phenomenon as lived. The assumption of this posture as a starting point is the sense in which phenomenology begins in silence.[2] There follows the famous set of moves called *bracketing*. These are attitudes or postures to the phenomenon through which a certain series of presuppositions, of taken-for-granted foundations of the object or world, are held in abeyance. For example, there is the bracketing of the natural attitude, the belief in the existence of the objects of consciousness. These bracketings are also called reductions in the literal sense that they lead back to the constitutive features of consciousness.

In executing the reductions our posture to the phenomenon is reflective rather than engaged. But this distinction is too sharply drawn here. The reductions are reflective postures in that there is a "stepping back from" the object.[3] In Merleau-Ponty's felicitous phrase, there is a "loosening of the intentional threads" to the phenomenon.[4] I do not seek to stay somehow outside of the phenomenon. The return to the things themselves is still operative. I still seek to stay with them but without becoming absorbed in them uncritically.[5] I stay with the phenomenon while continually maintaining a particular critical attitude which is the operation of the reduction. The reduction as a reflection precedes and guides the return. I return, for example, with a suspension of my belief in the existence of the phenomenon. This stepping back in effect allows me to be closer to, to be more open to the eidetic features of the phenomenon. I forget about the question of its being in order to arrive more directly at the "what" of it.[6] Precisely through the manipulation of these variable postures, the "levels of reduction" can be varied.[7] With these variations we can move from particular phenomena, to them as instances, to their general essence and the relations among essences, and to the parallels between the way we experience, the intending act, and what we experience, the intending content.[8] For example, from this table-as-perceived we are led back to the perception of something in general, the possibilities of the perceived, to perception as a universal type, and eventually to the perceiver.[9]

The reflective postures do not function, then, to disengage the investigator, to give him the externality of objectivity or the distance necessary for the operation of various traditional intellective acts. He does not step back to draw deductions or inductions or generally to gain the berth required for an application of logical modes of thought. In fact, part of the series of reductions functions contrarily to achieve a laying aside, a bracketing of just such inferential and syllogistic modes in regard to the phenomenon. Again, the stepping back is to better approach. Our return is governed by a systematic de-education, a stripping away of the sedimentations formed by culture, language, and even by method itself. The de-education is only a methodological tactic as there is no permanent casting away. All features, even (or perhaps critically) the most sedimented, are explicated and their role in the essential constitution of the phenomenon analyzed.

The method centers in the reflective but seeks to avoid the intellective. We must remain reflective to prevent reabsorption into the phenomenon, but we must avoid the intellective to guarantee direct access to it as lived. Husserl seeks a course between being beached again at the original, often forgotten, and essentially mute point of departure and being put off course by the conceptual or theoretical wreckages in the harbor that he felt historically had prevented such direct access. From his own description he is more wary of the latter hazard than of the former, and presents a more studied examination of the pitfalls of intellection.

In the context of the methodological task of the explication of essence or structure, Husserl is critical of intellection as an approach to the phenomenon, or at least of the adoption of an intellective posture at an early moment in the explication. Some of his reasons are reactive to traditional philosophical positions. An eidos is not an idea, an innate concept, or an a priori;[10] nor is it originally a derivative of thought. While it can eventually be captured in thought or described in words, it is *"prior to all 'concepts,'* in the sense of verbal significations" (his emphasis).[11] Contrarily, it is our concepts or verbal descriptions that "must be made to fit the eidos." [12] How is this eidos present in the original phenomenon, and what are the possible or necessary modes of its apprehension in the movement toward its eventual explication?

Structure as Intuited

For Husserl the eidos has an immediate presence in the original experience. Unfortunately, that presence is nonsensory or nonsensuous. We do not see or hear or even feel structure. The eidos is present in a way that parallels the presence of the rear of the house when I am perceiving the front. It is a part of the phenomenal field that is an "appresence";[13] it is present only as adumbrated. It is there only "as-meant," not as perceived. Given this original nonsensible appresence of structure, how can we explicate it? Husserl's strategy is the development of a procedure which would make it possible to posit that elusive appresence as an object, as directly focal and present. Only then would an unprejudiced description, a description not reliant on intellective mediation, be possible. Part of Husserl's method is the provision of a mode through which that original invisible can be known directly. He calls the mode *anschauung* and defines it primarily by its immediacy, by the absence in it of any intervening cognitive or thoughtful process. The immediacy of anschauung gives its object an apodictic or indubitable quality of self-evidence. Through this mode, the object, here eidos or structure, appears directly, through a form of presentification; it is not implied or represented. Anschauung can be translated, although only roughly, as "intuiting" or "looking at." [14] While clearly not perception, the mode is analogous to it. It is a kind of virtual perception akin to imagination.

The Method of Free Imaginative Variation

The method whereby this intuitive mode is eventually applied is straightforward. Husserl gives a relatively specific and illustrated exposition of the procedure.[15] The method begins with a reflective posture which is a reduction of a particular phenomenon to an example.[16] With this attitude, a now exemplary phenomenon can then be varied in a systematic fashion. For instance, a particular object of perception may be varied as to its shape or color without losing sight of the fact that it is a perception of something. Or a number of phenomena may be taken together as instances and looked through to the essential.[17] The perceived is relocated in a region of as-if, of possibility, or of "imaginableness." [18] Certain components are replaced or left off and found to be evidently essential or evidently inessential. An exploration of all possible perceptions allows the intuitive grasp of the eidos perception, a mode of consciousness.

Through this set of reductions we arrive at a presentification of the eidos. An aspect that has an appearance in the original phenomenon but only an intimated and appresent appearance is realized and made immediately, indubitably, and directly present in an intuitive mode. The essence appears as an entity although epistemological claims in regard to it are still bracketed.[19]

There are a number of aspects of this procedure that we would like to set off by contrast to the method of the present work. We have already alluded to the first, which is least problematic. Husserl utilizes a reflective stance, a "stepping back from" to gain a more direct access, an immediate presentation. More generally and paradoxically, he systematically adopts postures and applies them in effortful searches and variations and yet claims the immediate presence of the object of his search. The procedure seems to preclude immediacy, being itself rather a substantial mediation. However, the eventual presence of the eidos is immediate in the sense that it is not the product of an inferential or a generalizing act. The eidos appears in the way in which any posited object appears. It is more or less suddenly apprehended as there. There is no mediating move necessary. The particular reductive postures assumed, the lining up and the varying of instances, do not function as a mediation so much as they simply help to locate and to apprehend more directly what was already there but only intimated. It is like going to the corner of the house in order to see the rear of the house. The object of that view was already there from the previous vantage point but it was invisible. That shape is appresent in the original and can be directly apprehended given a set of moves which put the investigator in a position to apprehend it. Free imaginative variation is the requisite set of moves; eidetic intuition is the mode of apprehension made possible by the moves. The operational procedure is more a means of transportation than a mediating process.

It is in the description of the mode of apprehension itself that Husserl is less clear. How is the object of intuition present? Clearly, Husserl does not intend us to think that it is visible. What is grasped is an entity that was invisible in the original moment. Yet his language suggests that Husserl believed such entities could be made at least virtually visible. It is here, a critical juncture from our point of view, that Husserl's account is equivocal. The primary distinctions for him are that the intuited object appear without mediation and as a fulfilled or present rather than an empty intention. But he is vague about the mode of the presentification. When he does indicate a particular modality, it is the visual or rather the virtually visual. The terms "imagination," "looking at," and "looking through" figure centrally. However, often the language is neutral as to mode as when he employs the language of "being present." Perhaps intuition is not modality-specific and is fully identifiable merely as a sudden or immediate appearance.

Again, the language of the visual is dominant. For a number of reasons, Husserl relied on a model of perception as he approached the problem of eidos or structure. Given his concern with describing a method built on the immediate rather than the mediate and having established these features of eidetic intuition, he truncated his exposition of this mode of apprehension. From the present perspective, Husserl stopped short and indeed in part mistook this mode because he lacked an adequate phenomenology of the body and of action. The discovery of the intimate relation of these not only to a description of modes of apprehension of structure but to a phenomenology of perception itself awaited the work of Merleau-Ponty.

In Husserl we find a solution to the original invisibility of structure, not in a retreat to it as external to experience, but in a method modeled on perception. It is our view that in his development of the method of eidetic intuition, while Husserl took perception only as a guiding metaphor, he did think of the critical reflective mode as a kind of looking at. Although not visible, structure can be posited as the virtually visible, as the thin perception of intuition and imagination. The eidos was not constituted for Husserl by a living through either of the particulars behind which the eidos was said to appear or of the eidos itself. This is unfortunate in several regards.

It is limited, for it cannot give me either structures that are problematic or that are strongly taken for granted. A problematic structure, a structure that is present as precisely inexplicable, cannot be resolved by looking through instances of it. Nor can a structure that is so much a way that I live. I cannot simply put it or instances of it in front of me to look at or through. Even if I could, I do not know which of its features to vary. Such knowledge either begs the question or depends on the very postreflective descriptives I seek to bracket.

More generally, I am relatively too detached when I utilize Husserl's method. While the reflective posture is a stepping back in order to approach, the particular postures required by free imaginative variation too quickly objectify. I cannot so directly place a mode of consciousness, for example, or temporal horizon or other typically studied structure or eidos in front of me as an object. I have known them by living through them and I require a method that respects that original way of knowing them. Our model cannot be perception, particularly perception according to Husserl. A better wager is behavior since that is by its very nature a way of knowing that is a living through of phenomena.

In his concern to free eidos from a dependence on intellective and logical operations, Husserl sought to move back from these to their preconceptual ground. He found beneath the intellective the possibility of an immediate apprehension of the basic or universal shapes that are precisely the forms for or the framework of these intellective modes. His startling and revolutionizing discovery is that the starting point for this journey can only be our mundane consciousness of things as such, or as eventually broadened, our immediate experience of the world.

However, the description of this movement, this method, jumps too quickly from the object-as-seen to the eidos-as-intuited. The attractiveness for Husserl of the analogy between the immediate upsurge of perception and the immediacy of intuition yields a premature and an overextended application of the analogy. The procedure skips so that I am unconvinced that the eidos will emerge through the imaginative variation and the lining up of instances or that that which does appear is the eidos. The invisible is taken to be too much like the visible both in its appearance and in the mode of apprehension of that appearance. Further, even the too liberally applied model of perception is itself unsatisfactory, somehow thin. What is meant by the intuitive mode is unclear and mystifying. We will show intuition to be the endpoint of a long series of recoverable and describable moments. While the intuited object is at some point immediately apparent in Husserl's sense of immediacy, the work I as investigator have done to reach that moment is not simply the active effort of free imaginative variation. Any intuition that is not simply a direct recollection or a representation of an already constituted object of imagination, any intuition that arrives at a resolution of the formerly problematic, at a more or less sudden integration of the formerly unconnected or unorganized, requires that work. When I have little knowledge of that work or pay it little attention, my experience is of a period of incubation—a vague sense of a kind of quiet settling down process where the components of the problem form natural though often unexpected affinities, and hence resolve the problem. We will argue that that submerged process or work can be systematized and the modes of apprehension constituting it be intentionally adopted. The intuition will then still be an immediate appearance but the origin of that shape, the mode of its transport, the act of its formation and, in general, the intelligibility of both the product and its provenance will be enhanced. I cannot "see" the structure as I can see the rear of the house simply by changing my vantage point.

Husserl applies intuition prematurely, omitting the description of critical stages between it and the original lived sense of a particular structure. Further, even in the final stage where structure is posited as an object, he gives to intuition powers that it cannot sustain, for it is not a lived-through modality. We will describe a bodily reflective mode in chapter 5 which by contrast to intuition rendered as a form of imagination is more fitted to the task. In a sense part of our critique of Husserl's method is sympathetic to a structuralist critique of phenomenology. In his approach to structure Husserl is too close to the perceptual, to the surface, to sense qualities, to the phenomenal as mere appearance. But we have found, undoubtedly as Husserl would have, structuralism as a method too rational, too much dependent on logic and linguistic categories, particularly an imposed logic and a sedimented form of categories. In both Husserl and Lévi-Strauss we find an over-application of their respective metaphors. We side with Husserl and against Lévi-Strauss: structure has some preconceptual presence; it is not originally linguistic. While we further agree that eventually that presence is visible in what approximates an intuitive mode, the steps in the arrival at the intuitive are somewhat mysterious. The concrete description of free imaginative variation is insufficient and not compelling. We are left with the impression that the move to the intuitive is a leap, that it overleaps a number of intermediate modes or postures which are a kind of incubation for the emergence of the intuitive. Husserl's method defines a task for us by raising the question of the nature of those steps intermediate, most generally, between living a phenomenon and the eventual positing of its structure or essence. In like manner, but more grossly, Lévi-Strauss's method also jumps: it makes the rationalistic leap from the phenomenon as externally observed to an explicit discursive expression of its structure. Lévi-Strauss points us, then, by omission, to a different set of intermediate steps, a more advanced set—closer to the inevitable moment when structure is explicated in words. Further, as we have described, the role of isomorphisms in his work accentuates the importance of an understanding of similarity or equivalence in the problem of structure and in the problem of finding the words. Lévi-Strauss presents us with the task of providing a phenomenology of metaphor and describing its relation to a bodily mode of the apprehension of structure.

Neither Husserl nor Lévi-Strauss grasps the original mode of presence of structure. It is not originally present as the intimated backside of an object of perception, nor is it, at the opposite rationalistic extreme, simply without presence, being by its very nature a rule. In betting on behavior as our access to structure, we liken the original presence of structure to the presence of a behavioral field, that space of forces which is the concomitant of our acting in the world. The mode of our original abstraction of structure, an early step in its eventual explication, is a kind of virtual counterpart of behavior. This mode is a critical moment in both the intuition of structure and the basis of and then the discovery of metaphors sustained by a particular structure.

PIAGET

The Relation between Structure and Activity

With Husserlian phenomenology we have dealt with one system of thought that begins with and rigorously treats structure as intrinsic to phenomena. But we are critical both of its description of structure's presence and of the method of its abstraction and explication. Here we consider the work of Piaget in some of whose descriptions of a child's development we find evidence of a phenomenology of structure and possible modes of its apprehension, at their origin.

Piaget's work is transitional to our account for it is suggestive of the rich relation between behavior and structure. A reading of Piaget begins to uncover how action is an analogue of the structure of any situation, and how, then, variant modes of action are ways of knowing that both participate in the original constitution of structure and, in reflection, potentially provide the primary mode of its explication. Our thesis also finds support in Piaget's insight that the development of language and logic themselves have necessary origins and a ground in action. However, given Piaget's suspicion of phenomenal reality and his allegiance (for various reasons) to a dualistic ontology, to follow this initially thin line of action requires a momentary regression from the phenomenological end of the spectrum of concepts of structure under consideration. We must sidestep his peculiar ontology for it is a diversion from what, in this reading, is the main line of his contribution. I do so by distinguishing somewhat crudely between two Piagets, the grand theorist of structure as such and the more plodding, more concrete but ingenious delineator of particular stages in the development of the child's cognitive structures. As a structuralist Piaget tends toward a rational-empirical method and a notion of structure as extrinsic to and grounded in biology and logico-mathematical systems. However, while his general formulation of structure leans in this direction, the notion of structure that arises more directly from his stage theory of cognitive development at least suggests that structure may be located intrinsic to the child's immediate experience. My impression is that Piaget is sensitive to and orients himself to the immediate referent of structure in experience. As a result that referent shapes his exploration of the child, particularly in the early years of development, and informs his descriptions of various features of that development.

An Interactionist Theory of Structure

In his major work on the subject,[20] Piaget defines structure as "a systematic whole of self-regulating transformations." [21] He treats three main points within this definition: the notions of wholeness, transformation, and self-regulation.[22] Wholeness refers to the system's quality of structure, the definitive feature that we have termed "relations among parts" and "relations as such." Structure is holistic in that it cannot be reduced to its parts. It is an entity for which description at the level of atoms or elements, or even of additive combinations of these, is essentially inadequate. From Piaget's point of view, the problem is to locate and describe an organization of the whole that, while transcending any merely additive or associative relation of the parts, does not fall back on some gratuitous assertion of a vitalism or (the modern version of that) some principle of emergence that fails to specify the laws of its own operation.[23] The elements of a structure are subordinated to laws of the whole and these laws are "self-sufficient" or self-regulatory.

This "systematic whole" which somehow contains or consists in its own laws of organization is not a static form but a "system of transformations." A structure is "simultaneously structuring and structured." [24] It structures both itself and something outside itself, the world or an action upon or thought about the world. For example, the eventual object of perception and its field is a product in part of the transformation of "sensory given(s)." [25] Here we must invoke the dualistic language of his theory of intellectual development. The structure is a psychological or mental or cognitive entity through the operation of which the environment is transformed and organized or through which our actions on and perception of the environment are transformed and structured. A structure is an operation in that it acts on things or coordinates actions on things.[26] The laws of organization or of operation that transform the environment-behavior are implicit in the products of those transformations. Only the results of its operation, not the structure or operation itself, are present to the investigator and to the actor as well.

Structure is a system of transformations in the second sense that in organizing its object it itself is dynamic. The way it organizes its object is by being in systematic movement. A structure transforms itself in order to transform. The laws of a structure are laws of its own operation which in turn are the way it operates on the world. In Piaget's terms, when I grasp or add or "group," an "aliment" has presented itself to a psychological structure or a "scheme" for grasping or adding or classifying. That structure is not a static form but a dynamic potential. To organize my behavior so that I might classify, it moves itself.

Yet in its movement a structure is self-regulatory; structures are "self-sufficient" [27] and self-governing. How to grasp, add, and classify—these operations themselves—constitute a given structure. When a particular scheme moves so that I may add, it regulates its own movement, having recourse only to itself as sole knowledge of how to add.

However, there is a superstructure whereby each structure is regulated. Self-regulation is guided by or occurs within an over-arching biological context. Structures regulate themselves within the larger framework of adaptation to the environment. Adaptation as an invariant biological function is the ground of intellectual development. Given this ultimate grounding in the biological, any reliance on the experience of structure or of intellectual functioning is undercut. Rather, the investigator orients himself exterior to the phenomenon in much the posture of the rational-empiricist or the natural scientist.[28]

Adaptation involves two processes, assimilation and accommodation, which simultaneously regulate a given structure, providing a guideline for its self-regulation. The overriding conduct of the organism in regard to its intelligent behavior is in terms of a continual adaptation of its structures to the environment through these processes. Hence, their description in different developmental contexts is a resolution of the "really central problem of structuralism," [29] the explication of the development of a given structure. In general, a structure actively brings itself to bear, in a sense looks for occasions for its application. As it does so it is transformed through the process of assimilation-accommodation. It changes through the slight accommodation necessary to apply itself in any given situation. For example, the world presents itself to the child early in development as a series of objects to be grasped. By discovering what is required to grasp objects of different size or shape, the structure for grasping assimilates into itself a broader repertoire. It transforms itself through these variable applications of itself and in this limited sense actively constructs its own structure. Structure is a system of transformation in that at once it changes the world given to it and it changes itself as a particular operation through an adaptive process of assimilation and accommodation.

Piaget the theorist presents a general definition of structure that clearly places it within the structuralist band of our spectrum. To this point the formal analogy between his thought and that of Lévi-Strauss is striking. A certain region, roughly the environment or the sensory given for Piaget and social facts for Lévi-Strauss, presents itself as prestructural or as having only a surface structure. At a middle region, these data are organized and operated on, giving meaning and structure. The rules of this organization are guided by certain metarules, a metastructure or a deep structure that is invariant or innate or ahistorical. For Piaget these are biologically dictated adaptive strategies, while for Lévi-Strauss they are bipolar categories of organization. These constructions allow or justify a mixed rational-empiricist methodology.

Further, in both there is a distrust of the experiential, a refusal to give any direct presence to structure in the experience of the subject. As investigator, Piaget observes performance, infers constructs, defines tasks as operations of the constructs or structures, observes performance, and so forth. Observed performance has the same status as in a behaviorism. The investigator's observation, privileged as neutral and at the same time guided by presuppositions, here of certain universal biological processes, stands in the place of and, if necessary, in the face of the subject's—or for that matter the investigator's—immediate sense of the structure or meaning of that performance: "The 'lived' can only have a very minor role in the construction of cognitive structures, for these do not belong to the subject's *consciousness,* but to his operational *behavior,* which is something quite different" (his emphases).[30]

The statement that cognitive structure belongs to the subject's operational behavior requires further exposition, for it distinguishes Piaget from Lévi-Strauss in a way critical to our argument. Methodologically, this statement and one shortly following, that "structures are inseparable from performance," [31] simply buttress his focus as investigator on behavior or performance as distinguished from experience or the "lived." However, operational behavior or action is also central for Piaget in that through them the cognitive structures of an individual develop. The relation between structure and activity is not restricted to an investigatory strategy. Together with Piaget, we assert the centrality of action in the building up of structure. But Piaget, as the theorist of structure, does not go the further step of giving to the performing subject the possibility of knowing the world through his action, a "world" that implicates both its own structure and, correlatively, that of his action, his particular way of knowing the world.

Instead of this possibility of immediate inherence of the experiencing subject in a world directly meaningful to him, Piaget asserts an ontology common to a cognitive psychology. My knowledge of the world is not directly of the world but is an image of the world. Intelligence directs a process of internalization of the world in the form of an image or "picture" [32] of it. Adaptation is a movement toward congruence between internalized image and the world. As we will show when we turn to some particulars in Piaget's account of development, an individual's intelligent behavior dates from that moment when he first realizes the ability to form images.

In his general theory of structure, Piaget clings to an objectivistic notion of structure as explicit rule or law. While that rule may be inherent in the operation of the structure, it has no lived presence in the structure or in the world that structure intends. Piaget's presuppositions remain dualistic, his methodology cognitive-behaviorist, and his philosophy structuralist. Yet even within his theoretical writing there is a major tension that makes it transitional to a phenomenological position and that is uniquely Piagetian. At least according to one critic, Piaget's project is in part the same as the phenomenologist's: to find and describe structure in a region between a rationalism and a behaviorism or between an idealism and a realism.³³ Piaget's "interactionism" is transitional between structuralism and phenomenology.

For the structuralist, as we saw by taking Lévi-Strauss as proto-typical, structure is external to human action and to the world. While in his dualistic ontology Piaget can refer to both the structure of the physical world and to psychological structures, structures of mind, he largely houses structure within the mental. Unlike Lévi-Strauss, however, for Piaget the application of structure is always also the development of structure. This development cannot be understood as a unidirectional imposition from mental regions onto the world, whether the physical world or the cultural world. While retaining the dualism, with its classical problematics as to the mind/body connection, Piaget insists on an interactive bidirectional relation. Assimilation and accommodation are the principles of interaction, each operating in an opposite direction. Through accommodation the aliment, a given environment, affects the operative cognitive structure, while at the same time at least to some degree, the cognitive structure bends the aliment to it through assimilation. This cognitive structure–aliment interaction is the center of the intelligent way in which organism and environment interact.

As assimilation and accommodation operate simultaneously, the impression is sometimes given that the cognitive structure–aliment is one system with two poles. However, the dualistic language contradicts this impression; the two poles are two different kinds of things in the traditional Cartesian split. The structure is housed within the mind of the organism and outside of the world in which it actually acts. There is, then, a tension or contradiction in Piaget between keeping to a dualism and bridging it. In Piaget's own view, the assimilation-accommodation approach to a resolution of the dualism for assimilation is a species of rationalism, of mind operating on matter, while accommodation is an empiricism, an instance of the givenness of the physical environment influencing the formation of mind.³⁴ In an interactionism these can and do occur together.

Dualism aside and with the appropriate phenomenological reductions, Piaget's account of a bidirectional causality quickly approaches the mutual implication of coconstitutionality. Causality gives way to a dialectic in which structure-aliment is like the system body-world: the meaning of any moment being at once a meaning given to me, that is, which the world presents to me, and a giving of meaning, a taking up of the world by me in a certain meaning-giving way. Piaget's interactionism more generally at least intimates similar ambiguities, which phenomenology directly addresses and on which it builds what has been referred to as a philosophy of ambiguity.[35] Piaget's interactionist notion of structure reveals an impulse, never fully realized by him, to breach the dualism and locate structure in a region between the mental and the physical. Although he does not dislodge structure from its peculiar status as a cognitive entity, a somehow formless mental form, through his description of an interactionism and his focus on the development of structure through activity, he hints at structure's inherence in my immediate involvement in the world.

Given his distrust of the "lived," Piaget was disinclined to provide a description of structure that might be coincidental with a sense of structure as experienced. Particularly in the later stages of his developmental theory, he treats structure by reliance on external rules and systems from a logico-mathematical realm. Yet he did not fully accept the twin structuralist themes that structure is external to some superficial reality, and that structure itself is describable through explicit rules external to it. That this is the case is revealed when we approach Piaget, forgetting the three-tier structuralist framework and the dualism. This is more readily accomplished as we turn from his general theoretical writing to some of his voluminous descriptions of particular stages of development.

The Sensorimotor Period

We examine further the relation between action or performance and structure through consideration of Piaget's account of the first two years of life. While Piaget refers to the presence and importance of physical structures and to behavioral structures or reflexes particularly in the first few days of life, the primary vehicle of the development of intelligence is the psychological structure,[36] referred to as "scheme" in this period.[37] Much of the activity of the child is an occasion for the development and integration of various schemes, such as the grasping scheme and the scheme for visual following. Scheme does not refer directly to an act but to the organized pattern of an act or of that pattern common to a set of acts—the grasping of variously shaped objects. It is a cognitive or psychological structure that organizes an act and, by giving form to it, makes it recognizable as a certain way of acting on the world and a certain way of knowing the world. For example, at a certain period early in development, the child largely knows the world as a situation that does or does not offer something to grasp. In fact, he knows graspableness even before he distinguishes between an object to be grasped and the act of grasping. There is simply world-as-graspable, a fusion of the act and the possible object.

While a scheme is like a tendency or disposition to organize an act in a certain way, it is not a motive in the traditional sense.[38] There is no need or drive to grasp that impels the scheme so that it then organizes the act of grasping. The structure is self-motivating and self-regulating, being itself dynamic. Inherent in it are the inclinations to exercise itself, to complete itself, to generalize itself until it is adapted to the environment—until it can grasp what can be grasped within the limits of its physical structures and of its coordination with other relevant schemes. Like a sentient organism, the scheme seeks situations for its own application so that it may eventually more fully realize itself. Structure here in this stage is not constructed from outside itself in the sense that it functions according to rules imposed on it. If the structure is a rule or rules, they are inherent in it and give it or constitute its vitality.

In regard to its relation to action, the scheme is a psychological or mental entity which organizes acts, which gives them a common style or "mode."[39] Being that which finds and defines a situation as an occasion for a given action, it is intimately related to action. It guides the act and guides its own growth on the occasion of the particular act through its monitoring of the adjustment of the act to the situation. It tends to enact itself, to put itself into operation. A structure is an implicit or potential act of a certain kind.

Although the scheme is a psychological entity, an organizing scheme for a certain class and style of behavior, the child is not aware of it. He is not aware of the structure as such. The structure is mental but has no presence in experience nor any necessary presence postreflectively as an explicit rule of which the individual is aware.

Piaget's emphasis on the importance of action in the origin and development of psychological structure, that entity that is the site of intelligence, of meaningfulness, is a seminal insight. Piaget describes how structure is acted out through particular actions; how it interacts with the environment through action, action being a kind of "between" for the intelligent organism and the environment; how it is thereby transformed through action; how it enacts itself as a kind of action; and, of course, in the other direction, how at the same time that it depends on action, it gives structure to action. Yet despite structure's intimacy with action, it is as if it were a spirit rather than a potential embodiable act. Any particular act of grasping somehow is the embodiment of a *disembodied* structure, an incarnation peculiarly adjusted to the situation, since structure, a psychological entity, and situation, a physical environment, have license to intercourse despite their being different kinds of things. Piaget's ontology is dualistic but it is also lax. While elsewhere he insists on the precision of formal language to describe structures,[40] here his description is occasionally neovitalistic, the structure being like an organism; at other times it is described as an organ of an integrated biological organism which by nature acts to adjust itself to the environment; and at times it is the unknown instrument by which a person actively constructs a world for himself.

As we follow Piaget from the sensorimotor to the preoperational stages of his description of development, the critical role of action gives way to the critical role of images and operations on images as precursors of thought. However, the shift is more complex than an eventual substitution of thought for action as the "enactor" of psychological structures. While in the sensorimotor period, action is between organism and environment and structure is related to action in the various ways we have just described, the preoperational stage begins when images of the world are formed and structure stands between those images and the world. Structure in a sense takes up the former position of action. At this point in development, adaptation is the movement to congruence of image/world and is mediated by schemes. It is no longer as directly a function of an organism/environment interface that is mediated by action. The role of action is diminished and, at least for Piaget, the primacy of action is forgotten. While Piaget describes a fascinating developmental sequence by which action is internalized as image and image become flexible gives rise to thought and schemes for thought, he loses the sense in which structure is like an implicit

action. Without a notion of structure as embodied or, more generally, of consciousness as incarnate, as thought later in development becomes the dominant modus vivendi of the intelligent individual, Piaget moves to a more rationalistic and external notion of
structure.

Structure as the Internalization of Action

Here we will follow Piaget's description of some of the sequences
leading up to and constituting the bridge between the sensorimotor
and the preoperational stages in somewhat more detail, for eventually we can demonstrate through a more phenomenological
account of them how structure or scheme is related to action.

The grasp is originally a reflex occurring in the first months of
life. Like all reflexes, which for Piaget are simply early schemes,
in order to develop into a pattern of action with a broader repertoire, it must repeat itself. At first repetition is confined to actions
that the infant has already performed, in what Piaget calls the
"primary circular reaction." [41] There is as yet little variation in
the infant's behavior. In this invariability there is a primitive form
of imitation.[42] While in all schemes repetition of the acts they pattern constitutes a form of imitation, this scheme is related to imitation in the further sense that to grasp an object requires a rough
mimicry of its shape. After an initial period in which there is no
action/"object of action" distinction, the scheme comes to pattern
a prehensile act through which the child apprehends the form of
something. A grasp is an outline in the rudimentary sense of the
exterior shape of something, its line at the surface. In like manner
for Piaget, perception is a kind of grasp—an act in which the
person imitates the form of an object. This imitation of it constitutes the seeing of it.[43] While the scheme for prehension, like
all other schemes, advances through the simultaneous processes of
assimilation-accommodation, the grasp, in that it is essentially imitative or duplicative, has an overriding affinity to accommodation.
Through the exercise of this scheme the body or part of the body
takes up an object's form. Through the interaction of the scheme
and this embodying behavior, the shape of the object is inculcated
into the repertoire of the individual and becomes part of the scheme.
Through this growth the individual more and more comes to carry
the forms of the world. Form, in the rudimentary sense of the

"outline" of something, is known through action. The accomplishment of form through action is a theme of both Piaget's and our work. While form here has little yet to do with the notion of form as the living relations that constitute structure, an intimacy of action and structure is suggested. In Piaget's frame, in the grasp there is both a bodily and a psychological reproduction of the world; in particular, there is a duplication of similarities in form or shape. The sensorimotor grasp as a primitive active relation to the world predelineates the possibility of an action-oriented knowledge that is largely accommodative, that largely mirrors or imitates the world. In Piaget's terms it de-emphasizes the assimilative, that is the constructive, playful, or interpretative side of our constitution of the world.

However, in this stage grasping has a basic limitation in that it is an understanding, a grasp, only available in the presence of that which is the object of its knowledge. The child only grasps in the concrete presence of the graspable. While the scheme may be rich in its repertoire of shapes, each form requires a milieu suitable to its own evocation. This limitation eventually is surpassed through the further development of imitation, a phenomenon that itself has a primitive source in the grasp reflex.

Through its relation to one of the dynamic features of the operation of schemes, repetition, and to one pole of the basic process of scheme, accommodation, Piaget gives to imitation or finds in it a critical conservative role in the construction of the child's world. After several phases in the development of the structure of imitation, from its restriction to copies of his own movements, to a rough imitation of the movements of a model (providing these movements are already in his repertoire), the child acquires "deferred imitation" of the act of a model.[44] Piaget infers from this that the child now has at his disposal some kind of symbolic functioning. The child can evoke an imitation of the action of a model now absent. This development enables the child to maintain a sense of the "constancy" of a hidden object through internal representation of it. The "as if" presence of objects and situations in the form of images of them and of active reproductions based on these images allows the emergence of the belief, unshakable once established, in their continued existence independent of their presence to him.

These developments near the end of the second year of life

signal the birth of mental life in Piaget's view. While the child has had the intelligent use of schemes which are clearly psychological structures, prior to this point he has not had an access to this knowledge as positable or thetic. His knowledge was limited to direct enactment of those patterns of behavior implicit in the schemes. But the schemes, for Piaget, were not present in any mode of consciousness. Mental life is originally an immediate development of imitation, or rather is itself an advance form of imitation. For the first time a scheme or structure does not realize and develop itself through interaction with a concrete action but rather through some interior product. Piaget refers to this product as image or picture. Of course he draws evidence for the constitution of images exclusively by inference from observable behaviors.

Our explication is cumbrous here, for it matches Piaget's elaboration of his research. At the center of development we have schemes which are, within this first stage, possible actions; we have these actions which are at once the fulfillment of schemes and a kind of mediator between them and the environment, the source of modification of schemes; and now mental images enter which are initially internalized derivatives of action inferred from the observation of deferred imitative acts. Beginning with the grasp, which is inherently imitative, Piaget demonstrates graphically how action throughout its development has an imitative or accommodative pole. Objects in the world, the behavior of others, and even the child's own behavior are all known through imitative acts. As these imitations begin to occur without the immediate presence of the original, action tends toward the function of an incipient symbolization or representation. Piaget's insight and description of this process is a powerful discovery. Action, actual manipulation of the physical environment, emerges as a critical precursor of no less than thought and its structures, the integrity of the self, and language. Piaget complements a contemporary view of action as a modification of the environment[45] with the notion that it captures the environment, that it is a relative congealing of situations.

In the beginning, action is all there is to the world of the child. He is not yet a self-world system. The world is not yet an intentional object that implicates an intending subject. The subject-object or body-world does not yet form a mutually implicatory system; the two elements are more or less fused as action. Given this beginning, it follows that those systems must be a development out of action. With his usual patient and thorough observation of the child's behavior and his ingenious exploitation of its seemingly random vicissitudes, Piaget, more than any other worker, reveals concretely how this wedded polarity which is the body-world develops.[46]

The congealing of features of the world, implicit in an act of deferred imitation, points to the beginnings of a separation from the immediate physical environment which now no longer has exclusive claim to and dominion over the action of the child. This conservationist bent of action, that it now is that which the child can carry away from or preserve of a situation, a situation to which it and he were formerly chained and in which they had their exclusive existence, is also a rebellion, a separation. This relative independence of the child from the environment is the ground for the establishment of its permanence for him. Total immersion and constitution by action on an immediately and concretely present physical world had blocked a retentive grasp of that world as stable, as always there. This self-consuming relation to the world now gives way to the possibility of holding the world at arm's length. In being able to imitate the world more at his own whim, there are radical gains both in the child's integrity and in his constructive capacity. He can create situations through his own action, although from actions taken from previous situations. The accommodative power of action yields the flowering of assimilation and the power of playful construction.

For Piaget these developments—the separatist, symbolic, deferred, and abbreviated features of imitation and the permanence both of the imitated and the imitator—culminate in the internalization of the act of imitation. Abbreviated imitation carried to its extreme is a mental act, an action in which bodily motion is invisible or, given Piaget's dualistic presupposition, where it is disembodied, mental. Action so transformed is thought. At first, "thought" is largely in the form of images, relatively frozen pictures that represent a concrete situation. The child has available a represen- tation, a symbolization which, although a derivative developmentally of a concrete act, is now internal and inactive. While tracing in great detail the origin of the image in and through imitative action, having reached this radical departure, the mental, those sources are no longer formative. Once having accounted for the origin of a second world, an internal representation of the world in which action initially and unreflectively found itself, Piaget's description of the further development of intelligence largely abandons the role of action. Further, from this new plateau his portrayal of subsequent development loses claim to being an account even transitional to a phenomenology. From our point of view experiential referents become more vague and difficult to derive. Having taken action to the doorstep of a mental life which it originates, Piaget then leaves it outside. His description becomes more abstract and his view of the course of development more idealized. The description of this evolving intelligence focuses on the internal representation or image of the world and mental acts on that image. This account relies on and derives from a theoretical construction based on inferences from observed performance and deduction from a presumed superstructure, certain logico-mathematical systems. The critical role of active commerce with and in the world is forgotten as mental acts are disembodied, inaccessible, and abstract despite their origin in action.

The subsequent turn notwithstanding, in his account of the internalization of action as image, Piaget has provided a rendering of the birth of "mental life" that seemingly has no leaps. The attempt is formidable considering that, next to the origin of life itself, consciousness is the traditional stronghold of emergentism. He has shown consciousness precisely to be a development, that is, an evolution from earlier structures. The focus on action as the origin of mental life is fortunate and compelling. He has recognized in action the basis for a notion of structure as "between." Action neither simply executes a movement that is preformed nor is it in any simple fashion given by or a derivative of a present situation. Like action, structure cannot be understood either through a perspective of a prioris or preformations or through an empirical point of view. Like action, structure is dynamic and mobile. It is transformative both of that on which it operates and of itself. Although it is an organization or provides organization, it is itself changing, and the way in which it organizes is by providing particular ways of transforming.

As compelling as it is at certain points, Piaget's description of how action interiorized results in an image is unclear. He does not tell us how an action, even an abbreviated one, can become an object, in what sense that object is an image or imaginable, or how an object originally acted through can become an object upon which we perform operations or actions. If we infuse Piaget's observations and descriptions of this critical transition with an inwardness, with structure's sense of itself, that is, if we take up residence in structure's presence in lived experience, we can attempt to answer these questions and to find action's further and more radical implication into structure's domain. Also, by finding it prefigured here in Piaget's work, we hope to support our thesis that it is through modes of action that structure is both immediately present and explicable in reflection. In his isolation of the critical moment when the symbolic function originates through a development in the child's imitative actions, we find evidence of the mode of apprehension that we call forming. Behavioral imitation, condensed and separated from its source, becomes the condition for the possibility of what we call virtual behavior. The child in this period attains the ability, as it were, to perform in the mind's eye. By taking seriously behavioral imitation as the precursor of that mode of experiencing, we can begin to suggest that this ability can be and typically is utilized as a mode of apprehension of structure. We can indicate how behavioral imitation deals in rudimentary ways with the problems we have highlighted—the apprehension of relation as such, similarity or equivalence, and abstraction.

The Bodily Apprehension of Structure

Consider the following observations of Lucienne at age one year, four months:

Lucienne at first fails to free a watch chain from a matchbox in which Piaget has lodged it. After these initial efforts at groping with her fingers to reach the chain through the presently insufficient opening in the box, she looks at the slit for a moment and then "several times in succession, she opens and shuts her mouth, at first slightly, then wider and wider." With this she then immediately removes the chain by enlarging the opening.[47]

Here Lucienne is attending to a situation as a problem. In a sense there is nothing peculiar in this, for in Piaget's thinking all activity is a response to the problematic, being in the service of schemes which seek to stretch themselves before an environment that is a challenge to them. But here the problem is not only the general one of a scheme that cannot quite handle a present environment; rather, the situation itself is problematic. The child studies a situation as a problem. What aspects of the situation does the child need to understand in order to solve the problem?

The child must understand the workings of the matchbox. One part can be moved in relation to the other, resulting in a new relation between them, an enlargement of the opening between them. Further, the child must realize the relation between the matchbox and the watch chain, that the latter is in the former and is presently constrained by the given relation of its two parts. Finally, the child must understand that enlarging the opening frees the chain. It is evident that Lucienne needs to appreciate the structure of the situation, the various relations obtaining among parts.

How does she know that structure, by what mode? In the final moment of her study of the situation Lucienne employs a form of action, imitative behavior. She seeks to act out or enact the relations of the matchbox and chain problem. Her understanding is through bodily and behavioral imitation. She imitates the movement of the box through an analogous movement of her mouth. How is this possible? The workings of her mouth are a relationship that she knows intimately due to its importance in her survival and in her early exploration of the world. The child learns the structures of her body through her own movement and behavior. But further, before the age of two the child discovers that her body and her behavior can provide a copy of features of the world before her. Somehow she can invest in or finds invested in her body as she lives its parts and its mobility a natural correlate of any situation. It is as if how she knew a situation were inseparable from her bodily posture and action. Earlier we discussed a ground for this "natural analogy" [48] in the child's original embeddedness or situatedness in the world. Before there was a self to witness spectacles, there were only happenings and the climate of their occurrence. The child was of a piece with the world through her body.

Through attempts to manipulate the environment, the child begins to shift from being its appendage to finding the world at her fingertips. To do so, however, to coconstitute that world, she continues to rely on the discovery of bodily and behavioral analogies to it. This is seen not only in the grasp but in the omnipresent inclination of the child to form such analogies in play. Some additional descriptions from Piaget illustrate this common observation.

After observing her father's bicycle displaying a back-and-forth motion, Lucienne describes a similar motion with her own body.[49] After accidentally catching the feet of her toy clown in the neck of her dress and eventually extricating them, Jacqueline recreates that situation by crooking her fingers in the shape of the doll's feet and catching them in her low-necklined dress.[50]

In these instances, imitative action is advanced in terms of the object of imitation, the instrument of imitation, and their relation. Surpassing the rough mimicry of the grasp, the child is no longer confined to an imitation of the outer shape of an object. The motion of an object is readily copied by utilizing the expressive or gestural as well as the mobile possibilities of the body. Without the need for direct physical contact inherent in the earlier prehensile activity, the child mimics the movements and forms of objects with parts of her own body the relation of which to the object is now an analogy that is more like a metaphor than a homology. The child's swaying body or her crooked finger in her dress stand for, respectively, the motion of the bicycle or the shape and relation of the clown's feet to her clothing. While imitation originates largely within Piaget's accommodative function, in its later development it involves assimilation. While still bodily and behavioral, imitation becomes more creative, in a sense more artful, as the child's action is not so much a mirroring as a metaphoric rendering of a situation.

At the same time that the imitation is now accomplished by a literal separation from the object of imitation and by the creation through action of an analogy that makes the act a symbolic expression, imitation becomes abbreviated. The act is truncated in that the child reacts to familiar situations that formerly elicited certain full-blown actions now with only partial enactments of that response, that is, with acts that are abbreviated imitations of her own typical response. For example, Lucienne's mouth takes on the form of the matchbox's motion in opening and closing. This imitation later can be done with only a hint of the movement of her mouth. The kinetics have become almost mute.

As we have seen, at this point Piaget invokes the birth of the image to describe this apparent submersion of bodily activity. Our thesis posits a more direct and simpler progression—and one that is truer to Piaget's general description of this period than Piaget's. The culmination of the development of imitative behavior is the possibility of abstraction as we have defined that term. A mode partaking of the abstract intends an object in such a way that that object points to some original of which it was a part. Let us retrace Piaget's description of the development of imitation to show how an abstractive posture is a necessary endpoint.

The early imitative behavior of the grasp occurs exclusively in the presence of the original. It participates in it and with it. When the child can duplicate an object or situation in its presence, he has realized the possibility of actual bodily enactment. An example of this is when Jacqueline imitates the clown's swinging legs with her crooked fingers immediately after the former were caught in her dress. Following Merleau-Ponty, if we assert that to coconstitute a situation in the first place requires a bodily taking up of that situation, in bringing to bear some bodily duplicate or correlative of a present object, the child is becoming sensitive to that bodily coconstitutive pole. The duplication is here restricted to an actual enactment as the child actually moves. Further, the duplication is still participatory rather than abstractive. It does not occur at a remove. Duplication or equivalence is accomplished without yet giving up the "closeness" to the situation required in coconstituting it, without relinquishing the sense in which we must become the situation to live the situation.

Through the enhanced sensitivity to the bodily pole and, with that, the possibility of the actual enactment of that pole in the form of an imitative act, there is the further development of the postponement of enactment. When the child sees the playpen in which his friend had a tantrum the previous day and mimics it with his own outburst,[51] he lives this as a rejoining, as a participation in that situation anew. However, with further developments in the imitative act, that act partakes of the double story structure of abstraction. The act is no longer a moment of reimmersion in a previous situation. It recreates the original with a sense of distance from it. This is particularly striking in playful imitative behavior. For example, when Jacqueline pretends a fringe-edged cloth is her pillow and feigns sleeping with it,[52] clearly her amusement with her own behavior demonstrates an awareness that that behavior belongs elsewhere and is, hence, a part apart. Participatory imitation gives way to enactment which emphasizes a distance from the original. The child attains a growing repertoire of imitative behaviors which may be enacted in the contexts of symbolic play and of problem-solving where the original may be indicated without its actual presence. Imitation separated from the original and pointing to it assumes the structure of abstraction.

The final step from this mode, an actual bodily enactment of some feature of the original, to the possibility of forming is the abbreviation of the kinetic until it is mute. The resultant enactment, now virtual, signifies the completion of a gradual emancipation from the original situation while retaining access to the bodily coconstituting pole of it.

Beginning with the discovery that her body and behavior are a potential correlate of the workings of the world, the child's early education is largely a development of that correlative system. The body as potential enactment comes to be incredibly informed of the structure of situations. So informed, a person can "return" to situations as-lived through virtual enactment of the bodily pole of that moment.

If there is merit in this rendering of Piaget's original account, what is left of the role of image, what is the relation of image to knowledge as potential virtual enactment, of what eventually do we have an image? Here we return once more to Lucienne and the matchbox. The child confronted with the watch chain in the matchbox apprehends a critical structure of that situation through the mediation of the imitative act of opening her mouth, the body and its motion serving as an embodiment of the concept "enlarge." Later she can solve such a problem with only an abbreviated form of this bodily enactment. Eventually, the enactment is imperceptible. From this Piaget infers the sequence abbreviated action—interiorized action—image. He asserts that the result of the abbreviation and internalization of action is an image. In this example, of what would Lucienne eventually have an image?

Clearly, she would not imagine the matchbox and chain, for the action to be interiorized is an abbreviated form of a mouth being opened, not of a matchbox. Does she then imagine a mouth, her mouth, which is opening? Neither the eventual object of action, the matchbox, nor its bodily metaphor, the mouth, is interiorized, at least not as objects of the action. What is interiorized is an act, not the object of the act. The immediate experiential referent of "interiorized action" is that species of action we will describe as forming or virtual action. The child's mouth is not present in the virtual enactment as an object of that action since it is the instrument of it, that through which there is an enactment. Interiorized action is first an act, although a virtual act. It is not simply or directly an image, nor is it yet an operation on an image. There is a virtual motion or movement and the performer is engaged in that. The instrument of the act, here the mouth, and the act itself, here the act of opening, are present, to utilize Polanyi's distinction, only as a "subsidiary awareness." [53] I attend from them to their "object." What is that object? As we will describe in chapter 5, my virtual action has a product that I can posit as an object. That product is the path through space, an abstract space, that the virtual act articulates. It is that shape of which I can have an image, the product of my own virtual act. In the aftermath of her experience with the matchbox, the first object of which Lucienne would have an image is the immediate product of her own enactment. The object is not "a mouth opening" but "opening," for it is the movement, not its instrument, that carves the space to constitute a certain shape. Here the articulated space that is the product of the act of the mouth opening might be two lines moving away from each other: <

The implicit meaning of the image could be explicated as "becoming larger." There is no identifiable something that is becoming larger. The image captures only the motion of the act. The enactment embodies the concept "enlarge." From this it is clear that concepts can have a prelinguistic and preconceptual presence, a presence that is a necessary concomitant of a kind of action.

In that it is only the act that is interiorized, this rendering is again more faithful to Piaget than is Piaget. He has established that it is acts, particularly his own acts, upon which the child has been centered throughout this period of development. The motion of his own body has been focal. We claim that as the child begins to loosen his ties to the immediate concrete situation, a form of action leads the way for him through which he constructs an abstract preconceptual space. The stuff of which he constructs that first image, whether the imaginal mode be visual, auditory, or kinesthetic, is a byproduct of his own action. The first object of the child's imagination consists in a space shaped by his own virtual action.

If this is the basis of the onset of imagination, the hallmark of what Piaget calls the "intuitive" period, then the child's first "representation" of the world is more advanced than Piaget would have it. The object of the first image is not simply a variant of an interiorized percept, the child's view of the matchbox and chain: the object is the tracings left by the child's abbreviated action on that occasion.

As we have argued, that which the child enacts in her effort to resolve what is to her a problematic situation is a structure of that situation. That structure, certain relations among parts, is present as possible moves. Relations are dynamic and are known by living through those dynamics, by acting them out. Piaget's statement that structure is inseparable from performance is true in this further sense. The child's first image, then, is a product of an embodiment of the structure of a situation.

In order to posit that abstract space, the child must learn to carry it as a possible action or virtual enactment—the possibilities, respectively, of actually enlarging things by opening them, and of virtually articulating an abstract space which can be posited imaginally. The experiential referent of Piaget's "scheme" is an unfulfilled intention present as a bodily sense of this possible action.

Structure is carried and is implicitly present as possible action. Conversely, action is the mode of apprehension of relations between things; through it the world is originally built up, known as so built, further known and further built. I construct the world that I live in by modes of action and I can know that construction, that organization, by modes of action. The intimacy of the relation between structure and action may be more radically stated: Structure itself is possible action; it is the embodiment of living relations among parts. Again in the other direction, embodiment is form-bearing and is, then, the way in which we have, give, realize, and in a sense, are or exist structure.

Bodily and active modes are the noetic correlates of the noema, the structure of a situation. Following Merleau-Ponty, both in the original moment and in reflection experience is incarnate or embodied. The mobile body as correlative gives rise not directly to an image, for Piaget a mental life which then forgets its origin in bodily action; rather, it is the possibility of abstraction in the sense of taking a structural aspect from the whole. The body, in that through it I coconstitute situations, is, in Merleau-Ponty's term, the "informed body." [54] It allows me to carry from situations and to situations, dialectically, a sense of structures or forms which

are, as I shall describe more fully in chapter 5, the possibility of
action and the key to the initial, prelinguistically unprejudiced
moments in the explication of structure. In the act of abstraction
is the origin of and continuous potential for reflection, the method
of phenomenology. To abstract is to seize the bodily pole of
experience.

STRUCTURE AS LIVED

Before we turn to a description of forming, we will complete the
present account of the bodily or active apprehension of structure
with two brief returns to mundane experience. In the first, to
examine how it first appears to us, we begin with structure as if
it were located exclusively in the object. In the second we attempt
to find structure as it is already bodily carried.

  1. We begin again with everyday usage of the term *structure*.
With little or no scrutiny of the term, what do I refer to when I
speak of the structure of something? I assume only that our language
is consistent, that the structures of an object, situation, conversation, or a thought all have something in common that language
intends with that term. I am on the first of several tours of a newly
renovated building which will house the psychology department
and serve as a new working place for me. Even before I enter the
building I begin to be able to refer to the structure of the building.
It is a certain shape the building has or describes. Is it a kind of
outline of the building, as, perhaps, the building at its edges?
Clearly, it is not the material of the building but where and how
that stuff terminates. But the structure of the building is not the
outside, its exterior. I do not find the structure along some outside
edge. The structure of the building is not its contribution to the
skyline of the city. That skyline has a structure but it is not the
structure of the building and to try to locate it there would lead
me astray. The structure is given as a certain shape, but where
is the line that delimits it? It is not some silhouette of the building,
the character or style of its external edge. The structure of the
building is not so thin. It impresses me as having a body, as
having some weight of its own. Yet I cannot find the outside of
that body, let alone the body itself.

  As I enter the building and wander about its interior the sense
of the structure is stronger and begins to become more distinct.

I know more fully a certain shaped body. Is this because I am getting closer to the structure in the interior of the building? Is it the shape of the interior that is the structure of the building? The rooms have a certain shape which is given to me by a perceptual tracing along the baseboards and from one room to another. I can put these tracings together into a kind of blueprint or floor plan which I then may stop and imagine at any point in my tour. But again, while the blueprint, either the architect's actual copy or my own imagined one, has its own structure, that is not quite the structure of the building.

Now I must be more assiduous in my search. There is a certain shaped and hence delineated body that is the structure of the building. It is the same structure suggested by my view from the outside and strongly reinforced by that of the interior of the building. The most apparent outlines, however—those giving the silhouette of the exterior or a virtual blueprint of the interior—while consonant with my sense of the structure, do not directly reveal it or embody it. Structure refers to a less apparent, at least perceptibly apparent, kind of outline. We have somehow taken outline too literally, as out-line; or more accurately, we have presumed it to be directly perceptible. An outline of something is a body within a body, as a skeleton. The outline of an argument or thesis is its bare bones but it is also its framework, what supports it. It is the outline that largely gives the shape of the argument. Yet while it is intimately related to it, it does not directly give the substance of the argument. It is not the points themselves but some shape of their whole. The points of the argument are related to each other in various ways. For example, a particular argument has in succession three points of equal weight or scope, the third of which seems to return to and complement the first. A fourth point has less weight, is off the main line of the first three, and comprises two subpoints. There are then a number of points and subpoints which when I finish the argument are a certain pattern or organization of points. It is the "line of thought" or the "drift" of the argument that is the structure of the argument. As I go through the argument itself there is a certain movement; when I review the argument at the level of its structure, without directly positing the substance of the argument, there is again a certain movement which outlines this shape. The intimate relation of the movement and the shape of the argument are given in phrases like the thrust or the drift of the argument. Again, this

motion-creating shape is not somehow the out-line, the implicit
line that is the defining border between points in the argument.
The shape that I refer to as structure, whether of the argument
or of the building, is not this outer contour of entities. The sense
of structure is strong at boundaries not because it constitutes or
even highlights the places where one thing gives way to another.
That structure is more centered there has to do with its relation to
how things are together, how they are next to, below, within,
encircling, supporting, giving way to one another. Structure
concerns relations and a relation between two things is how they
stand one to the other. How they so stand is not separable from
their own individual being, yet it is their being "in relation" to
which structure refers. The example of an argument or line of
thought suggests that structure is a body within a body, as the
skeleton within your body. Our immediate experience of the
structure of a building revealed that it is strong at the boundaries.
How can we integrate these? The boundary is not the outer
contour. Where is the relation between parts, where is that
connection, that unifying border? Consider the doorknob and the
door, your arm and your shoulder, this present point and the
previous one, my relation to you. These are all pairs of entities in
relation, yet for none is the juncture of their joining an outer
contour. Do they then join within? But the joining of, for
example, that physiological joint, is not necessarily the relation
that I immediately experience as their structure. The structure is
not within as bones are in an arm or as anything is within another
thing. The structure of something is not visible as is an outer
contour nor is it potentially visible in the same way as the cadaver's
arm when dissected or the rear of the house with a change in my
position. It is not an actual framework but a living relation. It
is the being or style of a relation. It is an internal design consisting
of lines of forces, of pushes and pulls, of centers and epicenters,
of leanings and supports, of enclosing and being enclosed. The
architectonics necessary to know this living internal design is not
a measured vision or an application of physical or logical principles.
To find these lines of force requires a dehiscence, a sudden
bursting or splitting, an opening up which reveals the being of a
living relation. The structure of a building is a living body which
is known immediately and virtually by living it. All structures
have or are a set of dynamic relations. There are forces at work.
The structure of an English Gothic cathedral built in the twelfth

century remains a living set of relations. The flying buttress on
the exterior of the building still receives the lateral thrust from
the convergence of the ribs of the interior vaulting. To know these
living relations I must live them.

2. Even before it organizes an act, a structure is implicitly
present as a way of approaching the world. For example, I can
have a sense of the world as graspable or as to-be-grasped even
before I deploy that posture. As I turn to it directly at the other
pole from the world, that set has or is a bodily sense. It is present
as an unfulfilled intention to do something; it is a sense of the
style of an action, a sense of the general movement that is essential
to a particular kind of act. I can have that bodily sense in various
ways. When it is least available, being embedded in a host of
other possible moves, it is there only as ready to be called. When
it is called but still coiled, ready to be applied and looking for
its fulfillment, it is a certain tension of an act or operation about
to be done. When I am ready to grasp or ready to add or classify,
each has its own bodily sense which is a peculiar potential kinetic.
I approach the desk differently to grab my notebook, to sort an
accumulation of sundry papers, or to explicate in writing what is
only a half-baked thought. When I am in the act, the structure
is present as the fulfilling of an intention, as the general or typical
movement or way within a particular concrete act. When I finish
the act, I can walk away with a sense of the structure of that act
as once again a possible act. Sometimes I can sense how a particular
instantiation of that act stretched and slightly modified the unfulfilled intention the enactment of which partly constituted it. This
last is exemplified in a complex motor skill. I have a sense of a
basic four-ball juggling pattern and a possible variation on it
which I cannot yet quite do. Before I try the trick it is present
both as a certain way of articulating space and as a bodily sense
of an act the execution of which would articulate that space.
Following the act, if the attempt was an improvement, I now
have a clearer sense of the space it articulates and of the act, both
lodged in my body. I can walk away with this bodily sense relatively
congealed. At any moment I can call on that bodily sense. I can
actually act out the unfulfilled intention and do the trick or I can
virtually enact the scheme without props or apparent motion. This
last would be an instance of the mode of experience I call *forming*.

5

The Method, Part Two:

Reflection as an Enactment of Structure

INTRODUCTION

Forming is the centerpiece of the present method, for we claim
that being attuned to this mode and developing the ability to
adopt it in the course of the study of phenomena facilitates the
systematic grasp of their structure. With forming as a guide those
structures can be explicated. As we will describe, forming or its
product can provide the ground for the location or creation of
metaphors that evoke and meaningfully express the structures of
a particular phenomenon. We reach the present juncture after
an extensive detour in which we surveyed various concepts of
structure and methods of its explication. By this diversion we
have indicated how structure is originally known through the
lived body and unreflective action. Forming is a reflective mode
characterized by its peculiar access to and prolonged utilization
of just these bodily and active or behavioral features of experiencing.

Forming is a second abstractive mode; methodologically, it is
the critical one. It is a mode readily adopted through the abstractive
posture introduced in chapter 2. Like any other mode, an individual may assume it at any moment; yet it readily escapes notice.
In the course of events only the most reflective of us would point
to it through some second order reflection. It is taken for granted,
for in mundane living it is a transitional and transitory mode
which quickly passes over on the one side to behavior proper or
perception and on the other to intellection. It is also easily
mistaken for a species of imagination and its distinctive features

thereby overlooked. Even the phenomenological literature has not honed in on it and clearly has not realized its significance for method. While the claim is not critical to the efficacy or the originality of the present method, we assert that the mode properly deserves the status of sui generis.

In what follows we will distinguish it from imagination and perception while showing its kinship to behavior proper. A backdrop for this description is a critical examination of the proposition that as imagination is to perception, a kind of virtual spectacle, so, mutatis mutandis, is forming to behavior proper. Another organizing comparison is that as the mode that we designated within the abstractive posture as the affected body lifts, carries, and facilitates the explication of the texture of a phenomenon, so does forming collaborate with structure. To the degree that we find in forming a quasi-behavioral mode distinct from the quasi-perception of imagination, it follows, given the intimate relation between structure and activity, that this collaboration is not collusion or contrivance but natural affinity. While we expect to discover considerable features in common, forming is a more demanding mode than imagination, for to form we must engage ourselves in a kind of activity. To imagine a particular something, I need only have that intention and the intended object immediately appears. In forming I must form it through a peculiar activity undertaken in relation to that potential object—a relation that we must explicate below. To anticipate a phenomenology of forming, it is a mode that virtually enacts a behavioral space. However, that space is also the object of forming, as forming reflectively posits its own movement. Further, and critically for the present method, that virtually enacted space become object is the realization of an abstracted bodily sense of the structure of a phenomenon.

If there is any validity in this latter claim, it would follow that the description of a genetic phenomenology of structure is indistinguishable from the provision of a phenomenological method. Let me clarify how and why this is the case. The genetic phenomenology to be presented here is not of the development of a structure, whether a particular structure or scheme in the Piagetian sense, or of structure in general, or even of the development of the "ability" to structure. Rather, it is a description of the different ways structure appears in experience, beginning with an implicit

structure of a particular lived moment and culminating in a mode
of presence and apprehension of that structure which allows
me to explicitly formulate it. More particularly, I will trace from
an initial coconstituting involvement in a situation, to how the
lived bodily pole of that original moment is abstracted, to how
it is present as carried "in" the body or in a bodily way, to reflective
moments in which a virtual enactment of that bodily sense
eventuates both in an active formation of a space that is positable
as a scheme or diagram and in the "discovery" of metaphors
that share some of the structural features of the original. In the
course of this genetic phenomenology we will pause to present
a constitutive phenomenology of forming itself. This sequence
is the present method. The present chapter is organized in accordance
with it. (It may be helpful to refer back to figure 1 on page 55.)

CASTLES IN THE AIR

Before undertaking that account, some experiential referents that
approximate forming provide an initial orientation to it.

 1. As I sit at the typewriter the possibility exists for me to rise
and open the door. Of course, I may have this possibility as an
explicit proposition, "open the door." I say it to myself or, as
I look at the door, that statement seems to lodge itself some place
close to the knob or at the crevice between the door and its
frame. Or I may have the possibility as an image. I imagine that
particular door or a somewhat more vague, more schematic door
being opened. As I do so, the image eclipses the actual percept
for an instant.

 More typically, as I finish my work at the desk and begin moving
about the room with the intention of leaving, the way in which
I anticipate opening the door, prior to the act itself, is closer to
the mode of forming. The way in which I am already opening
the door is a certain virtual motion. That motion itself stands
out as an arc cutting through an abstract space. While it may
immediately give rise to a visual image, to an explicit proposition,
or to the actual fulfillment of my intention, at first there is only
a virtual doing and the space it articulates.

 2. When I watch a dance I may be with the dancer. I may
move with him, almost as him, being with him-as-subject, living
him. Or I may, no longer inhabiting his body, see it from outside

as a pole of action, as the center of intention which directs his
action. Or, another posture more exterior still, I may see his body
as an object, as a beautiful and skillful living thing. Finally,
however, I may forget the dancer even beyond taking him as
only his objectified body. I may apprehend the building up of
space by him. I do this in a grosser form when I observe a group
of dancers in such a way that their bodies themselves constitute
different patterns or shapes. However, when I take the body or
bodies not themselves as pattern but as designers of patterns,
when I appreciate the shape made by their gesture and movement,
the space realized is more articulate and refined. Of course, the
shaped space is not concretely there; nor am I simply visually
imagining it. I know the patterns as they are being formed by
moving as does the dancer—but without leaving my seat. I
trace the forms as he does, as it were, a step behind him, a step
quickly forgotten in the moment. I know the pattern through
a restricted, a virtual movement.

   3. There are a number of modes of apprehension of music in
which hearing the music is not the figural mode. Most often in
a tired moment or a reminiscent mood, we all have stopped being
present at the symphony and taken it as a vehicle to venture far
afield to a more fantastic setting. The music is assimilated to the
daydream.[1] Alternatively, we stop perceiving the symphony to
focus on its qualities as sound. We are at one remove from the
symphony, focusing rather on its sensuous qualities.[2] Certain
composers, Mozart more than Brahms, for example, facilitate yet
another mode which pushes even these sensuous qualities of the
music-as-heard into the background. I am listening to the music
when a certain emergent begins to appear. It comes from the
music but appears apart from it. When I focus on it I discover
that it is a spatialization of the music. In such a moment I am
no longer directly hearing the music. The score is present as a
background which functions to support and nourish an ongoing
articulation of itself. The space being articulated is given to me
as an isomorphic mimicry of the music. Much as the musician
transforms the notes on the staff to their musical equivalent, there
is this reverse transformation—a respatialization. My ignorance
of any conventional musical notation is no block. The shapes
being formed appear to come from the music. I know them by
enacting them. The enactment of the music is an immediate

and a continuous one. Something replaces or is being placed over the music at the same time that it so clearly originates in it, being a continuous equivalent emergent from it.

4. If I take my finger and trace a figure in the air, I can forget my finger as I forget my hand when typing. A figure in that moment when it is being formed has an appearance which is not yet an image nor yet a word, these latter being only implicated in that moment as the possibility of hearing is implicit in any moment of seeing. If I close my eyes I can undertake such action virtually and appreciate the abstract space it implies.

A GENETIC PHENOMENOLOGY OF STRUCTURE

The "Return"

The first step in a genetic phenomenology of the structure of a phenomenon, and hence in a method for the explication of such a structure, is to "return" to situations in which that phenomenon can be lived or relived. Traditionally, the investigator effected this return by the simple device of recalling examples of the phenomenon of interest. In a sense, the more general the phenomenon under scrutiny the more available are instances of it. At the extreme, in a study of a constitutive feature of experience its instantiations are unavoidable—any moment will do. As discussed earlier, contemporary phenomenological psychology has both developed and borrowed other extant devices to accomplish a return. Methods such as constructing "situations" evocative of the phenomenon of interest, conducting semistructured interviews, even rereading theoretical accounts, all intend to expand the possibilities for and contexts of a renewed engagement and participation in the phenomenon. In part a phenomenological psychology requires these methodological advances, with their turn to a kind of empiricism, because its target phenomena are often more particular than those of a project in philosophical phenomenology—for example, they might be restricted to a social class, to to a stage in development, or to a pathological way of being.

By definition, a phenomenon is already known at least tacitly; that is, it is already lived and available to the investigator or other individuals all of whom, then, through these devices are potential "subjects" in the study. A phenomenon is that which is typical in a situation or across certain situations. Any and all situations have both typical and unique aspects. In any experience the intended object appears both as a particular object and as an object of a certain type. Consciousness is a typifying agency.[3] The existential and the essential are two moments of any experience. In that a "situation" is coconstituted by my participation in it, by my living it, in that moment I am necessarily privy to its essential features, to those aspects which constitute it as a phenomenon. These essential features are structural in that they consist of relations among parts that are common to certain situations. I originally coconstitute and know them as structures, as the typical relations among the parts of an event or situation.

The return is an attempt to live through those aspects as they originally occurred. By and large the methodological account in this first step is well known and established. We described the way structure is present in the lived moment in the example of exploring the newly renovated building. What we add at this point is a criterion as to the effectiveness of a given return, effectiveness in the context of doing phenomenology. In the aftermath of both the original moment and any subsequent return, I can have "a sense of" those structural aspects. The presence of that sense and, more particularly, its robustness and potential for prolongation are criteria for the judgment of the return.

"A Sense of" Structure

Following the engagement through the vehicle of the return, a phenomenon's structure can be present in a distinctively different way which then becomes a second step in the present method. Hopefully, our explication of this moment and of its methodological importance will justify the selection of such a grammatically anomalous phrase for study. Common discourse provides an accurate referent for "a sense of." We are familiar with moments in conversation in which I am saying that I have a sense of what your basic situation is or of the thrust or gist of your argument. Sometimes a sense of your argument immediately gives way to the possibility of an explicit rendering of it in such a way that confirms it or you. In other instances my understanding is limited to "a sense of." I say that I *only* have a sense of your point. A sense of is an incipient understanding; it is a moment in which a structure that is not yet fully grasped is present. We need to show how sensing is the first of several modes in which a particular structure of a phenomenon lurks: how it is present without yet having been posited yet while not at that moment being lived. Such a moment, between lived and reflected experience, is most striking in problematic situations. Consider the following example.

I am working with a family in a first therapy meeting, a situation that presents itself to me with the question, "What is going on here?" Near the end of the session that question begins to gain my attention. I am struggling toward an answer to the question of how this family is put together and from that to a plan as to how I can intervene effectively. I do not immediately have an explicit conception of the family. I may spend a moment thinking to myself in a kind of interior monologue. Different concepts pop into mind and I seek variations of them that might be descriptive of the present family. But nothing quite fits. For another moment I try to "see" the family, to visually imagine it in the complex but vague way that it has been present to me during the hour. There is no sudden insight, no sudden coming together presented to me in a visual image. My sense of the family cannot yet realize itself in an image or in words.

Yet clearly the family is together or fails to be together within itself and with me as therapist in a particular way, and, as clearly, that (for me) problematic structure has a presence in the moment. In some as yet dim way I know but cannot yet posit such complex relations as a mother hovering protectively close to and over daughter, keeping father at bay; or a father providing a buffer against a potentially destructive confrontation between a mother and son turned away from each other gloweringly.

While I can neither posit these conceptually or imaginally, nor act upon them or further them through my own action in any responsibly knowing way, I have a sense of just that present complex of relations. In the aftermath of the meeting this sense of the family is available to me most apparently, most robustly, and, admittedly, most disturbingly when its nascent understanding refuses to be explicated or furthered in any way. It lingers precisely when something is and threatens to remain problematic. When I then attend to this sense of the situation it distinguishes itself as a first moment of abstraction. As I turn to it and attempt to stay with it, I discover that in general "a sense of" refers beyond itself to an original of which it was once "all of a piece" and from which it is now detached. In that part of the way it appears is as a part apart, this second moment has the structure of the abstracted. Of course, while achieving this extraction, this first remove, I am only doing so in the midst of a new situation in which that abstracted sense is now becoming figural in its own limited way. This nascent but unyielding understanding is something I now have. I can carry it away with me and I can turn to it in the absence of the original to which it refers.

To this point it is clear that a sense of the structure of a situation or phenomenon is a possible initial product, if you will, of an abstractive approach. But beyond this possibility of its abstraction and prolongation, how does it appear and how can its appearance contribute to the project of doing phenomenology? We have already indicated that it is referential but nonpositional. It is an intimation of a structure that is not yet posited or realized in any way, in any mode. "A sense of" neither symbolizes, nor envisions, nor articulates; it merely points. It functions as a marker which neither directly presents, nor represents, nor depicts. It refers to what was going on in the family meeting, its dynamic relations, without capturing them except as a finger that points toward something.

I locate this referential, only potentially positable sense in my body. "A sense of" does not appear in front of me, between me and the world like an object in imagination, nor am I already living through it as when I enact an intention. "A sense of" is a bodily sense. However, while it is bodily I do not have it as an object as I might attend to my knee, having bruised it. I am not positing my body or one of its parts as an object. But can "a sense of" be bodily without being a certain itch? The object of "a sense of" is not a thing but its potential realization. It is a nonintentional awareness in that it has not yet taken an object, being only the intention to do so. Such a preobjective feature of experience has been termed variously an "unfulfilled," "empty," or "incipient intention." [4] "A sense of" is an unfulfilled intention of a certain kind. My sense of an object to-be-posited is present as the potentiality of a bodily movement or action. The unfulfilled intention is an invitation to move in such a way that furthers the incomplete understanding, the incomplete grasp which is as yet *only* a sense of a particular structure. A problematic situation, one in which the structure remains implicit, cries out to be "done." That momentarily elusive structure evokes from me or in me an effort to act on it, to move it from its present amorphous shape to a more articulated form. A certain move would embody and thereby articulate the structure's implicit spatiality, the way its parts stand in relation to each other. Before I enact it I can have this only potential set of moves, carry them with me without yet fulfilling their intention to further understand. The tacit experience of a formerly lived moment is present as to-be-lived in the lived body. This aspect of the lived body originates in and unabatedly can refer back to the lived moment of its birth. This portable, referential, positable bodily presence beseeches me to become it, to take it up, to live through it, to let that bodily aspect I presently only have become the body I am.

The diver walks to the ten-meter platform to execute a "forward one and a half." The coach asks him if he is ready for the dive. He responds that he has it. He can locate this knowledge immediately. In the instant before his leap he can and indeed, to be successful, must have this knowledge without yet imagining it, describing it discursively as a set of moves or rules, or even enacting it virtually. He must have a sense of the dive, since given the limitations of time and the complexity of the act only "a sense of" can guide him, allow him to "find" it, and thereby actually to recreate it. He finds the dive by having it as a bodily potentiality.

Yet in mundane experience we often fail to posit this preobjective understanding as it quickly gives way to or is surpassed in its enactment or its thematization. Put another way, when the structure of a situation is unproblematic for me, it so resonates with my lived body that I miss it, overleaping it to an act, concept, or image immediately at hand. Yet it is always possible to attend to the sense of even a common situation, for the lived body hosts, since it is constituted by, a plenum of potential moves, all of which enacted realize a particular situation. At any moment, through this knowledge of structure, the lived body is more or less mobilized to co-constitute a situation. As we have indicated, when a situation or phenomenon is problematic to me, when I cannot quite grasp its structure, this first bodily mode of the apprehension of structure is more remarkable, more poignant, and more lingering. I am more likely to abstract just that horizontal potential modulation of space since in such moments it cries to be effected. Taking as his task the explication of structures that precisely are problematic, whether so because subtle or because sedimented and taken for granted, the phenomenological psychologist can and must pause in this bodily mode.

In an earlier chapter, we described how the lived body is the bearer of the way I am emotionally affected in a situation following that moment. For example, I can continue to feel the lilt of a marching band after the parade passes me by, as a certain buoyancy in my walk and carriage. In the way my body has been affected I carry the bodily pole of the situation. Through it I can gain access to the atmosphere or texture of that situation as-lived while within a reflective posture. Here we are adding that, less obviously, the lived body bears the structure of a situation in the aftermath of living it. This distinction between the bodily abstraction of milieu and of structure is critical, for the latter is the condition for the possibility of forming—a bodily mode through which we can posit structure as such.

Eugene Gendlin's work[5] corroborates the notions that there are modes of experience transitional between lived experience and reflected experience and that the experience of the body is prominent in these modes. For Gendlin, it is the bodily aspect of "experiencing" that provides the key to our reflective access to it. His description of how at any moment we can refer to, "focus" on, or locate the bodily pole of any situation as lived parallels the present exposition of "a sense of." His term "felt-meaning" is close to our "sense of" on the face of it. A meaning that is only felt and one that is only sensed both refer in common usage to that which I cannot yet have in words.

However, from our point of view, his description of felt-meaning collapses and thereby confuses at least two distinct modes. Felt-meaning is closer to the mode of abstraction that we have termed the affected body. The tension in my shoulders that I carry home with me after a long day at the office and first notice as I settle into my reclining chair is the same feature of bodily experience as the bodily felt lilt of the band after their performance. It is a bodily residual or continuation of a situation. That which gripped me or tightened me up during the day is still present in the tightness of my body. As Gendlin describes, when I later focus on it words can come from it. It reveals itself in general to be a concrete felt-meaning which is an as yet "undifferentiated apperceptive mass."[6] Continuing with our example, its immediate explication would be something like "a situation that tightened me up or something that I could not or did not want to assimilate at the time, or something that I wanted to protest but did not, or the like." This initial explication reveals the global impact of a situation, its atmosphere. It reveals how I lived in a bodily way and thereby coconstituted a situation that had the ambience of overloading me or restricting me. In practice, this explication may allow me to attend to my sense of that situation and hence to its structure. But more typically, focusing on the affected body and thereby explicating the impact of the day's events on me frees me to enter the evening with my workday settled and out of the way. In the clinical setting it gives the client access to his problem, for example, in a certain intimate relationship and eventually to how he lives such relations generally.

As we have described, there is a bodily aspect available that is the possibility of a more direct symbolization of the structure of a person's intimate relations. I carry another bodily aspect of my workday's tension or of a certain intimate relation which is not so much the impact of its atmosphere as my sense of the structure of that situation. There is the possibility of a direct enactment of that structure through the fulfillment of that "sense of." We are likely to attend to both of these modes when we have a problem, when we have something on our minds. But the problems are different. The problem of the first mode of abstraction is an affect-laden one. It is something that I have not dealt with or worked through. As Gendlin describes the situation, I am stuck or congealed. It is more likely problematic in a psychodynamic sense, that is, it is conflictual for me. The bodily aspect of the second mode refers to something that is problematic in that it is difficult to understand and hence to explicate. Such a problem cannot be carried as an impression or an impact on my body as can a mood or an affect for it is too complex. It is a set of relations, an implicit conceptualization.

In speaking of the "living body," Gendlin himself approaches such a position: "It also includes 'unfinished' or 'potential' patterns for certain preordered interaction with objects in the environment. These objects may or may not be present, yet the body order includes the patterns of interaction that could obtain if they were present." [7] In part because of their inherent complexity such potential patterns cannot be carried in the same bodily way that the atmosphere of a situation or an interaction with an object can be.

The diver on the platform is not guided in his dive by a feeling in his guts. He fulfills the intention to execute the complex move that is a "forward one and a half" with a phenomenologically distinct guide, a bodily aspect which is a sense of that dive—a "preordered interaction," a potential set of moves. He makes the dive not through but *despite* the feelings in his guts. Focus on the latter would give him the physiognomy of a world-as-barrier or as the possibility of failure. I can carry, locate, and explicate the gross impact of the family therapy meeting, its concrete impress on me, in the manner of Gendlin's felt-meaning. But the structure of that situation, that peculiar concatenation of dynamic relations, requires a bodily mode with more potential mobility.

The impact of atmosphere is felt; structure is sensed. An early stage in the understanding of an atmosphere is how it has touched me, while an early stage in the understanding of a structure is how I might enact it. My feeling about a situation and my sense of it are both tacitly meaningful, but common usage reveals a greater intimacy between "meaning" and the latter. My sense of a situation is how or what it means to me. The French term "le sens" suggests this association between sense and meaning, and, as well, between meaning and direction or, by extension, between meaning and a potential movement. Both feeling and sensing are bodily aspects and residues of my original living of a phenomenon, which is itself a bodily taking up or living through of that phenomenon. The residual sense of that assumption and engagement is more directly what I did, whether that doing was a perceptual or behavioral act; while the residual feel is the texture and the atmosphere of that deed and its correlative bodily impact.

The second step in the present method, following the "return," is the abstraction of a sense of the structure of a situation or phenomenon. A sense of the structure does not yet posit it in any modality, for the "object" of this peculiar mode remains pre-objective, only the potentiality of an object. How am I to realize this potentiality? Sometimes I cannot. Having become sensitive to this aspect of my lived body that bears structure as potential movement, occasionally I continue unable to "get it." When the problem is one of living, I am unable to live through and hence to effect a particular sense, for example, of a presently potential form of a current intimate relationship. As a result the development of the relationship stalls. When the problem is one of the explication of structure, as in a project in phenomenological psychology, I can return again to instances of the phenomenon of interest. I can do so until I can abstract a sense of structure that is so robust that it readily bursts its seam to fulfill its intention.

While in the immediate course of events a sense of the structure of a situation often is realized through action, thought, or imagination, the mode we term forming is another way of answering its call. It is the third moment in this series of bodily modes of the presence of structure.

Forming

Forming is a mode of experience that answers the call to be done implicit in a sense of structure by doing it. It is a *virtual* behavior which by virtually enacting the potential movement of the sense of a phenomenon's structure gives to that sense the object it could only intimate. The product of the act of forming is a direct embodiment of the structure of the abstracted original. I realize form through forming. This possibility establishes forming as a royal road to structure, as an unprejudiced, natural noetic correlate of the structure of phenomena. To unpack these statements beyond their exposition to this point, the following phenomenology of forming begins with a consideration of how any form of behavior is an understanding.

Knowledge through action. Following the lead of Dewey[8] and the more recent influence of Piaget and others, it is now a commonplace of contemporary education to emphasize the importance of experience in learning. It is said that we learn by doing. For example, we believe that we more quickly and fully understand physics by constructing an actual model of a thing, mathematical operations by dividing things among ourselves, and literature by performing the parts in a play. How seriously do we take this strategy of education? Do we really believe that doing something is a mode of learning distinguishable from perception and thought, or does it merely provide a fresh or a provocative or a lubricating condition or occasion for these latter modes? Within such an adjunctive role, doing something allows us to see more clearly and directly that which we would understand. When I do the thing, I am necessarily also seeing, hearing, and feeling it up close.

Pedagogically, activity's knowledge is no more than a composite of such perceptions. It is a ringside seat which takes us for a moment out of the bleachers of exclusively armchair thinking.

Further, in "doing" as against "thinking *about*" or "looking *at*" I am more directly engaged in the object of knowledge. "Doing" takes an object—I do the thing. To emphasize this and the value of experiential learning, we say colloquially, "I am doing physics or math or *Hamlet*." In "doing" I subject myself to what is to be known; I "get into" it; I have my being in or through it. This suggests that learning by doing distinguishes itself as a vehicle of engagement. In thought I only grasp the object indirectly and at a distance; in perception, I see something over there. Visual perception in particular is a distance sense.[9] But it can be the occasion of my immersion, my engagement to the point of identification with the object, as in the cinema. On the other side, in doing something I am sometimes alienated from myself and it as under certain conditions of labor or servitude.

While under certain circumstances activity can facilitate engagement or reengagement in an object of interest and while it can augment perception and thought, evidently these are not definitive. Yet in the present work we do take seriously the idea that knowing actually resides in modes of behavior. Through behavior I am inserted in the world in a radically distinct manner and can know the world in a particular way.

Consider the following instance: While I am doing gardening, I know about the garden beyond the sight and feel of the rosebush and the soil. I am learning a skill, pruning the rosebush. But my knowing is not limited to the practice of a set of manual operations, to a knowledge about doing gardening as distinguished from an understanding of the garden itself. In doing something to the rosebush, I learn not only how I work but how it works, how it is put together within itself and about its relations to other things and to myself. In doing something the sphere of my education is not limited to my activity as such; I also learn about the things upon which I act—in particular about their structure and the structure of the situation of which they and I are a part.

Yet when I learn about gardens by gardening, in that moment I do not posit the rosebush or the garden as object. This begins to distinguish activity from perception as a way of knowing. In behavior I am involved in an operation on a thing in such a way that

I am no longer positing that thing as an object. When I leave perception for behavior as a primary mode, while I do not leave the presence of the perceived object since I am still acting in a world common to it, I do cease to posit that object. When I prick myself while pruning the rosebush, I suddenly return to reposit the bush and now its thorn. But while I am pruning I work in or through the pruning shears and the rosebush to a different object—what I intend to do or a something done, the pruning of the bush or the pruned bush. Behavior does not take that which it immediately acts upon as an object in the way perception does. I see the garden but I do not "behave the garden." We reach a paradox. Following Merleau-Ponty's seminal description,[10] perception posits its object through a kind of doing in the sense that to perceive something we must be over at it, take it up, "inhabit" it. When I "act" on the rosebush at a distance through perception, I precisely posit it as really there, as there in the "flesh." [11] However, when I actually act on it, handle it, I cease positing it as there. A phenomenology of behavior suggests that that on which I act is not apprehended, that is, it is not at that moment concretely grasped. Behavior is a way of knowing that is not a mode of apprehension. Although I remain implicitly inserted in a perceived world, the focal meaning when I act is in the activity. I am engaged in the pruning and working toward a completed action with its "completed" object. Rather than posit the concretely present rosebush, I surpass it through my activity. Paradoxically, handling the bush in this sense forces its disappearance. It allows me to go beyond the flesh of that now only potential object to an involvement in how it works, an engagement in it as a set of relations. In modifying that upon which it acts, behavior lets me live in that act of effectance and forget the immediate recipient of the act. Of course, again, behavior and perception occur in the same common world, run into and implicate each other, and contribute to and are part of the same lived body–lived world. Yet in any moment of experience one or the other may be the primary mode; accordingly, we are learning in a different way.

Polanyi's work on tacit knowledge clarifies and furthers these points.[12] Tacit understanding is a structure of knowledge which he finds pervading such seemingly diverse ways of knowing as how we use tools, develop manual skills, use words, find intuitive solutions to problems, and apprehend physiognomies. In all of these Polanyi discovers a common structure which he refers to as the "from-to" structure of experience. He distinguishes dual levels of awareness or attention. For example, in the exercise of a skill there is an awareness of certain elements or parts on the level of muscular movements. On a second and "higher" level there is their integration into a complex patterned performance. For Polanyi the elements are a "proximal" term and their integration is a "distal" term. Together the two terms constitute tacit knowing in such a way that we attend *from* the proximal *to* the distal.[13] Our awareness of the proximal is a "subsidiary" awareness while we are focally aware of the distal. Our relation to the proximal is such as to direct us to the distal. The structure of tacit knowledge explicates a notion of intentionality in this way,[14] the "from-to" structure being precisely a kind of directedness. I know the parts by the meaning of the whole to which they direct me. If I shift attention to them they lose this integration and hence their meaning. The pianist can know the skill of his hand only by attending from it to the music performed. Those "parts" are not identifiable in any other more explicit or direct way.[15] For the proximal to have this intentional function we must "dwell" in them or "interiorize" them or "participate feelingly" in them.[16] This indwelling relation is distinguished from explicit knowledge and justifies the term *tacit knowledge*.

It is significant to our present concerns that Polanyi's primary examples of this structure of tacit knowledge are behavioral. This dual awareness is strikingly clear in complex behavior such as the way we know how to ride a bicycle. Following Polanyi, then, we can say that behavior proper consists in a subsidiary and a focal awareness. Dwelling in an act requires a shift in attention from it to an inherent product of the act—from the movements of my fingers to the performance of the musical composition, from the forgotten sensations of its impress in my hand to the shape of an object at the end of my blindman's walking stick. This engagement or dwelling in activity, this forgetting of the immediate "object" at hand, and this attention *to* some integrated product of my activity constitute how I know in "learning by doing."

Like behavior proper, forming is a kind of doing and shares these structures. As we will show, however, unlike behavior proper it is a reflective mode. Rather than being limited to an engagement that issues in the actual complex or integrated act of behavior proper, it turns back on itself in a peculiar way. Through this reflective and impractical turn it places in front of me an integration of parts or elements, an integration that is no less than the structure of a situation. A brief consideration of other variants on behavior proper provides further access to forming.

Virtual behavior. Unlike behavior proper, dance does not concretely effect or modify anything. However, what it loses in instrumentality, it gains in expressivity. Of course, all behavior is at least implicitly expressive in that it is meaningful. That it is so is how we distinguish it from movement. The response of my knee to a certain tap or of the infant's foot to a certain stroking of his sole are movements, not behaviors. They are closer to the leaf's reaction to the breeze then my response to a knock on the door. In that through it we say something, dance is like the gesture that often accompanies speech. In fact, S. K. Langer refers to dance as the art of gesture, of gesticulation.[17] When I dance, as when I posture and gesture, I create or recreate a particular situation by acting it out or enacting it. We shall refer to a form of action in which the primary intention is to express rather than to practically effect something as an enactment. As we have shown, enactment is possible because one way I know situations is as a set of potential moves.

Dance is a form of *actual* enactment. It occurs immediately and directly in the common world for it consists of a performance that is available to an audience. Through his actual enactments, the dancer constructs a space. That space is abstract in that it is not concretely anchored to anything. It does not constitute a concrete situation. While the space is abstract it is there in the moment of the enactment for both the dancer and his audience. This is more dramatically apparent in mime than in the more subtly patterned articulations of space of the dance. The wall that blocks Marcel Marceau even while he creates it is substantial although occurring in an abstract space. For his gesture to achieve the expression it intends, the dancer and no less his audience must attend from it to the abstract space it constructs. The dance is a form of behavior that must be realized not in itself but, as is the blindman's stick, in the telling undulations of the landscape. Through his gesture, the dancer shapes a world by carving out a space. His is a "space-shaping creation." [18] This combination of actual enactment and abstract spatiality constitutes the peculiar "illusion" of dance and

defines it as a particular art form.[19] Its movements must be actual
so that their dynamic fluidity can entice us and transport us to the
meaningful but abstract space they create. The abstractness of its
space, its lack of concrete encumbrance or entanglement, precisely
its impracticality, gives the dance its freedom of expression.

Forming is a virtual rather than an actual behavior, and its enactment occurs in an abstract rather than a concrete space. As
Piaget's account of the development of imitation suggests, behavioral imitation can be abbreviated to the point where its action
is apparent only to the imitator. I can imitate certain movements
and, as we have seen, can thereby embody certain structures without
actually moving. For Piaget this culmination of behavioral imitation's development is its internalization as an image. Imitation
gives rise to the mode of imagination. However, while undoubtedly
a derivative of this sequence, forming does not occur in the mind's
eye. It is a bodily mode, a kind of doing, a virtual movement, not
a species of imagination. While the product of its enactment can
eventually be posited as an image, in the moment forming engages
me actively in a way imagination does not, as we will describe below
in a fuller comparison of the two modes.

Given that its movement is virtual, the act of forming is not immediately expressive, that is, its audience is only implicitly present.
As the artist limits his audience while he paints to what he can
conjure of their view, so in forming my activity is initially an
enactment for myself. Like behavior proper and other variants of
behavior, forming engages me in a kind of activity, in particular
a set of virtual movements. I attend from their enactment to its
product. That product is an abstract articulated space. Forming
forms a space that eventually can be posited in other modes, that is,
directly apprehended. We must further characterize this space of
forming beyond the descriptive "abstract." We will show how the
character of its space makes forming a reflective mode in that
through that space I realize my own activity. In that that activity
is the enactment of an unfulfilled intention of an abstracted sense
of structure, the term "abstract" will be burdened with the "abstracted" as defined earlier—the portable bodily pole of a lived
structure.

Behavioral space. While that which I attend *from* in forming is
virtual behavior, that which I attend *to* is a variant of lived space

which we refer to as behavioral space. Provisionally, behavioral space is the shaped space that is the noematic correlate of a region potentially, actually, or virtually moved through.

The phenomenological literature on spatiality distinguishes between lived and objective space. The latter is a space conceived in reflection, for example, a space of the natural sciences or of a mathematics. One such space is the homogeneous, empty, ahistorical space of Euclidean geometry. By contrast, lived space is my immediate concrete living space. It is a prereflective oriented space in which there is a front and a back, a vertical and a horizontal, and a coordinating zero point—typically, my body or some body part, my home, or the center of the city. Lived space is a "filled and articulated space,"[20] which reflects and is organized with respect to my concerns. To illustrate, a feature of lived space is the vast and isolating distance between my apartment and my "neighbors' " in the anonymity of a large urban dwelling; while the objective distance in that situation is the measured distance, a matter of a few inches.[21]

Merleau-Ponty's philosophy provides a basis for these descriptions of a lived space, particularly in his phenomenology of the body and its constitutive role in perception.[22] While the present method is suffused with the thought of Merleau-Ponty, his ontology being implicit throughout, a few terms from his account of the body are helpful to introduce behavioral space. For Merleau-Ponty, a "theory of the body is already a theory of perception"[23] for to perceive something requires a kind of bodily act.

The object in perception occupies space and presents itself as situated among other potential objects of my perception which, in that they also possess space, limit, circumscribe, and thereby locate each other and the present object. Thus the perceived object appears in a concrete system. I know the present object and the system in which it is set by virtue of my body. Particularly through the mobility of my body, I "inhabit space" and "take . . . up" the object.[24] In Merleau-Ponty's phrases, objects "invite" me, "beckon" me to take them up.[25] At any moment, there is a myriad of such invitations which, as horizons to my present body, are at first merely "vague solicitations."[26]

Any object has a being that is a "motor significance."[27] It appears in a kind of atmosphere which is the possible moves to which it is liable. The object as a "pole of action"[28] or a "set of manipulanda" [29] can only appeal to a body that is itself a "motor power, a 'motor project,' a 'motor intentionality.' " [30] To see a house is already to settle into it. I cannot see it except through some such motor significance which I take up as a motor project, an intention to move with respect to it. Motor intentionality is my "grasp" or "grip" on the object. Of course in taking it up, in being appropriated by an object, I am not passive. A dialogue between the object and my lived body ensues, through which the situation is constituted. The couch and the typewriter invite me and I take them up according to my fatigue, my inclination to work, or the like. My "body is the potentiality of a certain world." [31]

The spatiality of perception must be a lived space, for to perceive I cannot remain somehow outside the world as if I were Archimedes with a lever. I cannot assay it with an objective measuring rod, one that does not implicate me or one that is not me. To size up an object I must mobilize my body, anchor it to the object, and participate in the system of which it and I through it are a part. The "operative intentionality," [32] the potentiality of movement discoverable through that anchorage, implies a human space, a "spatiality of situation," [33] a here sagging, there lifting, bent, curved space. Of course, for Merleau-Ponty perception has a "primacy" as a mode of experience for a number of reasons.[34] Since we are inserted in the world and have our being in the world, perception has the special status of that mode through which this essential and original relation is first realized. Hence lived space is generally a feature of all prereflective experience.

Behavioral space is a species of this vital hodological space of the lived body–lived world. Beyond the ways objects shape space by their differential weights, their exclusive occupation, their disclosing and hiding each other, objects also carve up space through their movement, whether present, anticipated, or remembered. The salience of these movements is more readily appreciated in behavioral modes, hence justifying the term behavioral space. While behavioral space is a horizon of various modes of experience, including perception, behavioral modes accentuate it by featuring movement more directly.

The movement of behavior proper is actual and the space it realizes is concrete. When I am actually doing something, I know and constitute the space of that present concrete situation. It is a space of instrumentality, of practical purpose. For example, consider the spatiality of my room when I get up in the morning. As I pull the shades, open the closet, make the bed, I am creating a space around these objects, a space of praxis. One meaning of this organization of space is the use of things at hand.[35] I know the space by actually moving the things. I do not need to see the shade to open it and so know its space; in fact, in the early morning hours I cannot. Behavior proper has its own form of spatiality which is anchored in things and effected by my action with respect to things, an action that is a product of a relation of reciprocal influence. But while it constitutes a peculiar space and has a kind of knowledge of it, the learning by doing that we have described, behavior proper, cannot posit this space. In the act I do not see or conceive or imagine its space; I can only practice it.

I cannot posit it for I am otherwise engaged. Consider the behavioral space of the following situation: In the midst of a squash game, when I see the ball after my opponent's shot, I immediately know my return. The court at that moment, as I make my play, already has the spatial configuration that is the arc my return shot will take, the position my opponent will reach to return it, and where I will be, then, to gain an advantage. Again, the behavioral space of behavior proper, like that of perception, is tied concretely to a present enterprise. Both partake of the same real immediate world. As this example shows, they often occur more or less together in experience. An adumbration of the shot I am about to make is one horizon of my perception of the ball immediately following my opponent's shot. That predelineation within the perceptual field and my actual execution of the shot, with its creation of the space of that sequence of plays, are barely distinguishable. In fact, my game is "on" to the degree that there is no gap between them, to the degree that the shot I implicitly see is the shot I make.[36] Through perception and behavior proper I am embedded and participate in the world in such a way that it is continually modulated or reshaped by my participation.

Again, while its action is actual, dance relinquishes the concrete space of both perception and behavior proper to step onto a stage of abstract space. Part of its being abstract is that it is relatively undirected and unsituated, while the concrete instrumental space of behavior proper is directed and historical. The latter's spatial articulations are functional paths, routes from here and now to there and then, purposive spaces to be traversed, covered, or conquered; or they are the instrumental regions of a machine or tool, the possible movement of any object for my use. By contrast, the leaps and turns of the dance are not going anywhere. Beyond the general frame of its orientation toward the audience, the space of a particular dance has no coordinates in a concrete situation through which it is given an orientation. The particular expressive space realized through a dance can take little of its bearings from its setting. More positively, being relatively free of a concrete situation, of anchorage in a practical project, it can create its own situation, its own context. As audience to the dance we are in some ways as "audience" to our own imaginal productions. Like the spatiality of the imaginal, as we will show below, that of the dance occurs in *front* of us, without implicating us fully or directly, without requiring our actual participation. With respect to us, part of its being abstract is that it expresses itself in a space relatively detached from our own immediate historical and situational context. While the behavioral space created by the dance is poignant and central to our appreciation of this art form, that space shares the spotlight with the actual behavior that is the execution of the dance itself. By contrast, we must show how forming consists more or less exclusively in the creation of a behavioral space. In forming what I am doing is articulating a space.

The reflective power of forming. In a fashion similar to the dancer's living relation to his behavioral space, forming requires me to live the behavioral space I create through it. In order to form it, I must enact it. As with other variants of behavior, I dwell in the doing and am directed from it to an inherent product of it. My awareness of my action is contemporaneous with my awareness of that to which it directs me, but it remains a subsidiary awareness. But while I must dwell in the behavior of forming, in that the act is virtual, any kinesthetic horizon is less salient than in other variants of actual behavior. My kinesthetic sense is mute in forming. The aesthetics, the competence, the integrity of my body are not at stake. Further, like that of the dance, forming's space is abstract. It occurs in a domain where it cannot concretely effect anything. It is not anchored to a concrete situation. Again, like the spatiality of the dance, forming's behavioral space is relatively unsituated and ahistorical. In place of the general frame of the stage its only frame is the intention to understand something—a generalized something, concrete instances of which are not immediately available. For these reasons, in that it is virtual, impractical, and relatively un-embedded situationally, and in that my body is not at issue, in forming I am free to attend to the creation of a behavioral space. The articulation of space by movement is the act of forming; it and only it is what the behavior effects.

The intentional object of forming is that space. It is that which I am making present to myself; that space is figural for me. That which in other modes of experience is a horizon, a surround that is part of how a posited figure means, is here the figure. The object of forming is a space-object, a space become or becoming object. Forming does not so much occur in a space; rather, the space it creates constitutes its object. In forming I am virtually performing an operation but the object of the operation is not already present; unlike the rosebush I am pruning, it is not con-cretely at hand. Rather, it is being presented under the auspices of my act.

But what is it that is being presented; what is it that is being formed? The emerging object of my attention is a behavioral space. That space is the path cut by my virtual operation. My oper-ation is inseparable from a presentation of that operation. My enactment, that which I am expressing through my action, is an embodiment of itself. The operation is a set of movements that, in being done, direct me to the certain space that they articulate. Hence, while I am directed from an operation, at the same time I am turned back to it for the path to which I am directed is nothing but an embodiment of my virtual movement. Forming is a species of behavior with the peculiar property of looking at itself. My act seeks to know itself in the only way it can, by living in itself and attending from it. But while a path through space is thereby formed, what is revealed in the path is the act. While behavior proper can tacitly recover itself in a certain modification of the object of its action, forming can reveal itself more directly as an articulated space which is an embodiment of itself.

To put this important but difficult feature another way, in a sense the character of the intentionality of forming, the way it takes an object, is a deceit, an indirect maneuver. Its directedness tran-scends itself to present itself, to return to itself. It does not get out of itself to take up residence elsewhere but to know its original occupation, a set of potential moves. It is an act through which, in

Polanyi's terms, the subsidiary is made focal. What appears in forming, its behavioral space become object, is more intimately related to the mode through which it appears than is "what is seen" to the "seeing of it." In forming what appears is that act, a way of doing something that is indistinguishable from the trail it blazes. Unlike behavior proper, forming is not a tacit mode of knowledge; it is a reflective behavioral mode for it posits its own activity. It points to itself by pointing beyond itself. It reifies itself by spatializing itself. It is like a verb that does not take an object but is producing one in the form of its own gerund. "To form," that act, yields a tracing of that particular act, a certain form, "a forming." The moves that constitute a given operation of forming are presented as an implicated path which is, then, an emergent object created by the act of forming and, as it were, in its own image.

The virtual enactment of structure. It is helpful to reset these points in the broader context of the genetic phenomenology of structure. Temporarily bracketing that context to simplify the presentation of a phenomenology of forming, we have been limiting our description to forming, the act and its immediate object—a virtual enactment that posits a behavioral space-object. While forming's object does occur in an abstract space that allows it to be relatively unsituated, the act is part of a larger project. While unlike other variants of behavior forming posits an object, namely its own action, like other behavioral modes it also has an overriding project, an end toward which it moves, and, as well, a guide to that end. I am working to understand something through the act of forming. My project is to make the heretofore implicit and problematic structure of a phenomenon explicit by enacting it. That which I seek to cultivate in forming are not things like gardens but relations among things, structures.

Burdened with that project, I return to situations in which that target phenomenon can be lived or relived. From those engagements, I abstract and carry a bodily sense of the structure of that phenomenon, present as the unfulfilled intention to realize a set of potential moves. That sense of structure guides me in the act of forming. By recourse to it I virtually enact that potential set of moves that are the sense of a structure lived through, bodily abstracted, and now prompting further work. In enacting those moves I realize directly the structure of those situations and of that target phenomenon. This is possible because structure is a set of relations, relations among and within objects or between an object and myself, that is originally known as a field of forces. Those forces are potential moves. As we have described, structure occurs in a region *between* things, a region that consists in how objects and parts are actively standing one to the other, in how they are relating. These relations consist in dynamics, in pushes and pulls, leanings and supports, enclosures and openings, that are inseparable from apparent motion. Structure refers to these relations as such that occur in this peculiar region of living relations.

Behavior and its variants also occur in such a region. Any act reveals, embodies, and describes a relation between things. The simple act of opening the door reveals and describes a relation between the door knob and the door, or the door and the next room. Further, while I open this door in a particular way circumscribed by my present position and the architecture of the door, in doing so I call on a more general move and embody a more general relation. Behavior is akin to structure in that it is relational and in that it is always typical; like structure it has to do with relations as such. Behavior is plastic both on the side of the agent and on the side of the object; yet any particular act bespeaks the general or the generic. It realizes a certain general style that is a relation as such.

In that a structure is a field of forces, a set of potential moves, it is already implicitly a shape, a certain form. Yet while structure already has a form, while it cannot but be a form from its beginning, it is a form that has not yet been posited. While behavior proper must live or move through the form of such structures as the condition of its bearing meaning or being meaningful, it cannot posit that form. It cannot know, except implicitly, that shape it moves through, which is to say that it cannot directly apprehend itself. Forming is a variant of behavior that can realize its own act precisely as the shape implicit in its own movement. The shape it presents is a structure originally known by living it, by taking up its kinetics.

That presentation, the product and immediately intended object of forming, is a first presentation. Its formal realization of structure is not a *re*-presentation, for no structure's particular provenance ever included such a direct presentation. I have known it only as

I originally lived it, and as I subsequently carried it—as an implicit bodily knowledge, an unfulfilled intention to realize a still tacit shape. Nor is it a representation of structure in the sense of an interpretation or symbolic rendering or transformation of structure. Rather, it is how structure appears, but now in its first showing. The abstract space-object of forming is the first direct grasp of the tacit but always potentially active bodily pole of a structure as lived.

But having formed such a space-object, is my grasp of it adequate to share it? How and in what form or forms can it provide or be the building block of a phenomenological description? Before we indicate two such products of forming, the schematic diagram and the metaphor, and through these trace the final two steps both in the present genetic phenomenology of structure and in the present method, we have one residual task. Through a brief comparison between forming and that mode to which it is most readily assimilated and hence lost, imagination, we can complete the present phenomenology of forming.

Forming versus imagining. While when I form what I form can then be readily imagined, forming is a distinct and prior act. As we will show here, while forming has some features in common with imagination and may be thought of as a hybrid between it and behavior proper, forming distinguishes itself as a quasi-behavioral rather than a quasi-perceptual mode. Both forming and imagination share confinement to an abstract space, as their respective objects are relegated to an "anti-world" [37] or a "world-frame" [38] rather than to the open, inexhaustible world overseen by perception and behavior proper. Correlatively, at the noetic pole both are virtual modes: if forming is a virtual behavior, imagination is a kind of virtual seeing.

In perception an object is given as present, as over there, as something that is an "ob-ject," [39] that opposes me in the sense that I could run up against it. The imagined object partakes of a different "type of existence." [40] Imagination posits its object as "not present" [41] and as nothing, as not a thing. In imagination I "see" that my friend Peter is not here. That its object is absent is part of the way an object is constituted in imagination. This is not to say that in imagination I posit an image; rather I have Peter in a particular way, as my friend who is not really here.

In like manner what forming presents is posited as "not here," as absent.

The object of imagination and the object formed are given as external to and apart from the real world cohabited by perception and behavior proper. To imagine is to stop seeing that world; the object in imagination eclipses the perceived world. In this sense it is unsituated. In an analogous way, we have described how the object formed, although abstracted from that world, is not concretely anchored to it. There is a sense in which even within their own respective "worlds," the imagined object and the object formed are relatively unsituated. In fact, the term "situated" is less apt to describe the setting of their respective objects. In the case of the imagined object, E. Casey refers to its "self-containedness." [42]

When I imagine Peter he appears in a certain way—tall, thin Peter with a letter in his hand. The imagined object does not appear in a field, in an actual setting of further possible aspects of itself or its surround. It does not invite further exploration like the object of perception. "The imaginative presentation, and thus its specific content, is *given all at once* to the imaginer" (his emphasis).[43] I imagine immediately just what I intend to imagine. There is no object concretely there with which I must or can sustain an open-ended dialogue. That which I imagine does not allow other points of view on it through which I could discover its various aspects. In this sense the imagined object is "frontal" [44] and "depthless," [45] complete in itself and already finished at its first appearance. It is "self-delimited" [46] in that what it presents is a function only of what the imagining self intends at a given moment.

In like manner the object formed does not appear embedded in a world of inexhaustible aspects inviting my exploration. It is relatively unsituated, free of the density of horizons, both inner and outer, of the perceived object. What appears is in a sense all figural, for any background is meager and vague. The emergent path of the object formed does not cut through any particular terrain. It is set against or in the same "hazy background" [47] as the object in imagination, that background being the real world. Although it refers to it, being originally abstracted from it, it appears in front of rather than enmeshed in that system of other potential objects. Given this depthlessness, this thinness of the

imagined object and the object formed, through neither can I be
in a world, even their own world, that approaches the rich
denseness of the perceived world. On the other hand, their
respective objects offer a certain fullness in that when I posit
them they are all that I have and I have them for that moment
all to myself. Both imagination and forming tempt me to be
self-indulgent.

In a similar fashion, the temporal background of the object in
forming is less thickly embedded in a layered structure of protensions and retentions. It has only a general and external connection
to other doings and happenings in my life. By analogy, while a
particular movie has its own internal temporality, for example,
the span of time its story covers, such temporal features are not
directly tied to my plans for the rest of the day. Even internally,
that is, within the abstract space being articulated, there is limited
temporal context since only one object is being formed, only one
space is being articulated. That space which is presently my
object fills my attention; other temporal comparisons are not
available. Being presently engaged in an act of creating an object,
that present occupation diminishes those thicker temporal horizons
both of perception and of reflective thought. I sometimes have a
similar experience when I play. When I finish the game I am aware
then of returning to the weight and temporal horizons of my own
history and of my own projects.

In addition to this temporal thinness with its predominant focus
on an object presently being formed, the object in forming has
a certain transience. That to which I am attending, the space being
articulated, is not permanently possessing or occupying space the
way an object of perception does. Forming is a movement through
space which carves it up and organizes it without yet filling that
space. Space is bent, regions having certain relations to each other
are suggested through lines that delineate without staking claim.
No chalk mark appears, only its demarcating effect. The path being
articulated and being appreciated is a geometry in motion, an
emerging system of lines of force. I know it as I am in the act
of forming it. Its poignancy appears in this transient ongoing
act, not in the permanence of its trailings. It is a space ephemerally
defined, more like that of the trail left by the skywriter than the
lasting scar of an etching or the fixed eruption of an embossment.
When I finish forming, its product quickly fades and I am left

again with a sense of a structure as only a potential act and its correlative shape.

In forming as in imagination there is a certain "discontinuity" [48] between that act and both acts in other modes and even subsequent acts in the same mode. By contrast, in perception I experience different views of a given object as belonging to a unified series of "intimately linked acts." [49] While an act of perception or behavior proper can occasion an act of imagination or of forming, as I undertake either of these latter I experience a certain break. As the space of their respective objects eclipses and appears in front of the space of the real world, so there is a relative temporal discontinuity in my experience of the act. Even subsequent virtual acts form only a "loose sequence" rather than the strict continuity of acts of perception or behavior proper.

It is easy to be misled by this description of the relative thinness of the temporal horizons of forming. Again, forming is part of a larger project—an effort to understand something. In a sense it occurs in that context and is thereby temporally situated. In the aftermath of the initial family therapy meeting, I find myself forming the retained sense of the problematic structure of that meeting or of that family. But while that problematic abstracted sense prompts me to form a certain space that refers to a past in which that structure was only implicitly known and a future in which I can anticipate a firmer grasp of it, in the act there is a certain temporal discontinuity and spatial disjunction. The act occurs in a time frame distinct from that of the original moment, and it realizes a self-contained space that is set off from the concrete space of the family meeting.

With all these similarities in the virtuality of their respective acts, the abstractness of the space of their objects, the divorced contexts of their occurrence, and even, given the transience of their objects, the ease with which one can yield to the other, forming and imagination are distinct modes. We need not confuse them. In imagination my intention to imagine something is already an act for that intention immediately realizes an image. In forming I first have a sense of a potential act, of a job to be done. When I imagine, its object is immediately completed. To form an object requires an ongoing act, one in which I am relatively engaged. The act of imagination does not busy me, nor does it actively implicate me. My involvement is limited to being lulled, to an

enforced passivity. While there may be an element of surprise in
the appearance of the imagined object, my surprise is at what I
had already intended, not at the product of my creation at that
moment. The imagined object "lacks that not-yet-discovered
character which is a precondition of discovery." [50] In imagination
I am watching that which is already appearing in front of me.
I am not called upon, as it were, to leave my seat or to direct
the action or even to keep watch. When I do not allow it its
general location in front of me, when I seek to tamper with it,
the imagined object disappears or is replaced by a different scene.
My mobility is frustrated and of no use.

Although when I am forming I am not concretely effecting
anything, to form something I must go through the motions of
an action. Forming requires me to live the space it creates as its
object; I am more like the dancer than the imaginer. In order to
form it, I must enact it. I am necessarily actively involved; I am
engaged in doing something. The theater of my operations is a
procedure, a preordered interaction, or a scheme in Piaget's sense
rather than a percept or an image. While I can imagine doing
something, for example fixing something, that imagined act is
different than the more self-absorbing, self-implicating, active
"up to the elbows" involvement of the virtual act of doing it.[51]
As we indicated in an earlier contrast between perception and
behavior proper, mutatis mutandis, here in the imaginative act
I sit back and my experience accentuates the sensual or the sensuous
features of its object. Again, this is part of the passive lulling
power of imagination. But it achieves this magic (magic because
sensuousness occurs without concrete presence), at the sacrifice
of relatively active hands-on involvement. Conversely, forming's
object is relatively nonsensuous, being an abstract space (not
merely occurring in one) and being realized by a kinesthetically
muted virtual action. However, what it sacrifices of rapture,
forming gains in understanding. Through its mobility, its active
engagement, and its work, it furthers a sense of a situation.
Continuing with Sartre's example of his absent friend, through
forming I relinquish any indulgence of my frustrated desire for
him for the possibility of reflectively articulating the form of
our relationship.

A noematic correlate of these noetic distinctions in quality of
activity and in degree of self-engagement of the two modes is the

difference in the forms of their respective spatialities. The imagined object covers a space without occupying or possessing it; it has extension without depth. It rents its space without appropriating it, without defining it through its own particular character. The imaginer does not or cannot bend or rend space. That he cannot is of a piece with his somewhat detached, inactive relation to the object he posits. The imaginer operates in a limited field of action, for what he presents (using Sartre's language here rather than Casey's) is an already interiorized object. Imagined space is unidimensional like that of a movie screen that flatly refuses to bend for it receives an already constituted projection. I cannot live through the imagined object because it owns no region, has no substantial claim. Of course, this can be put the other way: it stakes no such claim because I cannot involve myself in it. Its lulling but eventually frustrating ambience is part and parcel of the fact that its spatiality is not behavioral.

As we have indicated, to describe the spatiality of forming is to blur the distinction between object and space. Through my virtual action, when I form I create a space that is at the same time my intended object. When I form, a space-object that I have not known except in an unformed way is being built. The spatiality of forming is a behavioral space that receives its character exclusively from my own twists and turns as I am engaged in forming it. If the imaginer is a projectionist, the person who forms is a topographer, but one who somehow, having lost the surveyor's distance from the objective terrain, maps the implicit topological features inherent in his own travels.

As we have argued, positing those features is a first reflective presentation of the structure of an experience. By contrast to this function, Sartre argues that the function of imagination is to "presentify" what we have already seen or thought. "We learn nothing from the image." [52] It is always a review, a second showing, and a debasement of what we already have known. Casey's appraisal of the status of the imagined object is more mixed and more respectful. In agreement with Sartre, he states, "By imagining, we ascertain nothing that we did not know beforehand in some respect." [53] However, this is not to say that imagination's presentation is a debased form of what we already know. Rather, in a given specific imaginative production an unanticipated, a surprising, or even a novel aspect of something

already known may be presented. Further, imagination presents
its object in a way that distinguishes it as a mode. In imagination
we are not concerned with advancing understanding but in
"entertaining oneself with what is purely possible" (emphasis
deleted).[54] Possibility is pure that is not intermediary or instrumental. For examples, pure possibility is not a hypothetical device
in the service of understanding the actual or a preparatory device
to ready for a future event. It is possibility for its own sake.

Like the imagined object, the object formed is not a formation
de novo; it presents what was *toujours déjà là*. However, more
than an occasional sense of mild surprise, a concomitant of forming,
like that of Gendlin's "focusing," is an experience of advancing
or furthering an aspect of experience. What I feel that is furthered
in that moment is my grasp, my understanding of the structure
of an experience. Forming is the culmination of a sequence in
which a tacit understanding progresses to its explication. Through
the sequence of return, bodily abstraction, and the virtual enactment of forming, I move from the implicit living of a structure
to its reflective presentation. By embodying it in this way, ironically,
I extricate it from my body, from that vague apperceptive mass
of the lived body to place it in an otherwise empty abstract space.
I have it in that space—a space to which in the immediate afterglow
of the act, I am now pointed as the dancer might glance back at
the space he has just transfigured. From a blind living of a
structure, I move first to a dim bodily sense of structure, and
then to the reflective grasp of structure as such. Forming does not
present its object as pure possibility, but as the structure of an
experience once lived and now spatially mapped—as the freshest
and closest reflective grasp of pure lived structure.

Schematic Diagrams

Again, what is being "attended to" in forming is the behavioral
space inherent in the act of forming. That behavioral space-object
is in the act of being formed. It is one moment of that act which
creates it, being an immediate and ongoing presentation of that
act. We insist that this evanescent path in the making, this
transient articulation of space, is yet meaningful. In fact we have
shown that forming is precisely a mode of comprehension. That
which it gropes toward and that which it expresses is the organiza-

tion of a phenomenon. The way it means is as a schematic diagram means. Before it can yet be imagined and before it can be a vehicle for discursive description, the act of forming eventuates in a schema. I can actually draw its articulated space. In the same way that an artist can make explicit the border between two objects or two parts of an object with a line, whether or not that line was visible in some original, I can draw the implicit line of forming's space-object.

A schematic diagram symbolizes relationships, whether spatial or ordinal. To the degree that it is purely schematic it offers no representation of the particular character of the related parts. It limits itself to their organization. In this sense it is relatively contentless. We are all familiar with organizational charts and with flow charts which present, respectively, hierarchical and temporal relations with little or limited representation of the particular entities within the diagram itself. This relatively contentless feature of the schematic diagram requires that it be supplemented by an identifying legend.

The act of forming is a schematic diagram in the making, a "dynamic schematization." [55] Its virtual act can issue in an actual presentation of that schematization, that way of doing something that is indistinguishable from a living relation.

The meaning of this product of forming consists in a presentation of relations among parts with little or no attention to the identification of the parts. In this regard it is unlike an image. We must take issue with Sartre's phenomenology of imagination here. In doing so we can further characterize the kind of meaning that the act of forming bears and provides.

Sartre distinguishes the image from the sign in that only the image "make[s] an object appear." [56] By contrast, the sign does not "deliver its object";[57] it is not positional.[58] For example, the word *office*, a sign, bears no resemblance to an office although it can be the occasion of our envisioning one.[59] While an image directly envisions its object, although as absent, the sign points to an object and is itself forgotten. The image returns us to itself as an equivalent of the object.[60] Again, in imagination I have Peter present as an image, not an image of Peter. Sartre describes a set of variant objects of imagination which constitute the "image family." He builds this typology of "mental images" on analogy to their physical counterparts. The members of the image family vary in the ways in which they are equivalents. The portrait is a complex representation while the caricature is a more simplified representation that selects fewer features and accentuates them. In like manner, an image can present some generalization of a particular feature or features. For example, I can imagine Peter in a way that condenses several instances of our meeting.

At the far end of this spectrum Sartre describes a variant that minimizes representation. He calls this kind of image a "symbolic scheme" after A. Flach.[61] As the following three examples taken from Flach by Sartre suggest, this variant approaches the object in forming. Flach obtained the protocols by asking his subjects to try to understand the common concepts indicated:

Exchange: I gave my thoughts the form of a ribbon (bands). Here is a ribbon which represents the circular process of the exchange. The movement of the curve is a spiral because in the exchange the one acquires what the other loses. The inequality of the curves should explain the gain and the loss involved in every exchange. The ribbon appeared on the field.

Compromise: It is the association of two men. I had the representation of two bodies gliding towards each other, sideways. Their form was vague but it was two bodies—one on the right, the other on the left— which sucked up each other. The body was solid and had some protuberances which it pushed and which disappeared in each other. Then, there was only *one* body. But what is surprising is that the body did not increase much in size. . . .[62]

Altruism: . . . the representation of a direction, the fact of going towards another thing which is not given. . . .[63]

It is clear that the objects of these subjects' experience approach the schematic in the sense that they retain little resemblance to the original. As Flach puts it, they "have no meaning in themselves but only a symbolic one." [64] Their relation to the object and mode of forming is striking. They represent "conceptual relationships" largely through spatial relations. They rely largely on movement— "movement of the curve"; "bodies gliding towards each other"; "the representation of a direction, the fact of going towards." To varying degrees they minimize representation of the character of the object in motion. In *compromise,* the objects gliding toward each other are vague in form but they are two bodies, being solid and having protuberances. In *exchange,* although the object is identified (a ribbon), it clearly is simply a vehicle for forming curves, laying down lines, articulating a space. It appears on a "field," suggestive of the hazy background that we have described as the relatively contextless setting of the object of forming. In *altruism,* finally, there is really no identifiable object, merely its motion: "The representation of a direction, the fact of going towards another *thing which is not given*" (emphasis added).[65]

According to Flach, the symbolic scheme occurs particularly when one is trying to understand something for which a solution is not immediately forthcoming.[66] Subjects report no schemes when problems are very easy. The exact role of the symbolic in the act of comprehension is of concern to Sartre. He is critical of Flach's assertion that first the scheme appears and then thought works from that image to explicit conceptualization. The scheme contains the solution and it then may be thoughtfully deciphered from the image. This is in conflict with a central thesis of Sartre's work on imagination, that the "image teaches nothing." [67] Its function is only to present the already known, to posit the already constituted. It does not function as an aid to understanding. In fact, Sartre argues that through its aim of "producing the object" [68] imagination necessarily "debases" the "pure knowledge" of thought. He, then, reverses Flach's view of the symbolic scheme. This image cannot be the occasion of further thought; rather, the understanding it contains must precede it. Previous thought gives rise to the scheme which merely presents that understanding.

While we do not take issue with Sartre's claim, also by and large confirmed by Casey, that imagination is not central to advances in understanding, it should be clear from our comparison of the two modes that Flach's "symbolic schemes" are products of forming, not imagination. Forming's object is much like these in Flach's examples. Forming's space-object can be largely non-sensory for it does not "deliver" any already constituted object. It is imitative but of a living relation, not of an object. It occurs on an occasion when comprehension is problematic, when there is a searching for understanding. It is not accurate to say, however— as does Flach, according to Sartre—that any solution must await thought on the symbolic scheme. Forming's articulation of space into a schematic diagram is already a form of understanding. Forming is not simply the presentation of an understanding already thought out, nor is it an act the result of which allows thought to arrive at an understanding through a deciphering of the schema after the fact. Forming is itself a prelinguistic mode of understanding. It is a discrete moment in the broader act of explication. Forming is a mode of experience intermediate between the sign and the image, between discursive thought and imagination.

I find myself forming when that which I would understand can neither yet be verbalized nor directly envisioned. The designed space that is the product of forming's enactment is a first formulation, a significant form. That form captures diagrammatically the living geometry of its own motion, which is itself an enactment of certain abstracted relations as such. Neither reinvoking a phenomenon or situation nor designating it, the schematic diagram limits itself to that phenomenon's organization. To do so it cannot yet resort either to the absent flesh of the imagined nor the conventional sign system of language. The power of forming is that through this product it articulates form nondiscursively. It is an abstraction, not an interpretation. It is a direct expression of a natural form, a virtual relation, a form as lived.

In chapter 6, we will provide ample illustration of the use of schematic diagrams in the context of the explication of a particular phenomenon.

Metaphor

The linguistic turn. To arrive at forming's diagrammatic product, we have provided both an itinerary for the phenomenologist's journey, and, more critically, a description of the requisite vehicles for that travel: an abstractive approach to effect the return to the phenomenon as lived; in its aftermath, a sense of the structure of that phenomenon bodily borne as a possible set of moves; and a virtual enactment, a forming, that fulfills that intention through the articulation of a space, a certain scheme or form. Throughout the journey we have emphasized the importance of the delay of the "linguistic turn" in doing phenomenology. In part we have done this to furnish a corrective against a current rush in many quarters to establish the primacy and the pervasiveness of language. When radically stated, such views assert that from the outset, to the degree that experience is meaningful it is already a text, a linguistic entity. By contrast, following Merleau-Ponty, we would resurrect the primacy of the lived body in the meaningful upsurge of our experience of the world. We do so not as gospel but because our own mundane experience in the practice of phenomenological psychology demonstrates, negatively, how we are misled when words and categories come too early, and positively, the effectiveness of adopting and prolonging sensitivities that are bodily and prelinguistic.

However, delay as we might, the last leg of the journey must take us to a verbal description. We undertake this final step in the present method through a discussion of metaphor. We intend to show how the present bodily abstractive modes are both generative in the creation of metaphor and instrumental in the understanding of a given metaphor. Our thesis here is in two parts: (1) What is called the "ground" [69] of a metaphor (that which "love" and "rose" have in common in the metaphor, "love is a rose") typically is structure. (2) At least in the instance of a fresh or new metaphor, to select its predicate (rose), we must apprehend the structure of the subject of the metaphor (love) as lived, that is, as known bodily, as abstracted and carried bodily. Even as we turn finally to language, we contend, our faithful guide continues to be the lived body.

While avoiding for the moment and except where necessary the problematics in the prodigious literature on metaphor in philosophy, literary criticism, and psychology, some working definitions and terminology are helpful. A metaphor draws our attention to similarities between apparently disparate entities by asserting their identity (a person is a fruit). The apparent improper naming or deviant statement is an error in lexical or literal meaning that prompts, inspires, or intimates another meaning that is metaphorical or figurative. Although not unanimous,[70] scholarly opinion generally holds that this latter meaning has a claim to be true, to be a genuine insight into reality. Its literal disparity aside, a sentence that is a metaphor consists of a "ground," an implicit but verifiable resemblance, which ties its subject or "topic" or "tenor" (love) to its predicate or "vehicle" (rose). In addition to pure metaphor, there are numerous other figures of speech that bear it a family resemblance. For examples, a simile asserts similarity rather than identity (love is like a rose); a parable omits the topic (a rose bursts brilliantly into bloom, then matures slowly before it finally fades); "hedge" forms[71] include the ground explicitly (love is as beautiful as a rose). Within metaphor proper, there are two types, similarity and proportional metaphors. In the former, the "ground" is a shared attribute (the beauty of love and of a rose) while in the latter it is a common relation. Two or more features of both the subject and the predicate are related proportionally or analogously (love's joy hides its burdens as the rose's blossom conceals its thorn).

The literalness of phenomenological description. To begin to locate metaphor within the subject of our concern, in a general and possibly confusing way there is an ambiguity in phenomenological psychology as to whether its descriptions are literal or figurative. In a sense phenomenology's ideal of adherence to an explication of the as-lived cuts across such a distinction. In a phenomenology of grief, when I write that "in my grief, I was empty," do I intend this predicate literally or metaphorically? To the degree he can relate to this description, the phenomenologically uninitiated, a person who lives unreflectively within the natural attitude, likely takes it as a metaphor. He finds much phenomenological description evocative in a manner comparable to the poetic.[72]

For the phenomenologist the descriptive "I am empty" is directly expressive of the experience of grief. It is not literal according to the letter of the meaning of grief—there is nothing of emptiness in the dictionary entry. But it is literal in that "emptiness" does not refer to a second entity that resembles grief. Rather, it is intended to refer precisely to a constitutive feature of grief. I cannot be in grief without being empty in some sense that could readily be more fully explicated. I know the emptiness directly as a bodily sense of a certain space that is a feature of the world of grief. To explicate it as "empty," I stay with that bodily sense until "words come from it," as Gendlin has described.[73] I move directly from felt-meaning to explicit meaning without seeking or intending any second entity that is empty *like* grief and without taking "empty" as itself a second entity, as if it were, for example, a metonymy for "empty bottle."

There is another consideration that at first glance suggests that such a descriptive as "in grief, I am empty" is nonetheless metaphorical. Recall that the bodily sense of emptiness originates in some actual or recalled moments of living grief and presently appears as a part apart. As I explicate this bodily abstraction, is it not the predicate of a metaphor for which the original phenomenon as lived is the subject? But I have shown both that the abstracted bodily sense is present as lived in the original and that it had a coconstituting role in that origin. Although I explicate a part apart, it is not one of two entities related by similarity, but one of two poles of a lived moment, of a phenomenon. Again, we are led to the conclusion that in general a phenomenological description has a structure that, in keeping with definitions in the literature on metaphor, is more appropriately considered literal or non-metaphoric meaning.

The body as the ground of metaphor. If, in general, phenomeno-logical description is not yet metaphorical, the phenomenological methods under consideration here readily lead to metaphor. When I embody a grievous sense of emptiness it opens me up to situations, which while not part of the world of grief, not simply more instances of it, have this feature in common with it. Bearing that sense of emptiness I more likely find myself recalling imaginatively or actually being caught by, for example, a moment in the empty theater after the show. It catches me, for although not grief, it is a kind of loss that resembles it. Following this, I can explicate the feature of emptiness with the unambiguously metaphoric statement *In grief, I am in an empty theater.*

In a preliminary way we are trying to distinguish between two strategies of explication. In one a bodily sense of the thing itself directly yields a descriptive which we take to be a literal explication. In the other there is an intermediary step, yet a further delay of the turn to language. Lingering in a particular abstracted bodily sense can facilitate a return to or fresh encounters with situations that resemble the original phenomenon. They do so precisely in that they exemplify a feature abstracted from it and present bodily.

We will provide a fuller and more graphic demonstration of this second strategy below. To get us on our way, we must return to and qualify the relation between structure and bodily modes of its apprehension, in turn to show their relation to the creation of metaphor. At times we have referred to *the* structure of a phenomenon while, strictly speaking, we were dealing with *a* structure of the given phenomenon. It should be clear that the structure of a phenomenon is not exhaustible. We cannot live, locate, abstract, or explicate *the* structure in the sense of all those

structures constitutive of a given phenomenon. There are a number
of ways of indicating how and why this inexhaustibleness obtains.
While we have insisted that the structure of a given phenomenon
is relatively fixed or congealed enough so that we can meaningfully
do phenomenological psychology, all phenomena are embedded
in history. As fundamentally historical entities, they are changing.
As phenomenologists, our relation to phenomena is not exempt
from this historicity. Even as we explicate the structure of a
phenomenon, that contact changes it (and us, for we are defined
by our world). In that we must live the phenomenon to know it,
affect it to be affected by it, we are necessarily both historian and
history-maker with respect to it. Through this dialectic, the
structure of a phenomenon remains elusive and in this sense
inexhaustible.

The perspectival nature of reality also provides a ground for
structure's inexhaustibleness. Even while all of a necessarily
indeterminate number of possible points of view on a given
phenomenon take up just that phenomenon, any point of view is
itself coconstitutive of the phenomenon. While a phenomenologist's
general approach (his point of view) is to incorporate many
points of view, he can exhaust neither them nor, it follows, all
the structures coconstitutive of a given phenomenon. Of course, to
say that the structure is inexhaustible implies that we cannot get
our hands onto or our lived body "into" all of it. We cannot
carry *the* structure of a phenomenon; that which we abstract is
only a part apart in this further sense.

From the fact that the structure of a phenomenon is inexhaustible
it follows that different phenomena might nonetheless have a
structure or structures in common, even apparently highly disparate
phenomena such as love and a flower. But then how are we to
know whether a rose is a rose or a moment of love? Presumably,
while roses and other objects or situations may have a structure
in common with the phenomenon of interest, say, love, they also
have other constitutive structures that preclude their being taken
as instances of that phenomenon. We know them only as phenomena that share a particular structure or limited set of structures
with the phenomenon of interest. On the other side, any lived
moment or instance of the phenomenon of interest shares an
unlimited, inexhaustible set of structures with any other instance
of the same phenomena. Each time I am in love I know it as love;

although I also know why I am inclined to send flowers on such occasions.

For its part, the body becomes informed of structures. By the simple expedient of living situations, that is, by enacting moves that coconstitute the structure of situations, the body gains a sense of their structures. In this way it becomes informed—it has or is a set of possible lived structures. Further, as we have described, to do phenomenology it is helpful to return to and live through phenomena in a way that highlights and isolates that bodily sense of a structure of a phenomenon. What we are adding to our earlier description of the bodily modes of apprehension of structure is the idea that so informed, the body is the "ground" of metaphor—here in both senses of that term. Through the informed body and the possibility of the virtual enactment of its unfulfilled sense of structures, we can create or discover metaphor.

But let us approach this important point more slowly. There is a sense in which actual behavior, as distinguished from the virtual enactment of forming, is also involved in metaphor. When I use my canoe as a lean-to or when I suddenly discover myself using a rock as a hammer, I am creating metaphors through my action. When the problems and strains of my workday are forgotten in a headache, I have reified a part of my body as a metaphor. A symptom is a metaphor hidden from its unwittingly expressive bearer. In that my body can carry the significance of an earlier moment and in that my behavior can find similarities in different objects, through them I can embody, enact, and, in those senses, express metaphors.

R. Romanyshyn argues more generally and radically that "behavior intends its object in a metaphoric way." [74] The intention to find similarity lies "at the operative level of an embodied action." [75] If metaphor is a "carrying over of the sense or meaning of one reality to another," [76] it might be said that "behavior metaphors the world." [77] and that "the metaphors of behavior are the ground for the metaphors of speech."[78] While this position, only suggested by the author, is supportive of our thesis, we do not need to assert it to demonstrate the lesser claim that sensitivity to bodily modes is conducive of the generation of metaphor.

The search for metaphor as a strategy of explication. To provide a bridge from actual behavior as metaphor to metaphor's relation to virtual behavior and to a more precise description of how to create or discover metaphor through it, consider the following example.

In the film *Modern Times,* Charlie Chaplin's task on the factory assembly line, the tramp for once being employed, consists of one repetitious act, tightening an unending series of nuts with a wrench. The aftermath of this workday brings no release from its tedious singularity, for Charlie is doomed to find a world that offers only analogous situations wherein he is tempted or compelled to tighten more nuts or nutlike objects—the fire hydrant's bolted top, the buxom lady's ill-placed gewgaws, the buttons of the irate cop's vestcoat.

In the terms of our analysis, here actual behavior realizes a structure, a particular relation in and toward the world. The structure is a relation between bolt, bolted, and bolter. Evidently we can carry that structure as a bodily sense of a certain move. As we have described, guided by that sense we could enact it virtually, forming a space which we eventually could posit as a schematic diagram. But we can also enact it through actual behavior, as here. In either case the relation between structure and a possible move, a way of doing something, between scheme in Piaget's sense and behavior, is clear. In this example that relation is graphically dramatized, for in the scene Chaplin himself embodies a particular structure coiled to find and enact itself. Like Piaget's child who, once having discovered the grasp, experiences a world consisting predominantly of the relation grasper/graspable, Charlie finds a world that requires and hence invites the continued over-time application of his seemingly limited repertoire. It is as if he is primed: there is a certain readiness or inclination of his body to constitute and reconstitute the situation of his workday or anal-ogies to it.

But in what sense are his actions metaphors, even on that oper-ative level of embodied action? The fire hydrant is more like another instance of his assembly line task than a metaphor for it, for a larger wrench would actually fit it and tighten it. On the other hand the policeman's vest does not lend itself to being bolted. Between that scene and Charlie's work situation there is only a crude similarity, a vaguely similar initial perceptual gestalt. Certainly, the policeman is not impressed with or convinced by the similarity, Charlie's protests notwithstanding.

Clearly, being primed by a sense of a particular structure opens us to realize that structure in various settings. Given the presence of an activated scheme, a moment in which I carry a particular structure as if poised in readiness to fulfill it, there are various possibilities. There is as here the possibility of loose, relatively unconstrained applications of it, whether out of playfulness, compulsiveness, or, in a Piagetian development context, an inclination to exercise it. When the structure is an abstracted feature of a phenomenon under study, there is the possibility that acting it out, whether actually or virtually, can provide predicates for metaphors the subject of which would be that phenomenon of interest.

To show and characterize this latter possibility, we reset the methodological context with another example. In the midst of a phenomenological study of the elusive in experience, we are explicating a structure of an object that appears as elusive.[79] We are describing a sense in which the elusive object is both known and unknown and remains just that. While the unknown primarily frightens and secondarily attracts by making us curious, the half-known of the elusive impels. Consideration of this characteristic relation to the elusive object leads to the following extended trope:

The elusive does not simply pique our curiosity so much as it seduces us. It appeals to me the way a possible sexual partner does who keeps me pursuing but always only pursuing. . . . It holds me by remaining incompletely explicit, always clad in a way that suggests, but only suggests never promises, the unclad. I am captured because I already possess it but only an aura of it, not yet its flesh.[80]

At that moment in which the metaphor occurs to me, I have a sense of this structure of the elusive object. As we have been at pains to argue and to demonstrate, at that moment, although it is possible, I need not nor typically do I have an image of a particular instantiation of that structure. I have a sense of a structure in a bodily way which I can enact virtually, yielding an articulated space which, in turn, can be posited imaginally or actually presented as a diagram. That product and a verbal description of it constitute a first strategy of explication.

Alternatively, I can utilize the present strategy to find a metaphor for which the bodily sense of that structure would serve as "ground." To do so, I inhibit the act of forming and just this former sequence. In this way, I further prolong the sense of a present structure.[81] This savoring of the bodily sense of a possible move activates that scheme without yet realizing it even virtually. So activated, like Chaplin I am primed to find instances of that structure. Often I imagine an object or scene that surprises me, its appearance being unexpected in that present context. In our example, I am concentrating on an aspect of the elusive when I find myself imaginatively pursuing a sexual escapade. Again like Chaplin, perhaps working too hard issues in a certain irresponsibility. On second blush, clearly that scene is an imaginative fulfillment or is the product of a fulfillment of just that bodily sensed structure for which I was primed. It is a product of my direct responsivity. I then have a metaphor for an aspect of the elusive object: it appeals to me the way a possible sexual partner might.

Or do I? Do the appearances of an elusive object and a possible sexual partner have anything in common, as they must for the second to be a predicate of a metaphor for the first? They do if the latter is an instantiation of a structure of the former. This I can verify by living in that imagined sexual scene, abstracting a sense of its structure and noticing whether it is a structure shared with the original phenomenon of interest. Even meeting this condition we may yet not have created a metaphor if a possible sexual partner is simply another instance of an elusive object. If that were the case we would not have met the definitional criterion of similarities between disparate phenomena. Clearly, a sense of a structure of the elusive object as such can lead me to more instances of the experience of elusiveness. But on the face of it, elusiveness and possible romantic escapades are disparate phenomena. Further, that the connection of the second with the first in imagination surprised me suggests that they are unlikely bedfellows, that the second is more than only another context for the occurrence of the first.[82]

Explication of a present structure through metaphor. Given the bodily sense of a structure of the phenomenon of interest, we have recourse to three possibilities: forming that structure directly as a schematic diagram, returning to yet another instance of the phenomenon of interest, discovering or creating a metaphor. While the first is a move within reflection, the latter two shift from a reflected domain to a reengagement in lived experience. It is as if through them I seek a reconnection or reunion with the lived world. But the second is a full return in the Husserlian sense. Moved by and through it I arrive back home in the familiar but dense, multivalent matrix of structure and atmospheres of the original phenomenon of interest. By contrast to this homecoming, while the creation of metaphor also involves a return to a familiar lived experience, with it there is an overriding strikingness and excitement in the moment of the reunion. Of course, what gives metaphor construction a sense of being a "find" is that the connection between the phenomenon of interest and the emergent predicate is a fresh one. At least initially the novelty of that connection is highlighted by the fact that it is also a circumscribed, tight fit. For a predicate of the metaphor is an instantiation of a presently carried structure of the phenomenon of interest, of just that structure. The find is at once an unexpected and an indubitable fit, at once a dramatic connection and a return.

The "ground" of a metaphor typically is a structure in common. With their emphasis on bodily sensitivities to structure as lived and borne, the methods described here put us in a position to create metaphor. The affected body, another bodily abstractive mode, can play a complementary if subsidiary role through the creation of similarity metaphors, metaphors whose "ground" is an attribute rather than a structure. When I instantiate a structure as lived in a fresh phenomenon, I create a metaphor. In an analogous way, when I carry and linger in a particular way my body is affected; I can locate phenomena that affect me similarly. For example, when an atmosphere of a phenomenon under study is oppressive, I abstract a sense of my body as laden or heavy. Staying with this I am led to other phenomena with a similarly oppressive atmosphere. While structure contributes to atmosphere, it is this latter that the affected body bears. It is limited to guiding us toward the creation of a metaphor through a bodily texture and its correlative atmosphere. Originating in the atmospheric, such a "ground" is necessarily a relatively vague or inchoate basis of similarity. A similarity metaphor is a less articulated, less complex, and probably a less extended metaphor than a proportional metaphor. As its "ground" is a common relation or transformation, a way of doing something, a proportional metaphor requires the more flexible, articulate, and moving possibility that is the bodily sense of a structure.

In the context of contemporary views our reliance here on the role of bodily sensitive modes stakes out a position between an intuitionalist and a semantic or linguistic account of metaphor. The former omits a description of how we know the "ground," of how we move from subject to predicate; the latter claims to find that "ground" in a linguistic realm. Metaphor production begins with a bodily sensitivity, either of a structure or an atmosphere of a phenomenon. That bodily sensitivity is already a potential implicit resemblance. It already has a certain generality through which it opens us to an extensive range of its possible application. With that generalized sense we are ready, primed, to find predicates for that subject from which the bodily sense is an abstraction. By contrast to the linguistic account we discover such predicates before we know them as words. When we carry a bodily sensitivity with the intention of reconnecting us through it to a lived experience, we discover a predicate. At that moment the bodily sense is present as an implicit resemblance. It is not quite accurate to refer, with Aristotle, to a "perception of resemblance," but rather to a bodily apperception of it.

The bodily sense that formerly led exclusively from and to the region of the phenomenon of interest now brings another otherwise distinguishable and distant phenomenon close to that region. I feel their proximity in or through that bodily sensitivity, for at that moment it becomes the "ground" of a metaphor that conjoins them. At that moment I do not associate words for I do not yet have any words; nor do I intuitively leap from a subject to a predicate that it resembles for what I sense most strongly is their resemblance, the bodily felt "ground" of the emerging metaphor. When a metaphor's appearance seems more the sudden flash of intuition than the flesh of a common lived body, it is because I have become insensitive to that body. When the production of a metaphor is a function of word associations, it is likely an old and tired metaphor if not a dead one. To bypass the body is to utilize a conventional, an already established meeting ground.

Yet a predominant view within just this semantic conception contends that metaphors, particularly those metaphors that are "good" in a literary context, "create something altogether new." [83] We can and do allow this "transcendent" function, this role of metaphor as lexical extender or source of semantic innovation, without submitting to a linguistic account.

Discovery of additional structure through metaphor. In the context of phenomenological method our primary concern is the production of metaphor. Davidson's assertion notwithstanding, that "there are no instructions for devising metaphors," [84] we can describe how, given a subject, we select a predicate that makes a metaphor. On this production end there is already the possibility of novelty and emergent meaning but in a limited sense. While the two phenomena joined by a metaphor have been known as or through a common prelinguistic bodily sense, the fact of that commonality, not to speak of its explication through metaphor, heretofore has gone unnoticed. Again, the potential implicit commonality guides me to a predicate. But I must already have known that predicate precisely as that particular bodily sense to find its connection to the subject, else how would I find it? I have known both but not their resemblance. The discovery of that resemblance is the extent of the novelty in the originating moment of metaphor production. In that moment I have not yet sensed, let alone explicated, novel features, particularly structural features, of the subject or phenomenon of interest.

However, such further discovery is possible given the now explicit metaphor. As distinguished from the creation of a metaphor, the task of comprehending a metaphor takes on the open-ended life of understanding a text. The inexhaustibleness of the meanings of both phenomena, respectively indicated by the subject and the predicate, opens us to an ultimately indeterminate range of their resemblances. The originating "ground" can be surpassed in the discovery of new and additional grounds. The extent of such elaborations of the ground may be taken as an index in an evaluation of the metaphor. Through this development lexical meanings can be stretched and extended—the river comes to have a mouth. In this sense we concur with Black[85] that it is an error to reduce a metaphor to the particular structural analogy (or set of such) that "ground(s)" it. But we can and do point to the centrality of a common structure in the original production of a metaphor. Living in the bodily sense of a structure and thereby activating it is a relatively sure way to discover a metaphor.

Once created, that metaphor is part of an explication of a particular feature of the phenomenon of interest. But further, the location of a phenomenon distinguishable from the original allows the development of a comparative description—of features in common and features peculiar to each. Through this exploration of the predicate phenomenon in tandem with the phenomenon of interest, I can disembed structures of the latter that were to that point unabstracted. Of course, this exploration utilizes the same bodily methods we have described.

The primary purpose of metaphor production is to provide ancillary images and language for a particular phenomenon under study. Through this device we complement the language that issues directly from a bodily sense of that phenomenon and from that diagrammatic space resultant from forming abstracted structures. By instantiating a particular structure of the phenomenon of interest in a relatively novel domain, the metaphor expresses that structure dramatically. Beyond this rhetorical gain, such an instantiation has the methodological advantage of momentarily isolating a particular structure. While bodily abstraction and the spatiality of forming offer a kind of isolation, here a particular structure, as it were, can be followed for it is put back into play in a fresh setting which is a tropological space. Further analysis of that feature is then possible. Both these separations are critical methodological gains. For if the problem of more analytic methods is that their dissection kills the phenomenon as lived, reduces it well beyond a vanishing point to what is then an idealization of the phenomenon in the image of the method of its inquiry, the problem of phenomenological method is that in its concern to be faithful to the rich multivalence of the phenomenon as given, it has difficulty distinguishing constitutive parts. Here a particular constitutive feature can be known through bodily abstraction and can be instantiated in a fresh setting where it is readily on display. The cycle can then be renewed with respect to this singular feature as it is readily traced in a lived way, bodily abstracted, and formed.

The informed body bears a potential basis of similarity; through it I am a seeker of metaphor, a natural poet-at-large. What I bear is not a representation of that basis of resemblance but is a possible presentation of it, as the bodily pole of its potential instantiation. So informed, we readily find ourselves in the midst of metaphor, in a landscape rife with possible structural isomorphisms. We do so before we speak to others or even to ourselves.

The discovery of a metaphor is not the postreflective application of a rhetorical device. T. Cohen suggests that for one person to comprehend another's metaphor requires an intimate relation, as an invitation to probe beneath the surface of the latter's remark is accepted.[86] The creation of a metaphor involves its own kind of intimacy. To join subject to predicate requires a bodily cohabitation, a carnal knowledge of each, an empathic understanding of how each is similar in a bodily and embodied way. That congress can be both a creative fount, a way of exploring new ground, and a conservative, that is, a form-retaining, way to verbal description.

The production of metaphor is the final step in the present phenomenological method. In a sense, with it we reverse our direction. While the general movement of the method to this point has been from engagement to reflection as bodily abstraction and from the particular to the general, here we move from abstracted structure back to at least the possibility of concrete engagement. Having traced earlier how the bodily sense of structure can give us an image of its generalized form, here we move from that bodily sense to another lived phenomenon and hence to metaphor.

We have come full circle from the phenomenon as lived, to its abstraction, to language, to the possibility of reengagement. We have entered the various dialectics that constitute doing phenomenology: that between the subject and predicate of a metaphor as here, between engagement and reflection on the phenomenon of interest, between structure and atmosphere, and between felt-meaning and meaning. For all of these we have suggested how with the body as vehicle we can backtrack, begin afresh, stay our movement, discover additional structures and fresh grounds—in general, how we can enter these various dialectics at various points and move within and among them.

6

The Method in Practice

To review to this point, beginning with the indisputable assertion that the keystone of a phenomenological method is reflection, we have indicated how reflection has remained recalcitrant to efforts to describe it. Undoubtedly, there is some justice in this state of affairs. To explicate reflection we must take it as a phenomenon, but it is precisely not that. It is not a phenomenon but a way of grasping such that posits how a phenomenon appears to us. Perhaps we must be satisfied with knowing it only indirectly, only as we employ it. However, a review of recent gains with respect to other issues pertinent to a phenomenological method reveals that, more than simply deferring to the elusiveness of reflection, this literature begins to construct a different methodological center for phenomenology. To salvage its proper role, we have attempted to meet reflection's recalcitrance in kind. By recasting reflection in terms of the problem of structure, both structure's presence in phenomena and possible modes of its apprehension, we hope to clarify what reflection is and to reaffirm that it is critical to a phenomenological method.

Traditional investigations of reflection demonstrate that its movement toward the self and away from an embeddedness in a phenomenon is effected largely through an explication, of both the structure of that phenomenon and the coconstituting embedded self. We have argued that the structure of a particular phenomenon is present prereflectively, in the living of that phenomenon. In fact, in that I coconstitute the phenomenon through my active participation in it, that presence of its structure is bodily. Coconstitution by "living through" or participation and the correlative bodily presence are the ground for the possibility of reflection. This is because a bodily sense of the structure of a phenomenon is a residue of my participation. In what is a first moment of reflection, that bodily presence is abstracted and bodily borne. Further, reflection consists in positing that bodily awareness and correlative aspects of the original phenomenon as lived. In these bodily modes, any role of the visual or the imaginal, the conceptual or the linguistic, is minimal by contrast. If lived experience is embodied consciousness, reflection is built on the bodily and consists in the bodily recovery of that original embodiment.

We have tried to open up two fronts on reflection. First, after consideration of other recent contributions to phenomenological method and other treatments of reflection, we presented a phenomenology of reflection as a bodily abstractive approach to phenomena. This abstraction is accomplished by two modes, the first of which is a bodily sensitivity to atmosphere and a subsequent bodily bearing of that atmosphere. The second mode, the one critical to a phenomenological method, is more closely related to the structure of a phenomenon. We explicated this mode, forming, through a genetic phenomenology of the moments in its reflective journey to explication and through its comparison with other modes, particularly behavior, perception, and imagination.

The second phalanx we sent against reflection by way of its ally, structure. We critically considered several contemporary ways of conceptualizing structure, organized roughly to highlight a spectrum from its presumed externality to its internality to immediate experience. Through this critique, notably of Lévi-Strauss, Piaget, and Husserl, we attempted to locate structure as a presence in and hence as a potential object of experience. In this way we laid a groundwork for the phenomenology of modes that intend structure.

PROBLEMATICS IN THE PRESENTATION OF A METHOD

To show the present method in operation we need only select a phenomenon and do a phenomenology of it. However, this is more problematic than it appears. How will the description of a phenomenon that is the fruit of a particular phenomenological method show that method in action? And if the method does show through in its product, will not that be a critical shortcoming of the method which, after all, has as its goal the return to and the description of the phenomenon as lived prior to any influence of a method of its explication?

Strictly speaking, no method of inquiry while in operation includes a description of itself. Yet most nonphenomenological methods consist of a "phenomenon" different in kind from the target phenomenon of their study. A description of method is not simply another study involving the use of the same method turned upon itself. For example, in the experimental method of the natural and social sciences, the "methods section" is on another level of discourse than the study itself. Typically, the methods section presents a description of a set of procedures that are outside of the field of inquiry and, in fact, provide it with its borders. While the assumptive base of the science may be problematic, the description of the operations is relatively unambiguous. More importantly, the presentation of their application shows the method in a straightforward manner. The "results section" patently demonstrates that the results are the product of an application of *that* method or procedure.

Any phenomenological method that is truly that consists in acts, postures, and modes of experience. The method is of the same stuff we seek to know through its application. A methods section, then, must describe a phenomenon that is on the same level of discourse as the study proper. Although it may require a second-order reflection, a description of the method is itself a phenomenological study. As Zaner states, every epistemic contribution or knowledge-claim is also a methodological contribution.[1] But by what method shall that "study" proceed and how will we show it? If we proceed in this direction, how will we avoid this regress? Further, by the light of its own name, is not phenomenology necessarily a phenomenon-centered rather than a method-centered mode of inquiry? How far toward the description of a method can we proceed in a methods section when that method must await our engagement in the particular phenomenon under study? In the final analysis the method must be a coming to terms with that target phenomenon in or on its own terms.

Implicit in the present work is the proposition that a general method can be described that attempts precisely to allow these "terms" of the target phenomenon to be met, engaged, and borne away as such. We have already provided that general exposition: our description of forming is a reflection on reflection. Here we wish to display the method in the act of its application, but we are having trouble understanding what that project can be. Again, we must select a phenomenon and present a description of it. While that description cannot demonstrate directly the ways of experiencing that constitute the method of study, they will have an appearance in the phenomenon-as-explicated. Being certain ways, intending the object in a certain way, that object appears in a certain style—as does the description of it. However, this style of explication does not appear through or as a deformation of the particular phenomenon. To the contrary, it appears as the style of ways of locating, extricating, and staying with its particular form— the style through which I become informed precisely and only of it. It is the style of forming, not of deforming; of reviving and positing a structure already embodied, though latently, not of constructing or of deconstructing.

We intend to show that style through the following description of a selected phenomenon. In addition, however, from time to time in the course of that description we can at least point to the acts and modes that are fostering it. That in this final chapter we can only point is at once an embarrassment and a respectful gesture to the present method. While to locate and argue its effectiveness in doing phenomenology, we have provided numerous verbal descriptions, a major thrust of our argument has been the limited role of words in this reflective method. Here, then, is a way we can show it without describing it explicitly.

In the study below I have utilized some of the methodological devices of the empirical phenomenology that I reviewed critically at the outset. For example, as an adjunctive aid in the initial location of the phenomenon of interest, I conducted interviews with several individuals who were in this way taking the role of "co-researcher." [2] Further, in those interviews and in my own subsequent individual reflections, I employed other generative and evocative devices such as the use of imagined exemplary situations, and comparisons with neighboring or with antithetical phenomena. Of course, I also was open to the influence of more classical strategies such as etymology, variations in perspective, and variations in the phenomenon as it is being constituted, that is, a genetic phenomenology.

AMBIVALENCE

Selecting a Target Phenomenon

The domain of application of the reflective methods under investigation here is inclusive of any phenomenon. With them we claim the power to explicate any object of experience, and no less any aspect of an object, any way an object appears, or any way of intending an object. The attempt to explicate reflection itself, undertaken in the previous chapters, suggests the extent of their reach.

Given its inclusiveness, the present method offers no guidance in our selection of a phenomenon for study here. Informal considerations suggest that a phenomenological method is put to good use if it researches the as-yet unexplicated. A phenomenon may remain unexplicated because it is taken for granted or because its presence is in the shadows of our existence, flickering in and out of our awareness at its periphery, or because it has recently emerged to prominence among the shifting contours of the culture, or because it is camouflaged by the demands of a particular theoretical netting. A phenomenon becomes of interest to a phenomenological method, and, in return, "tries" that method, when it invites such a shock of recognition, or illumination, or extrication. Of course, at bottom, a phenomenon of interest is one that interests me. I could select a phenomenon from my own life. After all, to do a phenomenology of something I must be able to find it, to involve myself in it and to have ready access to it. Only if the phenomenon occurs for me, if I live through it, can I know if I begin to describe it. On the other hand, would not the selection of a phenomenon from my personal life be an indulgence, an inappropriate self-display, and an intrusion into my privacy?

But this discussion already gives me a suitable phenomenon. I know well this weighing of considerations, this leaning toward and away, this quick succession of attraction and repulsion toward the same object; this "on the one hand . . . but on the other. . . ." This personally salient phenomenon, ambivalence, at the same time has an important place in theoretical writings, particularly in psychoanalytic thought. In fact, the term is of recent origin, beginning with E. Bleuler and adopted with modification by Freud.[3] Currently its popular usage broadens the strictures of Freud's systematic rendering of the term. Because of its general currency, locating at least roughly the intended region of its meaning is not problematic. For this reason I can begin with an example of the phenomenon from my own experience.

An Example

For the past few years I have been aware of ambivalence in my life, whether at center stage or in the wings, to the point of considerable familiarity with its various guises. The persistent occasion of its appearance is my ambivalence about the present project, this study of the phenomenological method. As an introduction to the phenomenon, the following account of a repeated personal experience may establish an initial referent:

I am sitting at the desk in my study. This is the beginning of my time to work on the paper, always an important part of the day. I am reading the last section, the previous day's work, and am on the verge of being absorbed in it. This eases the way to the current work session for quite often I approach it looking forward to it but also tight, somehow not knowing what to expect. Undoubtedly, how that last section will read is part of my anticipatory anxiety. Sometimes in reading it, I lose myself in it pleasurably. When I come to myself again, I realize I have left the paper, been launched by it, and ridden it to its gala reception. Buoyed by this fantastic trip, the transition to the day's work is immediately there for me and I am readily in it. Its movement and my movement are indistinguishable; as the boundaries between us dissolve, I am my project.

At other times in this preparatory rereading, I am absorbed not in the work but, as it were, in its cracks. As I read it, I do not encounter an integrity that I can embody but rather I am taken in by the faults. Falling into these interstices, I live them as in a chasm. The work is split asunder and I cannot possibly put it back together. Finally, sometimes there is no engagement. The section of the paper does not carry me anywhere or any way; I cannot understand it; nor can I carry it as it stands; nor can I further it. Both the fissure I cannot bridge and this latter more general failed transport readily become a repulsion from all that is there. At a distance, I am hating what is there; there is nothing there of value; at the extreme, there is nothing there.

I catch myself at this fantasy turned nightmare and try to reflect out of it. Surely, I am just stuck momentarily; stay with the task, I exhort myself. But I cannot stave off the negativity. The phenomenon I sought to describe has slipped through my fingers. There is nothing there of it in my descriptions. More, the target phenomenon never did exist with the significance or usefulness as a contribution to method that I had attributed to it. My present ravings bear witness to and confirm that I have been trying to describe what I wished to be there.

But did I not try, and am I not trying? And have I not been even here, at this murky bottom, before? And have I not come out of that depth, as I am about to now? Is this not simply a struggle with the "courage to create"?

At this point I realize explicitly that I am ambivalent, that at this moment I am both loving and hating this paper. Almost simultaneously, I see that the occasioning context of this ambivalence is the issue of my esteem. A negative impression of yesterday's work had immediately implicated my view of myself as creative, competent, worthwhile. With this, I feel some relief for I can "work through" these "dynamics." While I may never transcend them entirely, I have some mastery of them. Although perennial, they are, after all, a garden variety hang-up. I am not really ambivalent. It is not really a question of loving and hating, of embracing and abandoning this particular work so much as it is of a gnawing foundational insecurity about myself. And it is not only my esteem—it is also guilt. How can I justify this work, this sequestering myself with my own thoughts while others struggle out there in the world with the real social and political problems of the day, or give their lives that others may live longer and better. In the midst of this world, I, the phenomenologist, "devote" myself to writing papers, to such problems as sorting out the difference in experience between red-orange and orange-red.

Another round: I am back to my feelings about the paper, about this project. It is ambivalence and it is robust. I am not presently resolving it. I am dealing with my ambivalence in one of the ways I do that—by being obsessive. Or is that one way of being ambivalent? Am I being ambivalent about ambivalence?

Thus I readily locate the region of ambivalence. Indeed I discover that it is a powerful phenomenon, one more readily located than, once located, kept at a distance. Once in it, when I attempt to shake it by shifting the object of consideration, or by jumping levels, or by reflecting on ambivalence itself, it pursues me doggedly.

Theories of Ambivalence

Let me take a cooler approach for a moment by reviewing certain conceptualizations of the phenomenon in the psychological literature. Elsewhere, I have discussed the possible fruitfulness of a dialogue between apparently theory-bound conceptualizations and a lived sense of the phenomenon as a way both of discovering the presumed experiential bedrock of the former and advancing the explication of the latter.[4] However, in this brief survey I will not utilize that methodological strategy. I will limit discussion to a clarification of these definitions of ambivalence on a conceptual level and delay further direct return to and eventual explication of the phenomenon of interest. That direct return through the evocation of instances of the phenomenon will lend itself most graphically to a demonstration of the present bodily reflective postures and approaches.

As Bleuler identifies a "group" of schizophrenias, in like manner he distinguishes several kinds of ambivalence: voluntary, intellectual, and emotional. Ambivalence of volition involves a conscious conflict over doing or not doing something; in intellectual ambivalence a person simultaneously interprets a phenomenon in a positive and negative light; emotional ambivalence consists in loving and hating the same object.[5] In general, Bleuler places ambivalence in a psychopathological context, as one of the "four a's" diagnostic of schizophrenia, along with autism and affective and associational disabilities.

Freud modifies and restricts Bleuler's definitions to make ambivalence a major beam in his own theoretical scaffoldings. In *Totem and Taboo,* he defines ambivalence as "simultaneous love and hate toward the same object." [6] He limits the "object" of ambivalence to a person and the mode to feeling; ambivalence is a peculiar complex of feelings toward another person. More critically, "feeling" need not be and typically is not conscious. Simultaneity of two opposite feelings implies neither awareness of their contradictory relation, nor even awareness of either feeling singly.

In contemporary psychoanalytic thought "simultaneous" is further qualified, becoming a necessary but not sufficient condition for ambivalence. For M. Klein, what is definitive of ambivalence is not the mere existence of opposite and unconscious feelings, but the failure of their integration.[7] By contrast, "ambiguity" is the unconscious recognition, if you will, of that connection. In this contemporary view, simultaneous presence of or expression of opposite feelings is actually counterindicative of ambivalence for the latter is restricted to the failure to tolerate opposed feelings. It is their lack of integration, their being "split off" from each other, that constitutes ambivalence. The failure of expression, or, more, the denial of both positive and negative feeling toward a primary object implies an unconscious ambivalent state.

In psychoanalytic theory ambivalence has or is a structure in that it refers to a relation among parts. These "parts" reside in the "ucs"; the structure is a structure of the unconscious. Ambivalence, then, is not a question of a way of being, of a way of intending the world, that shows itself in the object intended and correlatively in the mode of intention. To understand ambivalence requires an observer's inference from behavior or an interpretation of history to an underlying, hidden structure. Ambivalence may be inferred from the observation of certain defenses against the expression of mixed or ambiguous feelings. For example, a defense against mixed feelings toward the same object might involve the relegation by repression of one feeling to the unconscious. This repression might be buttressed by reaction formation in which, for example, an overconcern for the well-being of the "loved one" would be evident. Or, the unacceptability into consciousness of polar feelings might give way to the alternating expression in quick succession of loving and hateful feelings toward the same object, feelings that yet remain "disassociated" from each other. Or, one might express love for mother and hate for father, the latter being displaced hate for mother.

In this psychoanalytic perspective, which in another context we found to have an affinity with contemporary structuralism, it is assumed that structure and understanding are receding beneath immediate phenomenal reality. Here ambivalence does not inhere in the simultaneous expression of opposite feelings. Even behaviors inferred by the analyst to be defenses against such are only symptoms of an underlying structure which is where ambivalence "lives" beyond our—both therapist and client's—habitation. Freud locates such structures partly in a biological substrate and partly in intrapsychic residues of early familial history. In his view ambivalence originates in the conflict of two opposed instincts or of an instinct toward and an internalized prohibition against the same object.

The child's dependence for gratification on and hence his or her likely frustration at the hands of the same object, his or her mother, is conceived as a constitutional condition for the origin of ambivalence. The persistent use of certain defenses later in life are the consequences of and the evidence of such instinctive impasses or developmental failures. Psychodynamic principles, particularly that of the mediating role of anxiety, provide an explanatory linkage between these defenses and the unconscious structures. The expression of awareness of opposite instincts or prohibitions is threatening and must be defended against.

Contemporary psychoanalysis relies more on genetic, that is, early familial or historic, reduction than on a biological reduction for explanatory power. For the "object relations" school of British psychoanalysis, following Klein, ambivalence originates in the internalization and representation of "partial objects" which are split into the good and bad mother. "Alternate images" of the object in the unconscious replace the opposite instincts of classical analysis as explanations. Ambivalence is a structural defect in which these images are not integrated but split. Such structures are evidenced in certain literary forms such as the familiar portrayal in fairy tales of the witch and the fairy, and in an individual context from relations to objects that deny mixed feelings.

The concept of ambivalence that emerges from this psychoanalytic literature is one that obviously owes much of its shape to a certain theoretical jacket. Love and hate must align with some version of basic instincts such as eros and thanatos; the object of ambivalence must be a new edition of a historically primary relation. Beyond these thematic and historical demands, the way ambivalence is known or concealed both to the subject and the investigator partakes of a peculiarly psychoanalytic mode of experiencing and understanding. The "presence" of a phenomenon of interest is known by its distortion, its concealment. From its absence it is inferred to be operative in an unlivable and unobservable, hence only inferrable, region, the unconscious. While defining ambivalence as simultaneous love and hate toward the same object, we do not find the phenomenon there, present in such a moment.

But putting aside all that is problematic and even wrongheaded here from a phenomenological perspective, there is some gain and some guidance for the present project. This literature suggests that any description of the phenomenon of ambivalence must deal with the feature of simultaneity. Ambivalence will need to be distinguished from other variants of simultaneous opposite feelings, such as mixed feelings, ambiguity, indecisiveness, and the like. Further, it seems that direct explicit awareness or expression of ambivalence is, minimally, unlikely in that it typically is self-threatening to intend opposite feelings to the same object. The existence of such opposition is apparently an occasion for pathological distortions.

As an aside, from the analytical philosophical point of view, I suspect that the meaningfulness of simultaneous antithetical feelings is problematic. Is the statement "I love and hate you at this moment" a conceivable proposition? If I cannot be above and beneath a thing at the same time or be dominant and submissive toward you simultaneously, can I at once be happy and sad toward you? While inconceivability in the strict sense of an analytic philosophical inquiry is not a block to a phenomenological approach, here again we are alerted to the likelihood that that which we intend by ambivalence may not be the direct simultaneous, symmetrical presence or assertion or living of opposed inclinations toward one object. While not hindered by a concern with the logically offensive features of a phenomenon, a phenomenological inquiry is not open to resolve such by hiding the "phenomenon," by denying its presence in experience. To understand any phenomenon we cannot give it an absence that has no presence, nor can we refer it to an "invisible" inferred structure, nor reduce it to a biological substrate or a historical precursor. To understand we must stand under it; we must live that structure for it to be meaningful. If ambivalence by definition requires simultaneous feelings or thoughts or the like, they must have an appearance. We must locate some form of dual presence. Certainly the phenomenological investigator is uniquely and powerfully equipped to discover the rich variety and subtlety of forms of presence, including that of the simultaneous and opposed. Presence as appresence, the present as absent, and "presence realized in the landscape" [8]— in these we may find ambivalence. What is the peculiar presence of ambivalence; how does an object appear that I both love and hate; what is the structure of that moment; how do I live an ambivalent world?

Definitions of Ambivalence

The term *ambivalence* does not make its first appearance in Webster's dictionary until 1934,[9] with the following entry: "the simultaneous attraction and repulsion from an object, person, or action." While coming into vogue through the widespread influence of

Freud, accepted usage as reflected in this early entry does not
adhere to the theoretical constraints of psychoanalytic thought.
It seems a more general and apparently theoretically neutral definition, perhaps more akin to Bleuler's original description. The
intended object is not restricted to a person, freeing the term from
an exclusively interpersonal context and, presumably, at least
loosening the tie of any present ambivalence to an early unresolved historical origin. Further, attraction/repulsion is broader
in content and in mode than love/hate. The former polarity includes action or inclination as well as feeling. A more recent definition relinquishes even this broad polarity with the phrase,
"mutually conflicting feelings or thoughts." [10] Here the connection
of ambivalence to the instinctive underpinnings of love or aggression is abandoned while the more general psychodynamic
concept of conflict is central. Simultaneity gives way to conflict.

Etymological considerations support the greater generality of usage
implicit in these dictionary definitions. The term combines *ambi,*
meaning "both," and *valency,* the "capacity of an atom to combine
with other atoms." [11] *Valency* itself derives from "valere," meaning "to be strong, to be worth." [12] In ambivalence there are both
"sides," the two sides of a conflicting feeling or thought. Both
sides are strong, both have their own worth. The etymology emphasizes the power of both more than their oppositeness of meaning.
Each can combine with the other; they are reciprocally influential.
There is a coming together of strong forces, and in that sense a
kind of compatability.

A Phenomenology of Ambivalence

At this point we can turn to an attempt to locate and describe
constitutive features of ambivalence. Again, the primary purpose
and focus of this inquiry will be to show how to do phenomenology: the particular essential features of ambivalence will remain
a secondary concern. How do we gain access to any phenomenon;
how do certain of its features begin to break away from any given
instance of the phenomenon and coalesce as constitutive features?
How do these features appear? The "how" of that appearance will
consist of both noeme and noese. We must portray both the way
of coming into presence, the way the object, here "constitutive
feature of ambivalence," itself is constituted and the mode of ap-

prehension through which that objectification occurs. Of course, these modes of apprehension of structure are critical to the present method.

In the introductory example of ambivalence above, we began in the throes of ambivalence. Through an example we returned to a moment of blatant ambivalence, to a center of the region of ambivalence. That it is that is independently confirmed by the fact that most people when asked to locate ambivalence in their own life go immediately to a similar moment or region. It is a moment in which they are painfully being pulled in two directions at once. Often the context is a moment of decision, as if ambivalence were highlighted by the occasion of decision making.

We will begin with a return, with an attempt to be at ambivalence as lived. We return most readily by the re-evocation of an instance of ambivalence from our own life. However, here we will employ the additional device of returning to an edge of the phenomenon. Instead of reentering ambivalence when it is in full bloom, we seek a region where it is at the limits of its constitutive structure. We might likely find such a boundary or "limiting condition" in a moment when we first discover that we are ambivalent. In the onset of ambivalence we might most clearly grasp what it is, what we are invited to be at that moment when we are about to become ambivalent. Also, with this device we might clarify ambivalence by contrasting it with neighboring but distinguishable phenomena.

Again, I am sitting at the desk in my study. I have just turned to finish the preparation of a lecture. As I focus on the lecture notes, there is implicitly an anticipation of how it will go when I present the lecture later in the morning. That anticipation is variable: when the notes engage or stimulate and advance my thinking, that anticipation is of an organized presentation, one that provokes student participation and discussion. Such a projected future lifts me lightly, even buoyantly toward the hour of the class. Of course, the converse also obtains. Any particular way I am horizontally anticipating the lecture informs my present relation to the lecture notes. When I anticipate not quite reaching the students, I feel that distance in the way the notes presently speak to me. They appear as what I would write in a rough draft, before I concern myself with the problem of addressing a particular audience. I feel relatively alone with the notes.

The past also plays its part in this last-minute preparation. How yesterday's lecture went, the lectures as a whole to this point in the semester, my general sense of how I am developing as a teacher, and other apparently less directly related recent and remote past events and contexts make their entrance—such as how yesterday's handball game went. They all color the way the notes appear and give form to my present relation to them and to our anticipated relation during the morning's lecture. The particular coloration lent by the past is complex and variable, as is the extent of the predominance of its implicit presence as compared to that of the anticipated future. When the first two of three lectures on psycho-analysis have gone well, I sense that momentum in the way in which the notes and I readily take each other up and lead each other on with a rush.

Early Moments in the Constitution of Ambivalence

This is only a suggestion of the many possible variations in the way this focal object can be present and can support and be supported by various temporal and spatial structures and relations to me. Let us return now to a particular moment in which I am preparing for a lecture and keep access to the bodily sense of all of these. To accomplish the return I begin with the focal object in the way it shows itself to me in a moment I can recall. At first, the notes do not appear to signify. I see only a style of writing, an arrangement of margins. The notes are staying on the page. When I read a group of words I have trouble embodying them, giving them their or any intended meaning. When I do get some gist, I cannot give it adequate or appropriate gesture or voice. There is signification without significance or import. The meanings are not part of a progression; even when they have meaning it is "out of context."

There is a present horizontal bodily sense correlative to the way the notes appear in this moment to which I have just returned in memory. My body assumes a sense of mild disorientation, of being unanchored. As I stay with it, it is a sense of "being neither here nor there." When I enact the movement implicit in this bodily sense, which is inseparable from this peculiar relation to the notes, I find myself forming a space that is not directly oriented to that original object. It is then clear that the bodily sense of a kind of floating is in relation to an "object" itself only implicit in this appearance of the notes. Forming that space I recognize a more general structure, one that I have explicated often before under the heading "being distracted."

When I return again to the original sense of the notes as failing to invite or obtain my embodiment in an anticipated meaningful lecture, I realize that I am being distracted, although in a very peculiar and particular way. What is distracting me is another potential object for my attention, one about which I am ambivalent. A comparison of variant forms of distraction suggests itself to clarify further what is going on here and to approach eventually an edge of ambivalence. I will leave ambivalence for a moment in the expectation that I may begin to explicate it as a species of distraction. Tentatively, one way I discover ambivalence, an early moment in the experience of being ambivalent, or one way it is present before I posit either the object of my ambivalence or the fact of my ambivalence is as a kind of distraction.

When I am distracted another project or relation is pulling me away from a presently focal project or relation. I can readily return to such a moment which is clearly and more simply a moment of distraction. It is a moment when I am preparing for a lecture while I would rather be doing something else. Of course, as we have just shown, other concerns, whether thematically or only marginally related, color and inform any present focal concern. However, here such peripheral concerns do not simply infiltrate and influence the presentation of the focal object; in some way and degree they prevent its full presentation. The object, while focal, is at a distance; it is not fully graspable; it does not make "good sense."

At this point I shift from the object to the correlative sense of my body in that situation.[13] *This is the preferred strategy at the center of the present method. The bodily sense is itself complex in that I can distinguish both ways I am affected and possible moves. Further, with this shift, metaphors, taking as their "ground" a given sense, begin to occur to me. However, I can select and stay with the possible moves of my body, forgetting for a moment the way my body is affected and, as well, inhibiting verbal explications of any bodily sense. I stop being affected to effect, silently and without words, that field of forces in which I had become involved through*

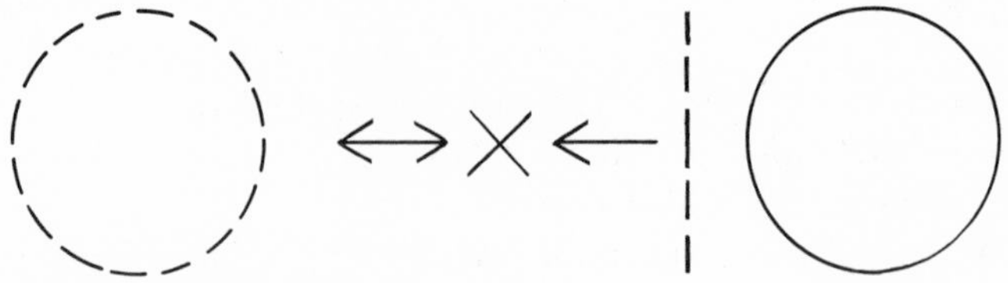

distracting ambivalent   self   focal
    "object"   object

FIGURE 2

the return and which now is present as an unfulfilled intention to
realize an abstract space through my virtual bodily motion. This
virtual enactment articulates a space which is a structure of the
evoked situation.

The correlative bodily sense here is a mixture: my affected body
is a sense of being stretched or elongated; there is also a sense of
straining toward. This latter immediately brings with it the metaphors—straining, as when I am trying to see someone through the
dark or to hear a message through the noise. But here I focus on
the bodily correlative of a certain field of forces. I realize a predominant force that is keeping me from my focal object, the notes.
There is no barrier as such; I do not bump into anything. It is
more that the space near the object thins out so that that space
cannot sustain my approach and I cannot quite grasp the object.
I am being pulled away from it. That force has more than directionality for while I have not yet posited any particular forceful
directing object there is an unposited shadowy entity pulling me
toward it. I can objectify the space that I have formed as shown
in figure 2. I take this, tentatively, to be a structure of distraction.
In particular, it is the structure of that moment of distraction
before I turn directly to the distracting object. It is the structure
of the way that potential disruption is present in that which I,
resistantly, am attempting to engage myself.

Once having formed and objectified this space I can move
through it, which is to say form it again. Recourse to the particular
original instance of it, the lecture notes, is unnecessary. As I do
so I find I can employ that space as a vehicle to generate further
instances. I can then return to these in turn, and begin afresh
the rough sequence: focal object and mode of its appearance,
bodily sense, and virtual enactment of structure.

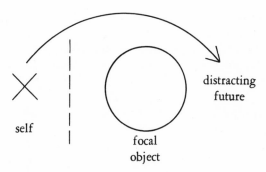

self

focal
object

distracting
future

FIGURE 3

At this point I could explore variations of distraction which eventually might fill out, provide limits for, and modify this first structure of a moment of distraction. For example, the significance of the relation between the modes of presence of the distracting object and of the focal object might emerge. When I am listening to someone I may be more vulnerable to other sounds than to a visual distraction.

In the present investigation I am varying distracting objects to highlight and to grasp the ambivalent object as distracting. A moment that at least begins to approximate an instance of an ambivalent distracting object comes to mind. I am in college taking my last exam before summer break. I am in the midst of the exam with ample time to complete it, yet my bodily sense is that I am racing through it. While I am still attending to the exam, it is as if I am too high, as if I am flying over it. Correlative to this bodily sense, the present focal object, a particular exam question, appears with a futural temporal horizon accentuated. I am not being pulled away from this question so much as I am pulled to "after"—to the moment when I will have finished it. Again, I am not yet positing that immediate future; it is present as a force pulling me beyond this present moment in time. I can focus on the sense of my body as racing and enact the implicit space of that force. As I do so a space is cut out, which I can then imaginally objectify and present as in figure 3. In this figure the arrow goes not to another as yet unposited object but to the anticipated end of the present project, the moment of my completion of the exam. At another moment before I actually complete it, I am looking through the windows at the sky, which, because

the windows are placed high in this huge hall, shows only above
the skyline. My body is no longer racing; now I am imagining
the heat of the sun as I lounge in my back yard. Having suc-
cumbed to the distraction, I am no longer distracted. For a brief
moment the exam is forgotten as the windows open to a daydream of summer. The pull of the end of the exam was merely a
stand-in for the powerful and distracting attraction of the coming
summer with its serene laziness and its respite from exams.

Here is one more example of a relatively unambivalent distraction. Again, I am reading my notes in preparation for a lecture.
The notes are not inciting me to work on them. My bodily sense
is of being logy. I am sluggish, heavy; I can hardly mobilize
myself, yet I have no apparent reason to be tired. The notes appear
a great labor which I cannot possibly undertake. As I reflect on
my inertia it appears that it is my own "depression" that distracts
me. My depressiveness is a bodily languor which so surrounds me
that there is no question of resistance. But there is more. A bodily
motion, a pull down, is implicit in this self-indulgent loginess.
Something is getting me down.

*As I try now to enact virtually this situation I do not intend
simply to somehow experience that drag on me more fully. Rather,
I seek to play out the kinetics, as it were, of the whole situation.
To do this I do not take up the role of all the actors in turn—
myself, the notes, the lecture, and the presumably distracting but
unposited object. I empathize with these but from a position external
to them. I am like the director who knows at once the movements,
the intentions, and the interconnections of all the principals in
the play. Like the director I can embody and hence can virtually
enact these as a unified dramatic design or pattern. Sometimes I
can enact that field of forces before I even identify the particular
roles.*

In regard to this scene I form the image shown in figure 4.
Something is pulling me down like a ball and chain, but it is not
the task of preparing the lecture. I now realize that that task
appears onerous only because I am already oppressed. That which
is already pulling me down has required me, tyrannically, to spread
a dark and heavy tone over all my endeavors. As I begin to locate
that object it appears heavy, dense, large. Finally I explicate it as the
project of writing this book in a period when I am discouraged
with it. As I do so a sharp pang of anxiety breaks through the

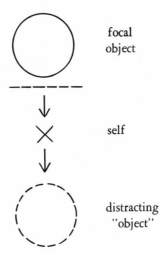

focal
object

self

distracting
"object"

FIGURE 4

depression. I had avoided the threat of turning more directly to
the prospect of a failed project.

To this point we have indicated a rough structure of distraction
and, through two examples, two variations on that structure. In
both instances I am pulled away from the present object: in one
the distractor lifts me forward toward an anticipated situation,
while in the second I am dragged down. Here we resume our
description of a moment in which I discover that I am ambivalent.
It is an instance in which the focal object is not an ambivalent
one but the distractor is. I am preparing for a lecture and the
notes appear in such a way that it is difficult for me to embody
them. While I am attending to them, that is, while they are my
focal object, I am not over at them. I cannot "get into" them;
but neither am I able to examine them intently at a distance by
assuming, for example, an analytic posture. There is a disaffection,
in the sense of an alienation from them. More than this, my bodily
sense is that I am mildly disoriented. I sense this generally and
indiscriminately, not simply in regard to the focal object. The
atmosphere of the situation is one in which there are no clear
landmarks; I am not sure of my bearings. When I attempt to
enact bodily the form of this disaffected relation to the lecture
notes and the general structure of this situation of "being lost,"

I begin to realize a variant of the spatiality of distraction. There is a peripheral concern distracting me that I had not quite noticed before. However, its "pull," the phenomenal space of its force, is not simply dragging me down or thrusting me forward. My being distracted is not a bodily oppressive heaviness or a euphoric lightness. The way I am distracted is in being disoriented. Now as I stay more directly with it, that disorientation appears as a sense of being "neither here nor there." Further, it is clear that the disorientation is a residual bodily sense. As I carried the lilt of the marching band after witnessing the parade, in an earlier example, here I bodily bear the effect of an earlier engagement with an object that is now peripheral, unposited, and distracting in a peculiar way. The present landscape now appears as a portable one. At this point, I can now enact the spatiality of this situation as shown in figure 5.

Here I have an incipient understanding of the texture and structure of a moment in which I first discover that I am ambivalent. When the ambivalent object is as yet unposited, I experience a certain bodily disorientation and a correlative landscape and atmosphere that effectively preclude the full presentation of and engagement in a presently intended object. As I turn to this particular variation of objects of distraction while still attempting to stay with its initial horizontal presence, instead of a shadowy entity pulling me toward it, there appears, as it were, a contradictory thing, something that at once pushes and pulls me. It is a monolithic entity from which issues a field of attraction/repulsion. I am not pulled toward it or repulsed, but invited at once to approach and retreat. Finding no resolution, I can only take it up as such. I readily recognize the bodily residue of dealing with this object

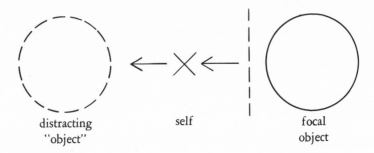

distracting   self   focal
"object"   object

FIGURE 5

in a sense of disorientation, of not knowing which way to go and losing my way.

As I posit it again now, I recognize that the ambivalent object, that which was distracting me, is the project of writing the present book. What further constitutes it as an ambivalent object?

Structures of the Object in Ambivalence

The powerful field of an ambivalent object. *One way to further explicate the ambivalent object in general is to return now to this particular ambivalent object. By beginning with it in its particularity as it appears when I am living it, working on the book, I can arrive at general structures of an ambivalent object. We shall do so in a moment. But it should be clear that the bodily modes of apprehension under scrutiny here do not require this move to the particular. In fact, in a sense, I am closer to the structure as such before I make this move. After all, I am already bearing the presence of both the texture and structure of an ambivalent object. It is this that we uncovered in the way that the lecture notes appeared and the way I was living that moment, a being neither here nor there. Already being bodily informed by an ambivalent object but having "forgotten" it, it had informed my world. Precisely this nonthetic, bodily presence most clearly and singularly accentuates the structure of the phenomenon. By lingering in it, I am closer to the shape of the phenomenon. It is at hand or in my hands for it is through the body that the structure is originally coconstituted. These bodily modes are most poignant when I bear the phenomenon but am not presently positing an instance of it.*

Again, the project is present as a task that at once attracts and repels me. While there are two distinct invitations implicit here, to move toward and to move away, as I first posit an ambivalent object the invitation is univocal. While all objects invite me to take them up in some way, to act in a particular way in regard to them, the invitation issued by an ambivalent object is problematic. As a result I readily find myself balking at its peculiar invitation. It requires me to act but it will not let me act. Our relation is stalled at the initial meeting stage for I am asked both to approach and not to approach. That in a singular act I cannot resonate with its implicit call highlights that aspect

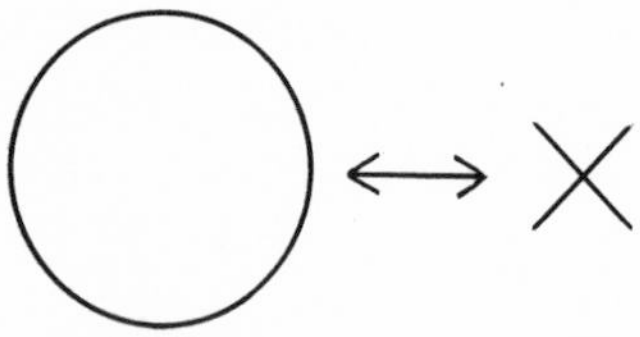

ambivalent   self
object

FIGURE 6

of the object that is its force. It is not necessarily more forceful, but its forces are relatively more figural. It is as if I approach the president or my boss—power predominates. At first, I know only it. Its prevalence is immediately felt, correlatively, as a modification of the space as I near the seat of power, and bodily, as I must inhabit that space. The relatively salient field of forces, then, is a simultaneous push and pull. When I take it up bodily I am tossed and turned as a ship on a turbulent sea. The generating moment of my subsequent sense of disorientation is clear. True to its etymology, the ambivalent object is power-laden; in its presence strength is salient (see figure 6).

As a way of defining the present methodology of bodily reflective modes in contrast to other methods, it is interesting to note a shift in the description immediately above. The paragraph begins with more dialogical, more personal, more personifying descriptions such as "invitation," "act," and "meeting." There is then a shift to a vocabulary of bodily sensitivity and to metaphors of impact and power and their spatiality. Of course, our inclusion of these latter is indicative of more than a stylistic penchant or even an allegiance to a certain ontology. Descriptives of body and space express directly the investigator's use of certain bodily modes of presence and reflection as a favored access to the structure of a phenomenon.

When I do lapse into the language of the former, it is sometimes to correct a certain unintended and unnecessary consequent of the description of body and bodily behavior. The use of bodily modes and the language of the body suggest that the lived body is merely reactive, that it is formed by the phenomenon, that if "I" consist of any agentic capacities, they are distinct from my bodily powers. To stress the role of bodily awareness in this method, I have re-

frained from saying "I feel" or "I grasp" or "I act." Yet to say the "body acts" seems awkward. Hence, occasionally I leave the unintended impression that the formative power is exclusively in the other direction—that the body is acted upon by the phenomenon. To clarify our intent, "body" here always is inseparable from "body-subject," an entity that, while it is embedded in the world, is the agent, myself. Our thesis is precisely that the body and the bodily are a primary locus of the active creation of meaning, that the body is coconstitutive of the structure of phenomena.

It seems that we have been describing that aspect of the ambivalent object which is, in Bleuler's term, the volitional. In the present example, being at once pushed and pulled accentuates a failure of will—of being unable to decide whether or not to complete the book. But while they are distinguishable, I cannot have the push and the pull without the attraction and the repulsion, the love and the hate. While I can write the book without loving it, to be pulled to the task is to want to do it and to be with it. "Emotional" and "volitional" ambivalence are of a piece, at least in this moment when I am first discovering the peculiar gravitational field of ambivalence.

As I now begin to surrender to this peculiar variant of distraction, I find the spatiality of push/pull and the bodily sense of being tossed and turned, of being neither here nor there, hard to sustain.

Again, I intentionally continue to inhibit positing the horizonal object, here the ambivalent object that is the whole project of writing this book. If I were to posit it or when I do, I typically am forced to take it up in its particularity. I am flooded by the concrete particulars of my ambivalence; the explicit pros and cons leap to mind. While I can move from them to the bodily sense of those arguments and hence, eventually, to the texture and structure of my relation to an ambivalent object, I can also approach that shape through a bodily enactment which stays at the more general level. Further, this inhibited approach with its affinity for staying with the generic, while it eventually embraces the same phenomenon, does so in a slowed motion that allows me to enact with more differentiation and articulation how we get together, what constitutes taking up an ambivalent object.

No longer spinning without direction, I am now split bodily. I feel my two sides, my left and my right, each with its own powers, jurisdictions, and inclinations. A sense of the symmetry of my carriage gives way to that of a split allegiance, of two different ways. Virtually enacting this yields a correlative change in the field—it is now divided. The prepotency of the field still clouds its source in the as-yet unposited object, but that field is now two distinct avenues, an egress from and an ingress to a concealed hub of power (see figure 7).

The ambivalent object as a dipole. With this I now succumb to an initial objectification of the ambivalent object as such. The field of force, once like the rings of clouds surrounding and obscuring its planet, breaks up and is partially absorbed as an inherent aspect of the object. Having turned to the object, force is less salient and I have a sense of the shape of the object. The contradictory complex of force has become an object with the simple structure of a regional bifurcation, effected by a slight invagination at its midline. There appears this largely indiscriminate object with the structure of a dipole, an object nascently separated within itself. While there is as yet no posited particularization of the object as a whole or of any contrasting regional characteristics, power has been transformed to or perhaps tamed by a sense of the differentness across the incipient divide. Any residual sense of power is the modulated and equal pull of both sides (see figure 8).

This now-posited ambivalent object invites me in a way that allows me to approach. I can act with respect to it as I could not, with respect neither to it nor the then-focal object, when ambivalence was only a horizonal and distracting presence. When living in the atmosphere of ambivalence, by contrast to the direct posited presence of the ambivalent object, the drive in or thrust of my life is muted. Being in that atmosphere I do not carry forward any other present project. Being stuck in the neither-here-nor-there

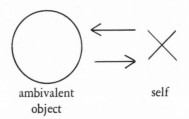

ambivalent   self
object

FIGURE 7

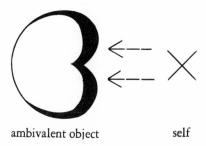

ambivalent object   self

FIGURE 8

of the presence of ambivalence that remains horizonal, I am un-
productive. Below, we will consider this as a way of living ambivalence, of dealing with it by failing to address it.

When I do take up the invitation to approach the present bipolar structure, I readily find myself living in the writing project
in a way that is characteristic of this initial stage of the assumption
of ambivalence. The modality of that experience is variable: usually
explicit thought, sometimes visual imagination. For example,
within a moment of my engagement, whether actual or virtual, I
have the explicit convictions that the project is a meaningful one,
that the target phenomenon is a way to do phenomenology, that
there is a potentially significant contribution to that field in the
project. These positive beliefs about the project are more or less
elaborated, again, sometimes in discursive thought, sometimes in
the form of imaginal fantasy. However, they give way to their
respective negations. The phenomenon and the method with it are
illusory; there is nothing there; I have nothing to contribute. The
negation is just that, the collapse of its positive. At this point it
does not sustain a fantasy—I do not see myself writing drivel or
embarrassedly receiving publishers' rejections. The project is simply
gone; again, there is nothing there. In this way various aspects are
explicated as "I can write" becomes "I cannot write"; or the
importance of writing becomes its unjustifiability.

In the positive pole, the affected body is that fullness and completion of self that we often feel when engaged in a meaningful
task, or, perhaps more saliently, when we momentarily leave it and
become aware that we still "have" it to return to. In the negation,
there is an emptiness, a sense of being left with nothing.

The sequence by which we effect the structure of this moment

FIGURE 9

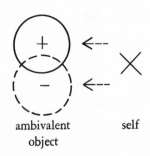

ambivalent   self
object

*in the experience of ambivalence is apparently at variance with
earlier methodological sequences. Here the typical experience for
which we seek the structure often begins in words, as the modality
of the engagement can be an explicitly thoughtful one. The content of various aspects of this particular instance of an ambivalent
object is the stuff of the lived experience. When the immediately
given is contentual, the possibility of utilizing an inductive method
is present. Of course, it could be argued from a Husserlian position
that even in the case of ideas, instances lined up reveal their common structure when we "look through" them and "intuit" them.
Still, the inclination to induce from these particulars to an inte-
grating concept is undeniably difficult to inhibit. A concept such as
"from a positive to its negation" may be arrived at in this way.
But this does not preclude the use of the reflective postures espoused
here. Whether the primary modality of my engagement in a phenomenon is perceptual, imaginal, behavioral, or explicitly thoughtful, there is a correlative bodily being affected and a bodily sense.
The presence of the positive and its negation and the movement
between them has a bodily realizable appearance.*

The peculiar movement through which I begin to particularize
the bipolar entity effects a change in its shape. The two poles are
not there both at once as in the case of an entity with a bipolar
organization; rather, one gives way to the other. Further, the
second is only there as the absence of the first. There are two
spheres, the one only the shadowy collapse of the other, its anti-
matter, a black hole (see figure 9). The movement between the
two does not advance or resolve anything. I do not settle on one
or the other; nor do I arrive at a reasonable, hence supportive,
hope which somehow integrates the two possibilities. The movement is between all and nothing. Both the nonprogressiveness and

the radical extremes with no middle term are hallmarks of various moments in the experience of ambivalence.

But eventually there is a progression here, and with it a modification in this space. The negation becomes a possible object in its own right. For example, the negation of the conviction that I might have something to contribute is now positively embodied as the possibility of enjoying my interests without necessarily being productive. Or instead of simply losing my conviction that I can or that I want to be involved in this largely solitary task, I form the positive intention of spending more time with my family. Sometimes I discover this shift from the second pole as negation to the second pole as a positive converse of the first in the midst of my engagement in the first. While at the writing desk, I find myself well ensconced in watching the birds in the field outside or imagining a hike through that field. This can happen numerous times before the day, pen still in hand, I am able to admit to myself that I would rather be out there than in here. With this recognition other particular negative aspects of the primary project give way to their respective positive converses, and a set of oppositions develops: working on the paper/playing with my child; structuring my day around the paper/letting things happen as they may. The two poles form a space now that is less connected. I occasionally enter into or live the one without a direct reference to the other. It is as if there are now two alternative objects or projects. For the first time there is some disjunction between the two, but beyond that newly found discretion it is not clear how they are related to each other through me—whether there is the possibility or perhaps the necessity of choosing between them or the possibility of doing both or neither. They only appear on balance as equally alluring. They are simply two possibilities for me; I am not torn between them (see figure 10).

The world of ambivalence. From this position I find myself exploring each. Again, I do so through any number of modalities—doing, imagining, thinking, inquiring of other people's experiences. Aspects, attributes, associations, eventualities, risks attendant to each appear as horizons which when taken up themselves constitute complex and ultimately opaque regions. Taking these together, I begin to constitute respective worlds out of each of the two objects; and, in that each is also a prospective place and way *I* might live, I constitute a prospective self or identity.

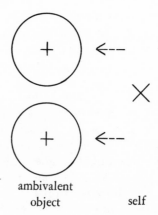

ambivalent
object   self

FIGURE 10

Committing myself to the completion of this long-term writing project, I would give up much of my spare time. Also, some of my other work would need to be pared down. I would discipline myself to stay with it, and I would structure my life around it. I would be a thinker, reader, scholar, academician, critic and assimilator of ideas, a contributor to a community of ideas. . . . I would be doing what I have thought I could do well and have enjoyed in the past.

Relinquishing the project's claim on me, I might constitute a second world in which I could be more with and more engaged in my child, my wife and her interests, the extended family. I might enjoy myself in a relaxed way, indulge myself, go on hikes, be out there with the animals and trees, do things for other people, be open to the developments of the culture around me, be a good citizen. . . .

I have presented these two explorations and subsequent world-creations as if they arose and were present independent of each other. To some extent such an independence is a common moment in the experience of ambivalence. As the second pole itself becomes a positive possibility and in that moment gains both some separation from the first pole and a more or less equal footing with it, there is a period when each can be embodied, differentiated within itself, articulated and made more substantial. I can realize the respective horizons and implications of each while "forgetting" the comparison between the two emerging worlds or at least keeping

that comparison in the background (see figure 11). Each appears
as a trip I might plan or a vision I might have, without reference
to the other. Each appears only as a *prospective* world and self.
When it occurs as I have just described, this moment is a respite
from the experience of ambivalence.

Ambivalence as world shifts. More often, however, as the two
worlds are constituted, they are so despite the continuing presence
in each of the implication of their respective counterparts. The
structure of this threatening and apparently contaminating mutual
insinuation can be explicated now.

In a moment in which I am exploring the possible world of
family or play (the second world in our example), I begin to
notice that I am distracted. At first the distraction has the structure
of the horizonal presence of an unposited ambivalent object. I am
feeling neither here nor there without explicating with respect to
what. As I move beyond the sense of that pushing and pulling field
of forces to a bimodal object the two regions of which pull me
equally, I realize that that distracting object is an *aspect,* a singular
feature, of this prospective world. The first explication of this
aspect consists of a positive belief, to wit, I can really live or live
fully by playing or being with my family; and its negation, I cannot
really live with those as center. The singular feature is the question
of the self-fulfillment of family life. As we have described, the
positive and its shadowy negation readily become two positive
and contending convictions: I can really live through family and
play; I can really live by writing.

In general, what is going on here is a working out of the earlier

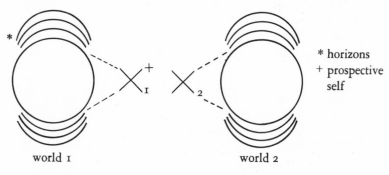

world 1   world 2

* horizons
\+ prospective
  self

FIGURE 11

sequence of structural changes limited to an intended object, although now in the context of two possible worlds. At any moment in the exploration of either world, an aspect of that world can be the occasion, mutatis mutandis, of the experience of a "new" ambivalent "object." To integrate that earlier description with its current extension in the context of the exploration of an aspect of two possible worlds, a fuller, although necessarily partial because ongoing, sequence might be as follows:

a. Original unambivalent intended object: I want to finish this writing project.

b. First negation: I do not want to finish this writing project.

c. Positive embodiment of first negation: I want to be with my family.

d. Aspect of positive embodiment of first negation: I can fulfill myself through family.

e. This aspect negated (second negation): I cannot fulfill myself through family.

f. Positive embodiment of second negation: I can fulfill myself by finishing this writing project.

It should be clear that when we return to the first world (at *f*), it is no longer the same world as when we left it (at *a* and *b*). We shall describe the potential progressiveness of world shifts in a section below. The shift here (at *f*) back to the first world is accomplished by the positive embodiment of an aspect of that evolving prospective world, here the aspect of potential self-fulfillment through that world. Obviously, there is an indeterminate set of such aspects, each of which can occasion a world shift. Any such aspect can go through a sequence that recapitulates, at the level of aspect and with respect to an evolving prospective world, that sequence with which we began at the level of unposited ambivalent object present as an atmosphere of distraction (see figure 12).

To reiterate, each world consists of horizonal aspects, each of which may be made thetic. Any one of these aspects can have the horizontal presence of ambivalent distraction. When taken up, each can yield a sequence through which ambivalence is realized and eventuates in a shift to that aspect's counterpart in the other world. This is possible because each world consists of a host of implicit aspects which themselves consist in a positive and a negative pole.

Ambivalent Aspects

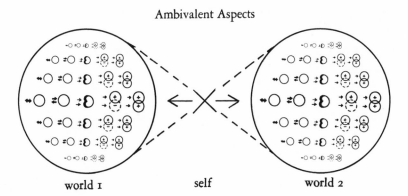

world 1   self   world 2

FIGURE 12

The positive is a positive embodiment of the negation of an original positive in the other world. The negative is a negation of this positive, and can be realized as a positive at a fresh level of the other world.

Ambivalence as a particular aspect at issue. A further possibility now reveals itself within the thickets of the structure of ambivalence. I can thematize any one of these aspects as such. Any and all aspects of my ambivalence about the writing project may be taken as an issue or concern—significance/happiness, risk/security, competence/incompetence, alone/together, work/play, thought/activity, verticality/horizontality. My ambivalence can come to center not on whether or not the writing project is significant, but on whether significance or happiness is more important to me, or whether they can occur together, or whether I have or will attain one or the other.

To illustrate this, at some point in the exploration of my ambivalence about the present long-term writing project, I discover another aspect of it which is the riskiness of undertaking this project as against the security of devotion to family life. A genetic phenomenology of this aspect by and large follows a progression similar to that of the question of fulfillment, and we need not present it fully here. In general, there are obvious contexts (economic, social) in which commitment to the project is a risk, while staying more centrally with my regular work round and family situa-

tion offers more security. Going back the other way on a different
level, however, there is a sense in which making family the center
is a new venture, while writing is a task in which, because of a
history of moderate success, I am quite secure.

In the later moments of this round, there is a strong sense that
the path being followed is a familiar one, that I am in a familiar
space. I have a sense that these moves back and forth between
riskiness and security, wherein the riskiness of the project gives way
to a sense in which it is secure and conversely with respect to
family, have been a common ground over which I have passed
in contexts other than this present ambivalence about the writing
project.

Through recourse to the familiar space and its correlative bodily
sense, I can recall a situation in which they were present. I recall
a relationship with a woman many years in my past. While I
can readily indulge a reverie of that time, when I direct myself
to the sense of familiarity, the common structure in that situation
can be clarified. After a period of being in love with this woman,
I began to have a distracting sense of something lacking. The
woman was exciting, stimulating, a challenge to me; she was also
unpredictable, utterly beyond my control, a high risk. The "something missing" was a more secure, more peaceful, and more ac-
commodating relationship, all of which I soon embodied in a
fantasy of another woman. To abbreviate the description of a
tumultuous period, I met a woman upon whom to play out such
a fantasy, and left the first. Then, discovering that another side of
security is boredom and self-deflation, I returned to the first. From
this "fresh" level, risk and excitement appeared as sustaining,
as a requisite condition for "securing" a relation. To the detriment
of my graduate work at the time, more world shifts ensued, first in
actuality, then constrained to my imagination, as variations of
"securing" risk gave way to risky security. The resultant dizzying
circle, a second-order structure, is the familiar space common to
my ambivalence about the writing project and that racy woman.
(Of course, I also now have the metaphor—riskiness is a racy
woman.)

To reiterate this feature of ambivalence, we have described how
a given ambivalent object consists of an indeterminate number of
aspects and how in a complexly lived but explicable way any one
of those aspects is demonstrably a constitutive part of two possible

worlds to which the ambivalence gives rise. I can explicate the sense in which both the possible worlds of a long-term writing project and that project's refusal, positively embodied in a more conventional clinical practice and family life, have their respective attendant risks and securities. In reflection, when I form the peculiar space that is the structure of this aspect, I recognize it as familiar and am led to discover that the given aspect is a feature of other ambivalent periods in my life.

With the discovery that risk/security occurs in a number of instances of ambivalence and that in each of those contexts it is lived as a similar set of moves and hence a certain structure, it is possible to take that aspect as a dimension, to find precisely it at issue. At such a point my ambivalence no longer is simply whether or not to undertake or complete this writing project: it is such questions as whether to live life dangerously or seek the safe harbor. The dimension risk/security is now the object of my ambivalence. By embodying the peculiar space that is common to the instantiations of risk/security, I can move, not to further instances of which it is an aspect, but to the issue of risk/security—to my ambivalence about that. Explicating this new ambivalent object, it may be followed or taken through a set of structures to eventuate in two prospective worlds—the worlds of risk and security. In turn, these could be explored as to their constitutive aspects.[14]

It is apparent, then, that typically in a late stage of the experience of ambivalence, there is a reversal with respect to the object occasioning the ambivalence and its constitutive aspects. The occasioning circumstance flips from foreground to background as aspect is dimensionalized and, itself focally at issue, becomes that about which I am ambivalent. Each aspect subtends a dimension which itself is a potential object of ambivalence. Of course, it should be clear that this is not to say that any particular dimension, like risk/security, is constitutive of ambivalence in general.

While to this point I have been largely faithful to the method under consideration, it would appear that here I backslide. With the explication of dimensions, am I not discussing themes or categories; am I not in the midst of language while I sought to explicate phenomena in a prelinguistic domain, arguing that there I am closer to experience as lived?

In everyday experience we thematize how we are living; we put into words what we are experiencing. As a way of experiencing, thematizing itself appears as a bodily sense. Our living of our language and the correlative bodily sense of words may be explicated through the application of reflective bodily postures. To the degree that it is meaningful to me, that is, to the degree that it evokes or embodies phenomena as lived, I can live a word and articulate its space. Although given in a different context, James's statement as follows is applicable here: "We ought to say a feeling of and, *a feeling of* if, *a feeling of* but, *and a feeling of* by *quite as readily as we say a feeling of* blue *or a feeling of* cold" *(his emphasis).*[15]

To summarize this presentation of the basic structure of ambivalence, several questions implicit in it may be gathered together. Earlier discussion of certain conceptualizations of the phenomenon in the psychological literature led to the notion that ambivalence consisted of opposite feelings simultaneously directed to one object. But is there one object of my ambivalence or two? Is the object(s) limited to a person; is the intended object limited to its concrete presence in a particular situation? What is the sense of "simultaneous" and of "opposite"; are these limited to feelings?

The object in ambivalence is complex and variable in shape, kind, and even number, for ambivalence is more like an unfolding drama than a single moment or a discrete event. As engaged audience, I have known ambivalence as a sense of being neither here nor there with respect to an object which has not yet made its first entrance, as a character who has power over me before I can yet identify him. But I have been ambivalent also with respect to an object that is more like a setting than a character. I have known ambivalence as two mises-en-scène that doom me continually to drop through a trap door to their respective counterparts.

Although in an early possible moment in its genesis I am ambivalent before I yet posit any object of my ambivalence, and although at a later moment I intend a single object which is beginning to reproduce itself as if by meiosis, still relatively early in a genetic phenomenology of ambivalence there is an emergence of a second object. Once I refuse to love her with all her faults, once I lean away from being with someone or doing something, the embodiment of that inclination quickly follows, even if only as an incipient nay-saying. When I refuse to assimilate the negatives into the positive, they begin to stand on their own as a second object. The simultaneous attraction and repulsion to one object,

the traditional definition of ambivalence, is an early and evanescent moment.

But, more critically, the concept does not embrace the general
structure of ambivalence, particularly its structure at the noematic
or object side. In ambivalence, there is always a bipolar system.
If I intend one object ambivalently, that object implies a second
which, in turn, implies the first: the relation of implication is
reciprocal. When the two poles are objects, they may be any kind
of object, from persons to tasks to dimensions, and they may be
present in any modality. However, the two poles need not be
objects. They can be ways of taking up objects, like two ways of
living; or they can consist of a certain type of "object," like two
evolving prospective worlds.

There is a dipolar system even when the second object is only
implied as a negation of the first. Even when the first object is
as yet unposited, there is always a presence of an implicit dipolarity,
a field of forces which itself implies two poles.

At the noematic side, ambivalence is a variable but delimitable
set of systems which have in common a dipolar structure. Whether
separate objects or worlds or whether parts of the same object or
project, there are two; and each implies the other whether by con-
taining it as the presence of an absence, leading to it, or temporarily
denying it or negating it. Each is a vital doppelgänger to the other,
as if their lives depended on each other.

Ambivalent Ways of Being

While we have explicated this basic shape of the object of ambivalence by recourse to a bodily knowledge, by a sensitivity both
to how it affects me bodily and how I tacitly follow its movement
as my own potential movement, in doing so we have largely faced
away, ironically, from the side of the subject. In the section to
follow I will attend more to the ambivalent person, to personal
differences as to style and pervasiveness of ambivalence. However,
it is already apparent that what is finally at stake in ambivalence
is myself. Even when I am living in one pole, experimentally or
forgetfully, even when the other pole is only a dimly felt lack,
what I already dread is an occasion of my redefinition. The polar
pulls, whether the vague intimation of another side or its sudden
numinous and disruptive upsurge, all tug at my integrity. On the

subject side, the correlative of the dipole is my "being between" the parts of that system. The tension of being caught between, that which I face when I turn to *my* ambivalence, is the necessity of a change in self. Whether the violent death of disintegration, the slower death of the inertia of indecision, or the creative or productive resolution of two possibilities, at bottom *I* am the issue.

The constitution of an object or system as ambivalent is a potential of any moment, object, or aspect of experience. As I have shown, the first order or interior structure of such a set of constituting acts at the object pole is a set of variable dipolar shapes eventuating in two evolving prospective worlds. The shapes of the paths between those worlds I shall refer to as second-order structures of ambivalence. Here I associate those interplanetary paths with attempts to resolve the tension of the dipole, as variable ways of dealing with being ambivalent. These attempted resolutions, which I will refer to as *positions,* consist of various self-dipolar system relations, variable ways I stand in relation to a given ambivalent surround. The resolutions may be entrenched like dispositions and hence describe a typology of the ambivalent personality; or they themselves may be a part of typical sequences of positions for any person. These, then, are not constitutive features of ambivalence but individual differences or developmental differences with respect to ambivalence.

Holding off. Given the discovery that I am ambivalent, I can take up a position external to the dipole. For that moment, I refuse to live through either pole, either possible world. We will describe the geography and topography of this particular self-implication as the "held-off" position of ambivalence.[16] In holding off, I am attempting to separate myself from the dipolar system. My mode of experience is logical, rational, and analytic. I decide between the two possibilities by transforming them into orderly lists or inventories, or a flowchart of branching alternatives. I weigh them and sort them, on the one hand and on the other, without dirtying my hands, through an inferential process rather than by directly grasping them. Keeping them at arm's length, external and distant, they do not weigh on me. I am not tossed about by them; I avoid being in the throes of ambivalence. The objects appear small as well as distant, for my attention is split between them and my method, how I am observing, inferring, and the like. Through this latter focus I prevent them from dividing me, from luring me nearer, from succumbing to their attractive but diverging display. There is a certain self-consciousness and self-confidence, an enlargement of myself relative to the objects.

I distance the two poles not only from me but from each other by identifying each with its own list of pros and cons, by keeping them on opposite sides of a ledger. I keep them separated by objectifying them, by refusing to take them up as two possible worlds, each of which, inclusive and opaque, would force me to meet the other on a ground and in a way I could not anticipate.

Holding off gives me control. That I develop both sides symmetrically, in balance, maintains them as equally weighted. I do not step into possible future worlds, nor am I "about to be" in a different way. The correlative of the objectification at the noematic pole is a sense of self as relatively unembedded in them, as uncontingent. I am the agent who will decide in his own time. By objectifying, by residing in an intellective process, I step out of the stream to enter only at my own will. The suspension of time, the suspension of feelings, the distantiation and objectification, all contribute to a stabilization of my relation to the ambivalent object. Further, it appears as a stability which I have constructed and which I can maintain until I resolve my ambivalence.

However, holding off sometimes is a position in which I get stuck and which does not lead to resolution. In that I systematize and categorize the two poles in a balanced way, their contradictoriness is highlighted and sustained. I neither allow either pole to move, nor do I follow either pole in a direction for which the other does not immediately and logically compensate. There is no momentary veering into space, no directionality in the movement of the system. Correlatively, I have no direction except keeping the two lined up. Bodily, my indifference is a sense of having no leanings. My only inclination is to utilize a sense of the symmetry of my body to hold everything straight, squared.

My cautiousness, my controlledness, my disinclination to move except to maintain the balance are self-protective against the way in which ambivalence is upsetting, particularly and often dramatically at its onset. Ambivalence is a dishabituation in which I am pulled from a present commitment to an object, a relation, a project, or a world. That coconstituting and coconstituted relation is now in question. The split in the object at once severs our relation and threatens to split me asunder by dividing my allegiance. Ambivalence is the experience of a seemingly unsolicited invitation to act, to take a new stand. It is at once the loss of a habit, of a sustaining structure, and an opening onto new opportunity. The initial sense that the now-ambivalent object would unground me, that any new possibility, being only a negation, would be unfulfillable and unsupporting, and the ongoing sense that any possibilities would be enduring bifurcations or seamless contradictions all occasion the present protective position. In holding off, I at least temporarily inhibit action, even that virtual action or that imaginative leap which are the acts by which I embody a possible future. Refusing to enter into the indeterminate space and unresolved future of the dipole, I construct a superordinate space which contains the system but at a distance. Within this new structure, I exercise a new habit which is a peculiarly inhibited and intellectualized form of exploration.

I explore without living through, without taking up possible moves. I come to know two sets of brachiating options without tunneling through them. At its pathological extremes, in holding off I am L. Salzman's obsessive, who lives in order to control;[17] or, more primitively, V. von Gebsattel's compulsive, who disavows at once the completion of any act, the fulfillment of even the most mundane intention, and the entrance into a future with its abandonment of self to find oneself anew.[18] In this psychotic compulsivity, action collapses into a set of ritual movements whose only intercourse is with each other; while in the obsessive posture, which is more directly akin to holding off, consideration reduces to a set of balanced categories that are fixed and laminated with respect to each other. When the position of holding off is not preparatory to some form of active participation, or when a decision is reached exclusively through this external consideration, holding off is a pseudo-exploration stabilized by the very condition that initially destabilizes—the fact of the dipolarity, of there always being two sides.

The refusal to participate in the life of the ambivalent object is also the refusal of the lived body, for it only lives by active intercourse with objects. The "on the one hand . . . on the other," which is part of the bodily sense of holding off, is a dessicated, vestigial sense of the lived body for it only knows the moves of a logic which serves to disengage me from the issue at hand. From

the point of view of the present method of bodily modes of reflection, holding off is the denial of the necessity for a phenomenology in the task of reaching understanding. It refuses to enter
the dialectic of the return, the living through, and the virtual enactment in order to know.

*In this description I have turned the present bodily reflective
methods against a relatively disembodied posture, a relation of
externality between knower and known, and an intellectualist
mode. This demonstrates that the relatively disembodied is incarnate and embodiable, which is to say that it has or consists in
an embodied sense of itself and its relation to its object. Again,
I can know and explicate even abstract or logical thought by virtual
enactment.*

Living in. On the other hand, I can take up a position in which I
am ambivalent largely by living in one or another of its object poles.
When I do so I am intimate with each in turn. I take up each
allowing myself to be absorbed in or to inhabit each. Through this
alternating living in arrangement I come to know each by trying
it out, by seeing how I fit in. But as I am a participating resident,
at the same time I am shaping it by my own occupancy, however
transient my stay. I can approach each object or world as an experiment in living. While I can actually live in one pole or the other,
I can also entertain them as possibilities through fantasy. In this
latter mode, I can be there and explore without reservation. I can
fully let any possibility go where it would.

To some extent, while I am in such, my sense of time is like the
temporality of play.[19] I am taking time off, time away; this time
does not count. Time is set off from that time remaining to the
completion of my actual present projects. But in that this fanciful
exploration is also part of being ambivalent, an anticipated future
is horizonal in which this present "as if" world will become a
more or less fulfilling project or relation. Each possible world of
ambivalence is like a camp whose activities temporarily catch me
and carry me along. I live in it presumptively as a complete setting, as a fulfilling surround that meets all my needs, precisely to
see if it does so.

Is a second camp present in the first and, if so, in what way?
While so exploring, in what sense am I still ambivalent? There
are various possibilities here within the "living in" position. At

one extreme, when I have not yet posited that I am ambivalent,
I am actually living in a world without recognizing that there is
another possibility. Or, having confronted that fact, I have now
conveniently forgotten it. In this latter instance, I sometimes actively deny any other possibility by seeing only the positive features of the present circumstance, in the manner of a hysterical
mode of experiencing.[20] The former is sometimes a setting for the
discovery of ambivalence. By contrast to the moment of discovery
already described, in which a slow and prolonged constitution of
the ambivalent object begins with its mildly nagging and distracting presence as an external horizon, when the presently engaging object is itself one side of the ambivalence, the other side
can suddenly and intrusively show itself.[21] This first appearance of
an alternative, and hence the initial onslaught of ambivalence, is
a dramatic entrance. For a moment, I cannot understand what I
had seen in the first side. If I continue in this hysterical mode
I can now delusively idealize the second and unceremoniously
bury the first. At this extreme I am "living in" alternatingly but
not experimentally. While I feel little of the tension of the bipolarity, there is also no carry-over or advance; failing to accept my
ambivalence, I am not moving toward its resolution. Refusing even
this occasional nonprogressive flip-flop, I can disown the bodily
sense of the other side and reify it as a bodily symptom. I know
the other side now only as the headache that is the occasional and
"dissociated" side effect of my present habitation.

At the other extreme, as the world shifts accelerate, I begin to
be shaken from the position of living in ambivalence. I have no
sooner set up camp when I find myself imagining that campsite
I just left or might discover farther down the river. I begin to be
unable to establish a complete setting, to take up even the most
transient residence. I lose the ability to explore a possibility, for
the other side immediately pulls me from it. As the movement
from one to the other becomes my chief occupation, I am no longer
living in ambivalence; I am now "in conflict," a new and distinct
position.

Conflict. While a danger in the holding-off position is that I can
become stuck in objectifications and thereby lose access to either
possibility or to the development of possibilities, in conflict I have
no egress, and no future. I am stuck in a vortex created in the

overlap of both possibilities as lived. In being intimate with both, there is the risk of being too open and of becoming subjected to them. They are not discrete poles but sprawling camps that have spread into each other. I no longer know either clearly for I am at their common periphery where they are mixed and indeterminable in character. If in the hysterical variation the two camps deny each other's existence by allowing me to live in either present setting as if it were my permanent family homestead, when in conflict I am never at home, being continually en route, being between them. Being in conflict highlights both the strength of both sides, that feature suggested by the etymology of ambivalence, and the way ambivalence places my self at stake. As the two camps displace each other in rapid succession, they appear to move closer to and be larger relative to a shrinking self. With the rapidity, I lose focus on either; they blur kaleidoscopically and I become dizzy. I can neither take up one or the other nor extricate myself by holding them off. I lose integrity and am out of control.

Beyond Ambivalence: Dialectical Experience

When the living-in position predominates without being extreme, I live in one camp, then another. Each is a living possibility, a potential context to be lived through. Each stay is adequate for me to become a member, to identify myself with the respective camp. I begin to know more and more about each as a possible way for me to live. But the other does not stand still while I reside in its counterpart, for the results of my exploration have a surprising efficiency. When I leave a first camp to live in the second, I enter it in a different place than where I left it. In this sense I learn that my exploration of the first results in a change of site of the second. Having explored an aspect of the first, my entrance into the second is at a point of complementarity. It is another way, a second convincing way when I live in it, of looking at the same aspect that was explored in the first. As this exploratory living in proceeds through subsequent shifts, I come to anticipate the one camp in the other, as another point of view. I welcome a subsequent shift with a certain curiosity as to how this new part of the landscape will look from the other side. And, again, since as resident I identify with the results of my exploration, the other camp is potentially moving me; I anticipate how I will change with or

through it. Both camps are movable abodes that reciprocally influence each other by their movements. They operate together for
me in a common exploration. I know and identify myself with
each as one moves or reveals more of itself and as I anticipate a
complementary progression in the other. With this there is a certain compatibility in size between self and the camps. I can fit
into them; I can enlarge with them. I feel confident that I can live
through each of them wherever they move. I accept that they may
continue to move and change in the future and that that change
is inseparable both from an act on my part, as I live in them, and
from subsequent change in myself.

In this there is the possibility of a genuine resolution of my ambivalence, both of a particular instance of ambivalence and of my
being ambivalent in general. When a particular instance of ambivalence has been either occasioned or crystallized by the necessity
for a decision, having lived through both possibilities in this way,
there is a sense of the acceptability of either way. While I must
choose to live one world in actuality, the second is known in
and through it. It is not known simply as what I could have done
or been—as an absence that pricks me. Rather, since its exploration as a possible world was part of the way I came to know the
world I chose, it is woven into the fabric of that present world.

More often, when a choice point is not apparently forced by
circumstance, as by a deadline, exploration by living in the two
poles redefines them. I hardly recognize the original alternative
for I am at a new place with its own incipient pushes and pulls,
eventually a new instance of ambivalence. The shape of change
here is spiral, a progressive circle that comes back at a different
place—by contrast both to the repetitive, fundamentally monoto-
nous circle of the holding-off position and the haphazard, ungrasp-
able and dizzying vortex of being in conflict.

When living-in is my typical way of dealing with ambivalence,
any particular instance of ambivalence is less critical, less trying,
less an emergency. Through living-in I come to expect a relation
of complementarity between both the two poles of a given object
of ambivalence and between them and myself, a relation of progressive change with which I can identify myself, of constructive
exploration, and of the possibility of the emergence of new possibilities, of options that transcend the original. In a sense, with
these expectations as background, the bipolarity of any moment of

ambivalence is no longer foundational. The sharpness of any particular bipolarity is dulled by a more general sense of a progressive inhabitation and exploration of a multifaceted, multipolar, inexhaustible reality.

We have suggested several second-order structures of ambivalence as a set of possible positions and movements of self vis-à-vis the dipole. The last position, living-in, fittingly leads back to a way of living, a way of knowing the world by living through it, by knowing it as it directly affects me, that has a certain sympathy with the bodily modes of doing phenomenology that we have been describing. A genuine resolution of ambivalence displaces it with a dialectic, demonstrating again, as it has been the burden of this book to show, that the dialectic itself may be explicated as a bodily way of living, abstracting, and understanding. The bodily application of dialectics to lived experience is a way to do phenomenology.

Notes

PREFACE

1   J. Derrida, *Of Grammatology*, trans. G. C. Spivak (Baltimore: Johns Hopkins University Press, 1976).

2   M. Merleau-Ponty, *Phenomenology of Perception*, trans. C. Smith (New York: Humanities Press, 1962).

3   M. Brown, "The New Body Psychotherapies," *Psychotherapy: Theory, Research, and Practice* 10, no. 2 (1973): 98–117.

4   E. Gendlin, *Experiencing and the Creation of Meaning* (New York: Free Press of Glencoe, 1962).

5   K. J. Shapiro and I. E. Alexander, *The Experience of Introversion: An Integration of Phenomenological, Empirical, and Jungian Approaches* (Durham, N.C.: Duke University Press, 1975).

6   K. J. Shapiro, "The Elusive in Experience," *Journal of Phenomenological Psychology* 6, no. 2 (1976): 135–52.

1   INTRODUCTORY CONCERNS

1   A. Georgi, *Psychology as a Human Science* (New York: Harper and Row, 1970).

2   T. S. Kuhn, *The Structure of Scientific Revolutions* (Chicago: University of Chicago Press, 1967).

3   R. S. Valle and M. King, *Existential-Phenomenological Alternatives for Psychology* (New York: Oxford University Press, 1978).

4   F. M. Buckley, "An approach to a Phenomenology of At-Homeness," in A. Georgi, C. T. Fischer, and R. Von Eckartsberg, eds., *Duquesne Studies in Phenomenological Psychology* (Pittsburgh: Duquesne University Press, 1971), 1:198–211.

5   W. F. Fischer, *Theories of Anxiety* (New York: Harper and Row, 1970).

6   A. Burton, J. J. Lopez-Ibor, and W. M. Mendel, *Schizophrenia as a Life-style* (New York: Springer, 1974).

7   J. H. van den Berg, *The Changing Nature of Man: Introduction to a Historical Psychology* (New York: Delta, 1975).

8   P. F. Colaizzi, "Psychological Research as the Phenomenologist Views It," in Valle and King, *Existential-Phenomenological Alternatives*, pp. 48–71.

9   G. Psathas and P. Becker, "The Experimental Reality: The Cognitive Style of a Finite Province of Meaning," *Journal of Phenomenological Psychology* 3, no. 1 (1972): 35–53.

10   R. Rosenthal, *Experimenter-Effects in Behavioral Research* (New York: Appleton Century Crofts, 1966); M. T. Orne, "On the Social Psychology of the Psychological Experiment: With Particular Reference to Demand Characteristics and Their Implications," *American Psychologist* 17 (1962): 776–83.

11   A. van Kaam, "Phenomenal Analysis: Exemplified by a Study of the Experience of 'Really Feeling Understood,'" *Journal of Individual Psychology* 16 (1959): 66–72.

12   R. J. Bernstein, *The Restructuring of Social and Political Theory* (Philadelphia: University of Pennsylvania Press, 1978), offers such a critique from several perspectives, notably that of critical theory.

13   While P. F. Colaizzi, *Reflection and Research in Psychology: A Phenomenological Study of Learning* (Iowa: Kendall/Hunt, 1973), makes important distinctions between empirical and individual reflection, these are distinctions between different objects of reflection. He does not attempt to describe reflection as a mode in itself.

14   Several papers at a symposium entitled "Applied Phenomenological Psychology" (American Psychological Association Convention, Washington, D.C., 1976) discussed this development.

15   Chapter 1 of Shapiro and Alexander, *The Experience of Introversion*, gives an extended example of this kind of reading of a theoretical text.

16   Colaizzi, *Reflection and Research in Psychology*.

17   H. Spiegelberg, *The Phenomenological Movement: A Historical Introduction* (The Hague: Martinus Nijhoff, 1969) 2:653–701.

18   R. D. Laing and D. G. Cooper, *Reason and Violence* (New York: Vintage, 1971).

19   For example, see chapters 5 and 6 of W. Kohler, *Gestalt Psychology* (New York: New American Library, 1947).

20   Derrida, *Of Grammatology*, pp. 52–53.

21   M. Natanson, *The Journeying Self: A Study in Philosophy and Social Role* (Reading, Mass.: Addison-Wesley, 1970).

22   R. Zaner, *The Way of Phenomenology* (New York: Pegasus, 1970), p. 36.

2 THE METHOD, PART ONE

1 H. Spiegelberg, *The Phenomenological Movement: A Historical Introduction* (The Hague: Martinus Nijhoff, 1969) 1:73.

2 M. Heidegger, *Being and Time*, trans. J. Macquarrie and E. Robinson (New York: Harper and Row, 1962), pp. 58–63. In this passage he introduces the possibility that a phenomenon may show or disclose itself.

3 W. James, *Psychology: The Briefer Course* (New York: Harper and Brothers, 1961), p. 28.

4 A. Giorgi, *Psychology as a Human Science* (Harper and Row, 1970), p. 176.

5 This is my reading of J. Derrida, *Of Grammatology*, trans. G. C. Spivak (Baltimore: Johns Hopkins University Press, 1976).

6 S. Sontag, *On Photography* (New York: Farrar, Straus and Giroux, 1977).

7 Ibid., pp. 15–16.

8 R. C. Ziller and D. E. Smith, "A Phenomenological Utilization of Photographs," *Journal of Phenomenological Psychology* 7, no. 2 (1977): 172–82, do indeed attempt to utilize photography as a method.

9 Sontag, *On Photography*, p. 24.

10 J. P. Sartre, *The Problem of Method* (London: Methuen, 1964) and *Search for a Method* (New York: Braziller, 1963).

11 M. Merleau-Ponty, *Phenomenology of Perception*, trans. C. Smith (New York: Humanities, 1962), p. 68.

12 Ibid.

13 D. Rapaport, M. Gill, and R. Schafer, *Psychological Diagnostic Testing* (New York: International Universities, 1968), p. 209.

14 J. H. van den Berg, *The Phenomenological Approach to Psychiatry* (Illinois: Charles C. Thomas, 1955), p. 62. "To write a treatise on swimming, he will first go for a swim."

15 J. Habermas, *Knowledge and Human Interests*, trans. J. Shapiro (Boston: Beacon, 1971).

16 See the critique of the "presumed virtue of pure description" in part 3 of R. J. Bernstein, *The Restructuring of Social and Political Theory* (Philadelphia: University of Pennsylvania Press, 1978).

17 E. Straus, "Aesthesiology and Hallucinations" in R. May et al., eds., *Existence: A New Dimension in Psychiatry and Psychology* (New York: Simon and Schuster, 1967), p. 148.

18 F. Saussure, *Course in General Linguistics*, trans. W. Baskin (New York: McGraw-Hill, 1966).

19 For a discussion of erasure or *sous rature*, see chapter 2 of Derrida, *Of Grammatology*, pp. 27–73.

20 For an introduction to J. Lacan, see *The Language of Self: The Function of Language in Psychoanalysis*, trans. A. Wilden (New York: Dell, 1968).

21 A. D. deWaelhens, *Schizophrenia: A Philosophical Reflection on Lacan's Structuralist Interpretation*, trans. W. VerEeke (Pittsburgh: Duquesne University Press, 1978), provides an application of Lacan's thought to psychosis.

22 The ontology implied in this statement is most fully explicated in Merleau-Ponty, *Phenomenology of Perception*.

23 M. Polanyi, *The Tacit Dimension* (New York: Doubleday, 1967), p. 4.

24 See the introductory remarks of N. Lawrence and D. O'Conner, eds., *Readings in Existential Phenomenology* (Englewood Cliffs, N.J.: Prentice-Hall, 1967), p. 14.

25 M. Scheler, "Towards a Stratification of the Emotional Life," in Lawrence and O'Conner, *Readings in Existential Phenomenology*, pp. 19–31.

26 Ibid., p. 28.

27 Ibid., p. 28.

28 M. Boss, *Psychoanalysis and Daseinanalysis* (New York: Basic, 1963), pp. 34–40.

29 Merleau-Ponty, *Phenomenology of Perception*, p. xiii.

30 E. Gendlin describes these terms and a therapeutic technique utilizing this possible access to the body in "Focusing," *Psychotherapy: Theory, Research and Practice* 6, no. 1 (1969): 4–15.

31 J. P. Sartre, *Being and Nothingness*, trans. H. Barnes (New York: Washington Square, 1971), p. 433.

32 Merleau-Ponty, *Phenomenology of Perception*, p. 62.

33 M. Merleau-Ponty, "The Child's Relation with Others," in *The Primacy of Perception*, trans. William Cobb et al., ed. J. M. Edie (Evanston, Ill.: Northwestern University Press, 1964), p. 119.

34 H. Ginsburg and S. Opper, *Piaget's Theory of Intellectual Development* (Englewood Cliffs, N.J.: Prentice-Hall, 1969), pp. 26–71.

35 H. S. Sullivan, *The Interpersonal Theory of Psychiatry* (New York: Norton, 1953), p. 29.

36 Merleau-Ponty, "Child's Relation," p. 125.

37 M. Mahler, *On Human Symbiosis and the Vicissitudes of Individuation* (New York: International Universities, 1968).

38 G. Bosch, *Infantile Autism* (New York: Springer-Verlag, 1970), p. 56.

39 Sullivan, *Interpersonal Theory of Psychiatry*, p. 9.

40 Ibid., p. 41.

41 Merleau-Ponty, "Child's Relation," p. 119.

42 Ginsburg and Opper, *Piaget's Theory*, p. 34.

43 Merleau-Ponty, "Child's Relation," p. 117.

215

44 R. Schafer, *Aspects of Internalization* (New York: International Universities, 1968), pp. 7–24.

45 See H. Kohut, *The Analysis of the Self* (New York: International Universities, 1971), pp. 40–43.

46 Merleau-Ponty, "Child's Relation," p. 135.

47 Ibid., p. 137.

48 Ibid., p. 118.

49 A. Schütz's discussion of Scheler is quoted in an editorial note to Scheler's essay, "Towards a Stratification," p. 21.

3 CONCEPTS OF STRUCTURE

1 Since Husserl, recent philosophical literature has further explicated structure by emphasizing its Gestalt nature. See Aron Gurwitsch, *The Field of Consciousness* (Pittsburgh: Duquesne University Press, 1964) and Richard Zaner, *The Context of Self: A Phenomenological Inquiry Using Medicine as a Clue* (Athens, Ohio: Ohio University Press, 1981). Zaner describes how any structure is a whole in which each part codetermines and is mirrored in the other parts. This mirroring notion is developed through the term "contexture" and is distinguished from context. Merleau-Ponty was also influenced by Gestalt theorists in his treatment of structure and is aware of this kind of reciprocal influence. Following Merleau-Ponty, in the present essay I primarily stay with a concept of structure as relations among parts. This is sufficient to develop my primary concern—the modes of apprehension of structure, for these constitute the method I propose.

2 Two introductory works on this broad intellectual movement are H. Gardner, *Quest for Mind: Piaget, Lévi-Strauss and the Structuralist Movement* (New York: Vintage, 1974) and M. Lane, ed., *Introduction to Structuralism* (New York: Basic, 1970).

3 P. Ricoeur, "From Existentialism to the Philosophy of Language" in C. Reagan and D. Stewart, eds., *The Philosophy of Paul Ricoeur* (Boston: Beacon, 1978), pp. 86–93.

4 Ibid., p. 90.

5 P. Caws, "What is Structuralism?" in E. N. and T. Hayes, eds., *Claude Lévi-Strauss: The Anthropologist as Hero* (Cambridge, Mass.: M.I.T. Press, 1970), p. 199.

6 Gardner, *Quest for Mind*, pp. 15–50.

7 Lane, *Introduction to Structuralism*, p. 27.

8 O. Paz, *Claude Lévi-Strauss: An Introduction*, trans. J. Bernstein and M. Bernstein (Ithaca, N.Y.: Cornell University Press, 1970), p. 6.

9 H. S. Hughes quoting Lévi-Strauss in "Structure and Society" in *Anthropologist as Hero*, p. 27.

10 B. Scholte, "Epistemic Paradigm" in *Anthropologist as Hero*, p. 112.

11 Caws, in *Anthropologist as Hero*, p. 207.

12 Scholte in *Anthropologist as Hero*, p. 110.

13 F. de Saussure, *Course in General Linguistics*, trans. W. Baskin (New York: McGraw-Hill, 1966).

14 Scholte quoting Lévi-Strauss in *Anthropologist as Hero*, p. 111.

15 Hughes in *Anthropologist as Hero*, p. 31.

16 Gardner, *Quest for Mind*, p. 122.

17 Paz, *Claude Lévi-Strauss: An Introduction*, p. 6. There is evidence here that Lévi-Strauss was influenced by psychoanalytic thought.

18 T. Reik, *Listening with the Third Ear* (New York: Harcourt Brace Jovanovich, 1977).

19 E. Strauss, "Aesthesiology and Hallucinations," in R. May et al., eds., *Existence: A New Dimension in Psychiatry and Psychology* (New York: Simon and Schuster, 1967), p. 157.

20 Ibid., p. 159.

21 O. H. Mowrer, "The Way the Mind Works?" *American Psychologist* 31, no. 12 (1976): 843–57.

22 R. N. Shepard and S. Chipman, "Second Order Isomorphism of Internal Representations: Shapes of States," *Cognitive Psychology* 1 (1970): 1–17.

23 R. N. Shepard and J. Metzler, "Mental Rotation of Three-Dimensional Objects," *Science* 171 (1971): 701–3.

24 M. Jay, *The Dialectical Imagination: A History of the Frankfort School and the Institute of Social Research 1923–1950* (Boston: Little, Brown, 1973), p. 47.

25 W. Luijpen, *Existential Phenomenology* (Pittsburgh: Duquesne University Press, 1972), pp. 17–89.

4 TOWARD A PHENOMENOLOGY
OF STRUCTURE

1 The two terms are only roughly equivalent. Husserl reserves eidos or the eidetic for the "essential" in the sense of a "universal not conditioned by any fact," for "pure possibility." See E. Husserl, *Cartesian Meditations*, trans. D. Cairns (The Hague: Martinus Nijhoff, 1970), p. 71. Since eidos refers to a more restrictive class within structure, we may safely assume that Husserl intends to capture structure or some subclass of structure. In the following sections on Husserl we will use the terms interchangeably.

2 H. Spiegelberg, *The Phenomenological Movement: A Historical Introduction* (The Hague: Martinus Nijhoff, 1969), 2:672.

3 R. Zaner, *The Way of Phenomenology* (New York: Pegasus, 1970), p. 136.

4 M. Merleau-Ponty, *Phenomenology of Perception*, trans. C. Smith (New York: Humanities, 1962), p. xiii.

5 Spiegelberg, *The Phenomenological Movement* 2:659.

6 Ibid., p. 691.

7 Zaner, *Way of Phenomenology*, p. 136.

8 Spiegelberg, *The Phenomenological Movement* 2:659.

9 Husserl, *Cartesian Meditations*, p. 70.

10 Spiegelberg, *The Phenomenological Movement* 1:105.

11 Husserl, *Cartesian Meditations*, p. 71.

12 Ibid.

13 Zaner, *Way of Phenomenology*, p. 156.

14 Spiegelberg, *The Phenomenological Movement*, 1:117.

15 Husserl, *Cartesian Meditations*, pp. 69–72.

16 Ibid., p. 70.

17 Spiegelberg, *The Phenomenological Movement*, 2:678.

18 Husserl, *Cartesian Meditations*, p. 70.

19 Ibid., pp. 71–72.

20 J. Piaget, *Structuralism*, trans. C. Maschler (New York: Harper and Row, 1971).

21 Ibid., p. 44.

22 Ibid., p. 5.

23 Ibid., p. 8.

24 Ibid., p. 10.

25 Ibid., p. 11.

26 Ibid., p. 19.

27 Ibid., p. 5.

28 See B. Levi, "Critique of Piaget's Theory of Intelligence: A Phenomenological Approach," *Journal of Phenomenological Psychology*, 3, no. 1 (1972): 103–4, particularly.

29 Piaget, *Structuralism*, p. 9.

30 Ibid., p. 68.

31 Ibid., p. 69.

32 H. Ginsburg and S. Opper, *Piaget's Theory of Intellectual Development* (Englewood Cliffs, N.J.: Prentice-Hall, 1969), p. 42.

33 Levi, "Critique of Piaget's Theory," p. 99–111.

34 Ibid., p. 105.

35 A. D. deWaelhens, *Une Philosophie de L'Ambiguité: L'Existentialisme de Maurice Merleau-Ponty* (Louvain: Universitaires de Louvain, 1951).

36 Ginsburg and Opper, *Piaget's Theory*, p. 22.

37 See footnote in Ginsburg and Opper, *Piaget's Theory*, p. 20, for usage of "scheme" as against "schema."

38 There are interesting parallels here between Piaget's concept of scheme and both Sullivan's "dynamism" (*Interpersonal Theory of Psychiatry* [New York: Norton, 1953]) and R. White's "intrinsic motivation" ("Motivation Reconsidered: The Concept of Competence," *Psychological Review* 66 [1959]: 297–333).

39 E. Erikson, *Childhood and Society* (New York: Norton, 1963), p. 52.

40 This is particularly the case in his description of later stages of cognitive development.

41 Ginsburg and Opper, *Piaget's Theory*, p. 39.

42 Ibid., p. 40.

43 Ibid., p. 77.

44 Ibid., p. 65.

45 See, for example, J. Macmurray's description in *The Self as Agent* (London: Faber and Faber, 1953), pp. 91–103.

46 However, see also Merleau-Ponty's account in "The Child's Relation with Others," in *The Primacy of Perception*, trans. W. Cobb et al., ed. J. M. Edie (Evanston, Ill.: Northwestern University Press, 1964), and G. Bosch's description of a possible failure of this development in *Infantile Autism* (New York: Springer-Verlag, 1970).

47 Ginsburg and Opper, *Piaget's Theory*, p. 64.

48 The fortuitous phrase is S. K. Langer's, *Feeling and Form* (New York: Scribner's Sons, 1953).

49 Ginsburg and Opper, *Piaget's Theory*, p. 76.

50 Ibid., pp. 75–76.

51 Ibid., p. 73.

52 Ibid., p. 79.

53 M. Polanyi, *Knowing and Being* (Chicago: University of Chicago Press, 1969), p. 140.

54 Merleau-Ponty, *Phenomenology of Perception*, p. 238.

5 THE METHOD, PART TWO

1 S. K. Langer, *Feeling and Form* (New York: Scribner's Sons, 1953), p. 168.

2 S. Todes, "Comparative Phenomenology of Perception and Imagination," *Journal of Existentialism* 7 (Fall 1966): 3–20, argues that an initial focus on sensuous qualities is one moment in the constitution of any object of perception. Further, he describes how we can stay with or prolong that focus

through an "inhibition of perception" which prevents the object from appearing as an existent.

3 M. Natanson, *The Journeying Self: A Study in Philosophy and Social Role* (Reading, Mass.: Addison-Wesley, 1970), p. 26. This work, following particularly Schütz, provides a phenomenology of typifying consciousness, and of the part of typification and roles in the constitution of self.

4 E. Husserl, *Logical Investigations*, trans. J. Findlay (London: Routledge and Kegan Paul, 1970), Fifth Investigation, 2:533–660.

5 See particularly E. Gendlin, *Experiencing and the Creation of Meaning* (New York: Free Press of Glencoe, 1962).

6 Ibid., pp. 27–29.

7 Ibid., p. 25.

8 For example, see chapter 12 of J. Dewey, *How We Think* (Boston: D. C. Heath, 1910).

9 E. Strauss, "Aesthesiology and Hallucinations," in R. May et al., eds., *Existence: A New Dimension in Psychiatry and Psychology* (New York: Simon and Schuster, 1967), p. 159.

10 M. Merleau-Ponty, *Phenomenology of Perception*, trans. C. Smith (New York: Humanities, 1962), particularly pp. 67–72.

11 This term is particularly prominent in Merleau-Ponty's unfinished work, *The Visible and the Invisible* (Evanston, Ill.: Northwestern University Press, 1968).

12 *The Tacit Dimension* (New York: Doubleday, 1967) is a briefer statement of this idea; or see M. Polanyi, *Personal Knowledge* (New York: Harper and Row, 1964).

13 M. Polanyi, *Knowing and Being* (Chicago: University of Chicago Press, 1969), p. 141.

14 Ibid.

15 Ibid., p. 146.

16 Ibid., pp. 148–49.

17 Langer, *Feeling and Form*, p. 174.

18 Ibid., p. 186.

19 See chapter 11, "Virtual Powers," of Langer, *Feeling and Form*, especially p. 185.

20 E. Strauss, "The Forms of Spatiality," *Phenomenological Psychology*, trans. E. Eng (London: Tavistock, 1966), p. 32.

21 O. F. Bollnow, "Lived Space," in N. Lawrence and D. O'Connor, eds., *Readings in Existential Phenomenology* (Englewood Cliffs, N.J.: Prentice-Hall, 1967), p. 180.

22 See Merleau-Ponty, *Phenomenology of Perception*, Part I.

23 Ibid., p. 206.

24 Ibid., p. 102.

25 Ibid., p. 206.

26 Merleau-Ponty's phrase quoted by R. Zaner, *The Problem of Embodiment* (The Hague: Martinus Nijhoff, 1971), p. 160.

27 Merleau-Ponty, *Phenomenology of Perception,* p. 143.

28 See discussion of this phrase in Zaner, *The Problem of Embodiment,* pp. 162–3.

29 Merleau-Ponty, *Phenomenology of Perception,* p. 105.

30 Ibid., p. 110.

31 Ibid., p. 106.

32 Ibid., p. xviii.

33 Ibid., p. 100.

34 See M. Merleau-Ponty, "The Primacy of Perception and Its Philosophical Consequences," in *The Primacy of Perception,* trans. W. Cobb et al., ed. J. M. Edie (Evanston, Ill.: Northwestern University Press, 1964).

35 M. Heidegger, *Being and Time,* trans. J. Macquarrie and E. Robinson (New York: Harper and Row, 1962), pp. 135–38.

36 For a popular but interesting discussion of how to develop effective approaches, attitudinally, to sports, see W. Gallwey, *The Inner World of Tennis* (New York: Bantam, 1979).

37 J. P. Sartre, *The Psychology of Imagination* (Secaucus, N.J.: Citadel, 1972), p. 194.

38 E. Casey, *Imagining: A Phenomenological Study* (Bloomington, Ind.: Indiana University Press, 1976), p. 50. In the following comparison I have relied both on Sartre's classic work on imagination, *The Psychology of Imagination,* which by contrast to the exalted status given it in romantic literature as the seat of the creative impulse, treats imagination as a debased or inferior form of thought, and the more recent and more temperate description by Casey.

39 See this entry in the *American Heritage Dictionary of the English Language* (Boston: Houghton-Mifflin, 1969).

40 Sartre, *Psychology of Imagination,* p. 261.

41 Ibid., p. 17.

42 Casey, *Imagining,* p. 35.

43 Ibid., p. 91.

44 Ibid., p. 93.

45 Ibid., p. 92.

46 Ibid., p. 88.

47 Sartre, *Psychology of Imagination,* p. 53.

48 Casey, *Imagining,* p. 89.

49 Ibid., p. 90.

50 Ibid., p. 93.

51 Compare this latter to the type of imagination termed "imagining-how" in Casey, *Imagining*, pp. 44–48.

52 Sartre, *Psychology of Imagination*, p. 10.

53 Casey, *Imagining*, p. 7.

54 Ibid., p. 119.

55 While H. Werner uses this phrase in a somewhat different context, his theory centers on the development of action systems akin to the informed body. See his *Comparative Psychology of Mental Development* (New York: International Universities, 1948).

56 Sartre, *Psychology of Imagination*, p. 25.

57 Ibid., p. 33.

58 Ibid., p. 31.

59 Ibid., p. 29.

60 Ibid., p. 30.

61 Ibid., p. 139.

62 Ibid., p. 140.

63 Ibid., p. 142.

64 Ibid., p. 139.

65 Ibid., p. 142.

66 Ibid., p. 139.

67 Ibid., p. 147.

68 Ibid., p. 138.

69 We shall distinguish "ground" here from that term's more common philosophic usage elsewhere in the text as foundation, or "condition for the possibility" by retaining the quotation marks.

70 In the minority, D. Davidson holds that metaphor has no meaning or sense beyond its literal meaning. See his "What Metaphor Means" in S. Sacks, ed., *On Metaphor* (Chicago: University of Chicago Press, 1979).

71 Defined by R. Verbrugge and N. McCarrell, "Metaphor Comprehension: Studies in Reminding and Remembering," *Cognitive Psychology* 9 (1977): 494–533.

72 The social scientist with an objectivistic bias reads phenomenological description more critically as *only* metaphoric, as an unacceptable, or at best, a preliminary form of understanding. To advance his understanding the objectivist seeks a more readily operationalized and hence observable level of analysis and with it, eventually, a more concrete, objective, and literal level of description. Of course, from the phenomenologist's vantage point the imposition of an operationization, a measurable and observable version of the phenomenon of interest, between that phenomenon and its subsequent

description makes the latter itself a kind of metaphor. It is necessarily a description of an apparently disparate entity substituting for an account of the original phenomenon.

73 E. Gendlin, "Focusing," *Psychotherapy: Theory, Research and Practice* 6, no. 1 (1969), p. 4.

74 R. Romanyshyn, "Metaphors and Human Behavior," *Journal of Phenomenological Psychology* 5, no. 2 (1975): 450.

75 Ibid., p. 447.

76 Ibid., p. 451.

77 Ibid., p. 442.

78 Ibid., p. 452.

79 K. J. Shapiro, "The Elusive in Experience," *Journal of Phenomenological Psychology* 6, no. 2 (1976): 135–52. Here we necessarily join a phenomenological investigation *in medias res*. This prevents the reader from participating in the discovery of metaphor and hence, to some extent, from directly experiencing the relations between bodily modes and metaphor under discussion. In the next chapter we will provide that opportunity through a fuller illustration of the present method in practice, by tracing a project from its inception.

80 Shapiro, "The Elusive in Experience," p. 138–39.

81 It might be argued that the possibility of the meaningful bodily prolongation of experiencing is the ground both of symbolization and of self-consciousness. Through it, the related ideas in psychoanalytic thought of delay, in Derrida of the trace, and in structuralism of isomorphism between culture and mind all might be found.

82 Of course, it is possible that the pursuit of a sexual partner is an instance of the elusive even given such surprise. If the sexual partner allowed me to end the pursuit successfully but I still was missing something, something still eluded me, then it would be clear that I had burdened the sexual with something it could not deliver—that sexuality was confabulated with elusiveness for me. However, here sexual pursuit, not sexual completion, is likened to the pursuit of the elusive.

83 K. Harries, "Metaphor and Transcendence," in S. Sacks, ed., *On Metaphor* (Chicago: University of Chicago Press, 1979), p. 71.

84 D. Davidson, "What Metaphor Means," in Sacks, ed., *On Metaphor*, p. 29.

85 M. Black, "How Metaphors Work: A Reply to Donald Davidson," in Sacks, ed., *On Metaphor*, p. 192.

86 T. Cohen, "Metaphor and the Cultivation of Intimacy" in Sacks, ed., *On Metaphor*, p. 7.

6 THE METHOD IN PRACTICE

1 R. Zaner, *The Way of Phenomenology* (New York: Pegasus, 1970), p. 36.

2 For a general discussion of this kind of use of "subjects," see R. Sardello, "A Reciprocal Participation Model of Experimentation," in *Duquesne Studies in Phenomenological Psychology* (Pittsburgh: Duquesne University Press, 1971), 1:58–66.

3 See A. Holder, "Theoretical and Clinical Aspects of Ambivalence," *Psychoanalytic Study of the Child* 30 (1975): 197–220, for a historical review of usage of the term.

4 K. J. Shapiro and I. E. Alexander, *The Experience of Introversion: An Integration of Phenomenological, Empirical, and Jungian Approaches* (Durham, N.C.: Duke University Press, 1975), chap. 3.

5 E. Bleuler, *Dementia Praecox, or the Group of Schizophrenias,* trans. J. Zimkin (New York: International Universities, 1950).

6 S. Freud, "Totem and Taboo," *Standard Edition* (London: Hogarth Press, 1955) 13:157.

7 Discussed in M. Merleau-Ponty, "The Child's Relation with Others," in *The Primacy of Perception,* trans. W. Cobb et al., ed. J. M. Edie (Evanston, Ill.: Northwestern University Press, 1964), pp. 102–3.

8 J. H. van den Berg, "The Human Body and the Significance of Human Movement," in H. Ruitenbeek, ed., *Psychoanalysis and Existential Philosophy* (New York: Dutton, 1962), p. 107.

9 *Webster's New International Dictionary,* 2d ed. (Springfield: Merriam, 1934).

10 *American Heritage Dictionary.*

11 *Oxford Dictionary of English Etymology* (Oxford: Oxford University Press, 1966), C. Onions, ed.

12 *Webster's New International Dictionary,* 2d ed.

13 In the description that follows I will continue to attend to both the target phenomenon, ambivalence, and to the method of its explication. While I intend to interweave both concerns in the text, when an extended statement that is predominantly a description of method occurs, I will set it off in italics for clarity and emphasis, as here.

14 A further complexity is that the two poles of this enworlded dimension themselves occur at different levels or poles of other constitutive dimensions. For example, when I feel stronger or more competent, I am more ready for risk.

15 W. James, *Psychology: The Briefer Course* (New York: Harper and Brothers, 1961), p. 29.

16 This position and the two that follow are more fully developed by V. J. Wallins, "The Phenomenology of Ambivalence," unpublished undergraduate thesis, Bates College, 1976.

17 L. Salzman, *Treatment of the Obsessive Personality* (New York: Aronson, 1980).

18 V. von Gebsattel, "The World of the Compulsive" in R. May et al.,

eds., *Existence: A New Dimension in Psychiatry and Psychology* (New York: Simon and Schuster, 1967).

19   A. van Kaam, "The Addictive Personality," in *Duquesne Studies in Phenomenological Psychology* (Pittsburgh: Duquesne University Press, 1971) 1:237–38.

20   See D. Shapiro's description in *Neurotic Styles* (New York: Basic, 1965), pp. 118–24.

21   Often it does so in a form suggestive of Jung's description of the law of opposites: the more dominant, more exclusive, and one-sided is a conscious attitude or function, the more its unconscious counterpart will "irrupt" with the untamed and archaic character of the numinous or demoniacal. For example, see C. G. Jung, *Psychological Types*, trans. H. Baynes (London: Routledge and Kegan Paul, 1923), pp. 541–42.

Index

Abstract space, 15, 111, 112, 119, 121, 133–34, 137, 138, 140, 142, 144, 146, 148, 182

Abstraction, 41, 46, 92, 112, 127–28, 152, 155, 162, 164, 165, 168; defined, 13; and imitation, 106, 108–9; of phenomenon texture, 52–55

Abstractive posture, 52, 109, 117, 118, 124, 153; and bodily modes, 42–47; defined, 30–35; and linguistics, 31; as paradox, 37

Accommodation, 42, 49, 94, 95, 97, 101–2, 103, 107

Action, 42, 110–12, 115–16, 129–32. *See also* Structure, and activity

Affected body, 52–53, 118, 126–27, 161; as abstractive mode, 42–47; and ambivalence, 181–82, 191

Aliment, 48, 94, 97

Ambivalence, 171–209; conflict, 206–7; definitions of, 177–78; as dialectical experience, 207–9; holding off, 202–5; living in, 205–6; love and hate, 174–78; phenomenology of, 178–80; risk/security, 198–99; structures of object in, 187–201; theories of, 173–77

Anschauung: defined, 86–87

Approach. *See* Posture

Architecture: structure of, 112–15

Art, 31–35

Assimilation, 49, 94, 95, 97, 101, 104, 107

Behavioral space, 134–40, 147, 148

Behaviorism, 5, 17, 72–73, 74, 95

Berg, J. H. van den: and abstractive posture, 36; and neurosis, 3

Black, M.: and metaphor, 163

Bleuler, E.: and ambivalence, 171–74, 178, 189

Bodily mode: defined, 13

Bodily sense, 14–15, 19, 31, 111, 115–16, 118, 154–55, 159–60, 162–65; and ambivalence, 180–86, 192, 198, 200, 203; of structure, 140. *See also* "Sense of"

Body, 40, 46, 52, 106–10, 112, 119, 120, 124, 135–36, 139, 148, 188, 189, 191; and ambivalence, 180–87, 203; capable of reflection, xi; child's, 48–50, 106–8, 109–10; as ground of metaphor, 155–62; informed, 164; knowledge of, 42; and meaning, 38–42; as unified object, 49–50. *See also* Affected body; Body-subject; Informed body; Lived body

Mental life, 112; development of, 103–5
Merleau-Ponty, M., xi, 11, 12, 17, 80, 84, 108, 153, 215 n. 1; abstractive posture, 36; behavior, 54; body as basis of reflection, 46; child's discovery of body, 59; informed body, 112; lived body, 41, 153; perception, 88, 131, 135–36; prepersonal union, 47
Metaphor, 16, 17, 53, 92, 119, 152–65; and ambivalence, 181, 198; body as ground for, 117, 155–57; child's imitation as, 107–8, 110–11; and forming, 117, 142; geologic, of structure, 59–60, 67; of return, 23; structure, 78; text, 163; virtual behavior, 158
Mime, 42, 133. *See also* Chaplin, Charlie; Marcel Marceau
Modes of experience: defined, 13
Music, 42–43, 120–21, 186

Natanson, M.: and lived experience, 19
Noema, 10, 112; defined, 12; and noeme, 53, 178
Noesis, 10, 15; defined, 12–13

Object relations: school of psychoanalysis, 176
Obsessive, 173, 204

Pain. *See* Symptom
Phenomenology: defined, 12
Phenomenon: defined, 12, 121–22
Photography: as posture, 27–28
Piaget, J., 25, 42, 50, 72, 109, 118, 134, 144, 158, 159, 168; ambiguity, 97; behaviorism, 96; body, 103; dualism, 93, 96–98, 99, 104; interactionism, 93–98; intuitive period, 111; isomorphism, 51; learning, 129; perception, 101; preoperational stage, 100–101; prepersonal union, 47, 48; schemes, 99–103, 146, 218 n. 38;

sensorimotor period, 49, 98–102; structure, 83, 93–94; structure and activity, 92–112
Play, 49, 101, 107
Polanyi, M., 41, 140; subsidiary awareness, 111; tacit knowledge, 131–32
Positivism: and early phenomenology, 1–2
Posture, 3, 16, 23–30, 49, 174, 200, 205; abstractive (*see* Abstractive posture); of analyst, 68–70; of anthropologist, 65; of bracketing (*see* Bracket); defined, 24–25, 26–32, 35–36; habituated, 26–28; objectivistic, 26; linguistic, 26–27; organizing, 25; and photography, 27–28; and reflection, 29; reflective (*see* Reflective posture); as return, 25; and time, 26
Preoperational period, 100
Prepersonal union, 47–52
Prereflection, 5, 22–23, 27, 136
Presence, 61, 86, 88, 91, 110, 119, 125, 167–68; and ambivalence, 176–78, 180, 188; defined, 12; of structures, 15
Problem solving, 106, 109
Proximal, 132

Redoublement: defined, 62
Reduction, 84–85, 87, 97, 176
Reductionism, 6, 41, 75; and early phenomenology, 1
Reflection, xi-xii, 5, 9–11, 18–20, 23–24, 29, 31, 35, 37, 46, 54, 92, 106, 112, 119, 132, 134, 147, 161, 165, 168, 170; and ambivalence, 171–173, 188, 192, 205; being and knowing, 24; as bodily abstraction, 41; defined, 13; elusiveness of, 167; and enactment, 38, 117–65; phenomenology of, 21–24
Reflective posture, 9, 24, 79, 84, 85, 87, 89, 126, 192
Return, 5, 7, 16, 22, 23, 29, 36, 37, 52, 55, 81, 84–85, 109, 121–22,